The MAYA

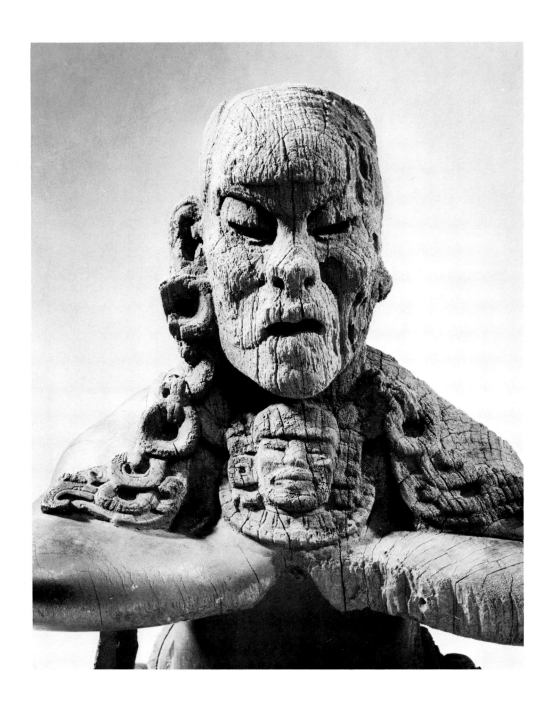

MICHAEL D. COE

The MAYA

Fifth edition, fully revised and expanded

With 153 illustrations

THAMES AND HUDSON

Ancient Peoples and Places
FOUNDING EDITOR: GLYN DANIEL

Frontispiece: Wood carving of a Maya lord from Tabasco, Mexico.
See ill. 51 for whole figure.

First published in Great Britain in 1966 by
Thames and Hudson Ltd, London

Second edition published in the United States of America
in 1980 by Thames and Hudson Inc.,
500 Fifth Avenue, New York, New York 10110
Third edition 1984
Fourth edition 1987
Fifth edition 1993

Library of Congress Catalog Card Number 92-63273

Printed and bound in Singapore

Contents

Preface

This book was originally conceived as a companion to *Mexico*, both volumes intended to present to the interested reader – including travelers and students – a concise and up-to-date introduction to the native civilizations of Mesoamerica. I first wrote *The Maya* because I believed that these fascinating people should be allowed to tell us about their own way of life and outlook on the universe. In the ensuing years, that goal has come far closer with the accelerating pace of decipherment of the hieroglyphic script: the ancient Maya can now speak to us across the void of time in their own words. They have now become the only truly historical people of the Pre-Columbian New World, as I hope that these pages will show.

The Maya first appeared in 1966. The past quarter-century has seen great advances in our knowledge of Maya civilization in both the Preclassic and Classic epochs, often in ways that earlier generations of scholars would not have approved. From a picture of the Maya that emphasized peaceful theocracies led by priest astronomers, ruling over relatively empty 'ceremonial centers,' we now have highly warlike city-states led by grim dynasts obsessed with human sacrifice and the ritual letting of their own blood. Although traditional 'dirt' archaeology has contributed to our current view of the ancient Maya, the contributions of epigraphy and art history have been, in my opinion, truly revolutionary.

I would like to acknowledge the advice I have received in the preparation of this new edition from my former student, Professor Stephen Houston of Vanderbilt University, many of whose suggestions for changes and additions have been incorporated in these pages. Chapters 2 and 3 have been considerably expanded to include new data on the Preclassic Maya of the Pacific coastal and Petén lowlands, and I would like to thank John Clark and Dr Richard Hansen for being so generous with their published and unpublished data.

I have added an entirely new, final chapter on the contemporary Maya, since the story of these remarkable people does not end with the Conquest. It has not been an easy one to write, and I think that most scholars find it difficult, as I have, to keep their judgment from being clouded by the tragic events of our own time.

A few words should be said about the pronunciation of Maya names and words. The system of orthography used here comes to us from the early Spanish friars who were attempting to record the native language of Yucatán, so that most vowels and consonants are as in Spanish. However, the good priests were plagued by the fact that many Maya sounds were unknown to

Europe and so had to devise new ways of writing them down. The letter *x* is used, as in sixteenth-century Spanish, to record a phoneme like English *sh*; *c* is hard, no matter which vowel follows it; *u* before *a*, *e*, *i*, and *o* is pronounced like English *w*. The Maya languages make an important distinction between glottalized and non-glottalized consonants, the former being enunciated with constricted throat. In the orthography of Yucatec Maya these would be as follows:

Non-glottalized	Glottalized
c	k
ch	ch'
tz	dz
p	pp
t	th

Glottal constrictions or stops may also occur between reduplicated vowels, although these are ignored in most dictionaries. Linguists and many epigraphers now use a revised orthography, in which the Classic site of Uaxactún, for example, would be written *Waxaktun*, but I have avoided this as non-specialists would find it difficult to recognize many familiar place names and personal names if they were put in this system.

Some of the words relevant to this book are in Nahuatl, the national tongue of the Aztec state, which was used as a great trading *lingua franca* at the time of the Conquest. Nahuatl names were transcribed in Roman letters in terms of the language spoken by the *conquistadores* of the sixteenth century; they have not been accented here, since they are regularly stressed on the penultimate syllable, whereas Maya and Spanish names have been given their accents.

There have been important advances in the accurate correlation of dates derived from radiocarbon determinations with those of the Christian calendar. Dendrochronological studies of the bristlecone pine now show that before about 700–800 BC there is an increasing deviation from 'true' dates back to a maximum of some 800 years at radiocarbon 4500 BC. In this edition, unlike earlier ones, all radiocarbon dates have been calibrated to take this into account. Radiocarbon dating has no real bearing on the chronology of the Classic Maya period (*c.* AD 250–900), which depends upon the accuracy of the correlation between the Long Count calendar and the European-Christian calendar. My colleague Dr Floyd Lounsbury has provided incontrovertible proof that the calendar correlation first advanced by the late Sir Eric Thompson (the 584285 constant, for specialists) is correct, and that is the one used here. All Christian equivalents are given in terms of the Gregorian Calendar.

DATES (Calibrated)	PERIODS	SOUTHERN AREA		CENTRAL AREA	NORTHERN AREA	SIGNIFICANT DEVELOPMENTS
		Pacific Coast	Highlands			
1530	Late Post-Classic	Aztec Xoconochco	Mixco Viejo	Tayasal ↑	Independent states	Spanish Conquest Highland city-states
1200					Mayapán	League of Mayapán
	Early Post-Classic	Tohil Plumbate	Ayampuc		Toltec Chichén	Toltec hegemony in Yucatán
925	Terminal Classic	Cotzumalhuapa	Quen Santo	Bayal/ Tepeu 3	Puuc, Maya Chichén	Toltec arrive in Yucatán Classic Maya collapse, Putún ascendancy
800	Late Classic		Amatle-Pamplona	Tepeu 2 1	Early Cobá	Bonampak murals Height of Maya civilization Reign of Pacal at Palenque
600	Early Classic	Tiquisate	Esperanza	Tzakol 3 2 1	Regional styles, Acanceh	Teotihuacan domination and influence
250	Late Preclassic	Izapan styles ↑ Crucero	Aurora Santa Clara Miraflores	Matzanel, Holmul I Chicanel	Late Preclassic	First lowland Maya dated stela at Tikal Massive pyramid-building in lowlands Spread of Izapan civilization, calendar, writing
AD / BC						
300						
	Middle Preclassic	Conchas Jocotal	Las Charcas Arévalo	Mamom Xe, Swasey	Middle Preclassic	Earliest lowland Maya villages
1000	Early Preclassic	Cuadros Cherla Ocós Locona Barra				Early Olmec influence on Pacific Coast Beginnings of social stratification Origins of village life, pottery, figurines
1800	Archaic	Chantuto		Belize Archaic		Hunting, fishing, gathering
3000						

1 Major topographical features and cultural areas.

1 · Introduction

The Maya are hardly a vanished people, for they number about six million souls, the largest single block of American Indians north of Peru. Most of them have resisted with remarkable tenacity the encroachments of Spanish American civilization, although in the past few decades these have taken an increasingly violent and repressive form. Besides their numbers and cultural integrity, the Maya are remarkable for an extraordinary cohesion. Unlike other more scattered indigenous peoples within Mexico and Central America, at the time of the Conquest the Maya were confined with one exception (the Huaxtec) to a single, unbroken area that includes all of the Yucatán Peninsula, Guatemala, Belize, parts of the Mexican states of Tabasco and Chiapas, and the western portion of Honduras and El Salvador. Such homogeneity in the midst of such a miscellany of tongues and peoples testifies to their relative security from invasions by other native groups – the Aztec, for instance, never extended their empire to include any part of Maya territory, although they had important trading relationships with them.

There are few parts of the world where there is such a good 'fit' between language and culture: a line drawn around the Maya-speaking peoples would contain all those remains, and hieroglyphic texts, assigned to the ancient Maya civilization. It would be an error, though, to think of these peoples as existing in some kind of vacuum. An earlier generation of archaeologists, which included the late Sylvanus G. Morley of the Carnegie Institution of Washington, thought of the Maya as *the* great innovators and culture-givers to the rest of the peoples of Mexico and Central America. A later generation, which included myself, came to view this fundamentally 'Mayacentric' outlook as wrong: the ancient Maya had received much more from the non-Maya Mexican civilizations than they had given. I must now admit that Morley may have been more right than wrong, for reasons that will be made clear in this book.

In pre-Spanish times the Maya belonged to the larger grouping christened 'Mesoamerica' by Professor Kirchhoff. The northern frontier coincided approximately with the limits of aboriginal farming in Mexico, the desiccated plateau beyond holding out only the possibility of humble collecting and hunting. To the southeast, the Mesoamerican border ran from the Caribbean to the Pacific across what is now Honduras and El Salvador, although in late pre-Conquest times it is apparent that northwesternmost Costa Rica was thoroughly Mesoamerican in culture; the southeastern frontier generally divided the civilized Maya from simpler peoples of foreign tongue.

All the Mesoamerican Indians shared a number of traits which were more

1

or less peculiar to them and absent or rare elsewhere in the New World: hieroglyphic writing, books of fig-bark paper or deerskin which were folded like screens, a complex permutation calendar, knowledge of the movements of the planets (especially Venus) against the background of the stars, a game played with a rubber ball in a special court, highly specialized markets, human sacrifice by head or heart removal, an emphasis upon self-sacrifice by blood drawn from the ears, tongue, or penis, and a highly complex, pantheistic religion which included nature divinities as well as deities emblematic of royal descent. Also in all Mesoamerican religions was the idea of a multi-tiered Heaven and Underworld, and of a universe oriented to the

137 four directions with specific colors and gods assigned to the cardinal points and to the center.

While there are profound differences between the subsistence base of the lowlands and that of the highlands, the ancient foursome of maize, beans, chile peppers, and squash formed then, as it still does, the basis of the Mesoamerican diet, but of course these foods were widely spread elsewhere – from the southwestern United States to Peru and Argentina in pre-Conquest times – wherever native cultures had advanced beyond a level of semi-nomadic simplicity. In Mesoamerica, none the less, the preparation of maize is highly distinctive: the hard, ripe kernels are boiled in a mixture of water and white lime, producing a kind of hominy (*nixtamal*) which is then ground into unleavened dough on a quern (*metate*) with a handstone (*mano*, from the

130 Spanish *mano de piedra*), later to be fashioned into steamed *tamales* or into the flat cakes called by the Spanish term *tortillas*. The latter, perhaps introduced into the Maya area in late pre-Conquest times from Mexico, are characteristically toasted on a clay griddle which rests upon a three-stone hearth.

The importance of the *nixtamal* process cannot be overstressed. Maize is naturally deficient in essential amino acids and in niacin (a member of the vitamin B complex): a population whose diet consisted solely of untreated maize would develop pellagra, and would be malnourished. Cooking with lime (in Mesoamerica and the American Southwest) or with ashes (in North America) enhances the balance of essential amino acids and frees the otherwise unavailable niacin. Without the invention of this technique, no settled life in Mesoamerica would have been possible.

Given the similarities among the diverse cultures of Mesoamerica, one can only conclude that its peoples must have shared a common origin, so far back in time that it may never be brought to light by archaeology. Yet there is some consensus among archaeologists that the Olmec of southern Mexico had elaborated many of these traits beginning about 3,000 years ago, and that much of complex culture in Mesoamerica has an Olmec origin. It is also reasonable to assume that there must have been an active interchange of ideas and things among the Mesoamerican elite over many centuries, a state of affairs which can be documented in the Terminal Classic epoch thanks to recent research; this in itself would tend to bring about cultural homogeneity – for example, it might explain why both the Classic Maya and the very late Aztec held a snake-footed god to be the supernatural ruling their respective royal houses. It was out of such a matrix of cultural evolution and diffusion that Maya civilization was born.

The setting

There can be few parts of the globe as geographically diverse as Meso-america, which includes almost every ecological extreme from the snow-swept wastes of the high volcanoes to parched deserts and to rain-drenched jungle. The Maya area is situated in the southeastern corner of this topsy-turvy land, but actually is somewhat less varied than the larger unit of which it is a part. For instance, high-altitude tundra is not found, and deserts are confined to narrow stretches along the upper Río Negro and middle Río Motagua. It is also true that tropical forest is more extensive here than in Mexico outside the Maya area.

There are really two natural settings in the land of the Maya: highlands and lowlands. In geology, in animal and plant life, and in the form that human cultures took, these are well set off from each other. The Maya high-   2
lands by definition lie above 1,000 ft (305 m) and are dominated by a great backbone of volcanoes both extinct and active, some over 13,000 ft (3,960 m) in altitude, which curves down from southeastern Chiapas toward lower Central America. This mighty cordillera has been formed principally by massive explosions of pumice and ash of Tertiary and Pleistocene age which have built up a mantle many hundreds of feet thick, overlain by a thin cover of rich soil. Millennia of rain and erosion have produced a highly dissected landscape, with deep ravines between hog-back ridges, but there are a few relatively broader valleys, such as those of Guatemala City, Quetzaltenango, and Comitán, which have long been important centers of Maya life. Not all of the highlands are so recent in origin, however, for to the north of the volcanic cordillera is a band of more ancient igneous and metamorphic rocks, and beyond this a zone of Tertiary and Cretaceous limestones which in the more humid country bordering the lowlands take the fantastically eroded appearance of a Chinese landscape. Isolated to the northeast are the Maya Mountains, a formation of similar antiquity.

Highland rainfall is dependent, as in the rest of the New World tropics to the north of the Equator, upon a well-defined rainy season which lasts from May through early November. In effect, this follows a double-peaked distribution in both highlands and lowlands, with heaviest falls in June and in October. For the highlands, the highest figures are registered along the Pacific slopes of Chiapas and Guatemala, a zone noted in pre-Conquest days for its cacao production, but in general total precipitation for the Maya highlands is no greater than for the temperate countries of northern Europe.

The highland flora is closely related to soils and topography; on the tops of slopes and ridges, pines and grasses dominate, while further down in ravines where there is moisture, oaks flourish. Compared with that of the lowlands, the wild fauna is not especially abundant, but this may be due to a far denser human occupation.

Native farming practices in the highlands are quite different from those of the lowlands, although inhabitants of both regions depend upon the burning of unwanted vegetation and upon rest periods for farm plots. The moderate fallowing practiced in the highlands depends upon the position of the field on the slope, with only about 10 years of continuous cultivation possible in higher fields, after which the plot must be abandoned for as much as 15 years, while further down up to 15 years continuous use with only a 5-year rest is practicable. In densely populated areas of highland Guatemala, almost all the available land may be cleared or in second-growth. Several kinds of maize are planted over the year; tilling is by furrowing and, after the sprouts have appeared, by making hillocks. In these maize fields, or *milpas*, secondary crops like beans and squashes, or sweet manioc, are interplanted, as well as chile peppers of many sizes, colors, and degrees of 'hotness.' In summary, while it utilizes the same kinds of plants as in the lowlands, the highland system of agriculture seems to be well-adapted to an area of high population with good, deep soils where the competition posed by heavy forests and weeds is not a major problem.

But it is the lowlands lying to the north which are of most concern to the story of Maya civilization. A greater contrast with the highland environment can hardly be imagined, as every tourist flying to the ruins of Tikal from Guatemala City must have realized. The Petén-Yucatán peninsula is a single, great limestone shelf jutting up into the blue waters of the Gulf of Mexico

2 Lake Atitlán in the Maya highlands, Guatemala. This view, taken by E. Muybridge in the 1880s, shows native traders carrying loads of pottery to market.

3 Lacandón Maya in the Chiapas rain forest.

which borders it on the west and north; its reef-girt eastern shores face the Caribbean. These limestones have risen from the sea over an immense period of time. In the older Petén and Belize region of the south, the uplift has been greatest, and the topography is more rugged with broken karst hills rising above the plain. As one moves north to Yucatán itself, the country becomes flatter – it looks like a featureless, green carpet from the air – but this is deceptive, for on foot the pitting of the porous limestone is all too apparent. In the northern reaches of our peninsula, about the only topographical variation of any note is the Puuc range, a chain of low hills no more than a few hundred feet high strung out like an inverted 'V' across northern Campeche and southwestern Yucatán.

Unlike the sierra to the south, there are few permanently flowing rivers in the lowlands, except in the west and in the southeast, where extensive alluvial bottom-lands have been formed. The great Usumacinta with its tributaries is the most important system, draining the northern highlands of Guatemala and the Lacandón country of Chiapas, twisting to the northwest past many a ruined Maya 'city' before depositing its yellow silts in the Gulf of Mexico. Sizeable rivers flowing into the Caribbean are the Motagua, which on its path to the sea cuts successively through pine and oak-clad hills, cactus-strewn desert, and tropical forest; the Belize River; the New River; and the Río Hondo which separates Belize from Mexico.

The lowland climate is hot, uncomfortably so toward the close of the dry season. In May come the rains, which last through October, but compared with other tropical regions of the world these are not especially abundant. In much of the Petén, for instance, only about 70–90 inches (178–229 cm) fall each year, and as one moves north to Yucatán there is a steady decrease from even this level. Nor is there total reliability in these rains, for in bad years there may be severe droughts. Really heavy precipitation is found in the far south of the Petén and Belize; in the Lacandón country of Chiapas; and in the Tabasco plains which are covered with great sheets of water during much of the summer and for that reason were largely shunned by the pre-Conquest Maya.

Lakes are rare in the lowlands, especially in the Yucatán Peninsula. The absence of ground water in many regions makes thirst a serious problem. In the Petén of northern Guatemala, there are broad, swampy depressions or *bajos* which fill during the summer but are often dry in the rainless winter season. Smaller and similarly seasonal water-holes called *aguadas* are found in some places in Yucatán, but there the major source of drinking (and bathing) water for the inhabitants is the *cenote*, a word corrupted by the Spaniards from the Maya *dzonot*. These are circular sink holes, some of great size, formed by the collapse of underground caves. Because they are perennially filled with water percolating through the limestone, they necessarily have served as the focal points for native settlement since the first occupation of the land.

The relative dryness of the northern half of the peninsula presented especially grave problems to the inhabitants of the Puuc area, where *cenotes* are largely nonexistent. According to Nicholas Dunning and Jeff Kowalski, the water table is at least 210 ft (65 m) below the surface, and while deep caves may be a source of drip water, they could never have supplied the needs of the dense populations of the Puuc. As a response, the Maya excavated and constructed thousands of underground, bottle-shaped cisterns called *chultunob* (sing. *chultun*), the entrances of which were surrounded by broad, plastered aprons to catch the water which fell during the rainy season.

A high monsoon forest (now badly destroyed by unrestrained lumbering, farming, and cattle-ranching) covers the southern lowlands, dominated by mahogany trees towering up to 150 ft (45 m) above the jungle floor, by sapodillas, which gave wood to the ancients and chewing-gum to ourselves, and by the breadnut tree. In the middle and lower layers of this formation grow many fruit trees important to the Maya, such as the avocado. The forest is only partly evergreen, however, for in the dry season many species drop their leaves; but in a few places favored by higher rainfall, there is real, non-deciduous rain forest.

Interspersed in the monsoon forest, particularly in the Petén and southern Campeche, are open savannahs covered with coarse grasses and dotted with stunted, flat-topped trees. There is no real agreement on the origin of the savannahs, but modern opinion is against the idea that they were created by the ancient Maya through over-cultivation of the land. On the other hand, they are certainly maintained by the hand of man, for while they are avoided by farmers they are periodically burned off by hunters so as to attract game to new grasses which sprout in the ashes. When Cortés and his army crossed these grasslands on their way to the Itzá capital of Tayasal, they came upon a herd of sacred deer that had no fear of man, and thus allowed themselves to be easily slaughtered by the *conquistadores*.

To the north and west, where there is a profound drop in the annual rainfall, the forest turns into a low, thorny jungle, finally reaching the state of xerophytic scrub along the northern shore of the Yucatán Peninsula.

There is a rich fauna in the lowlands. Deer and peccary abound, especially in Yucatán, which the Maya called 'The Land of the Turkey and Deer.' Spider monkeys and the diminutive but noisy howler monkeys are easy to hunt and well-favored in the native cuisine. Among the larger birds are the ocellated turkey, with its beautiful golden-green plumage, the currasow, and the guan. More dangerous beasts are the jaguar, largest of the world's spotted cats, which was pursued for its resplendent pelt, and the water-loving tapir, killed both for its meat and for an incredibly tough hide employed in making shields and armor for Maya warriors.

Of more importance to the development of Maya civilization is the agricultural potential of the lowlands, which is by no means uniform. While some of the soils of the Petén, for instance, are relatively deep and fertile, those of Yucatán (except for the Puuc area) are the reverse. The sixteenth-century Franciscan bishop, Diego de Landa, our great authority on all aspects of Maya life, tells us that 'Yucatán is the country with least earth that I have seen, since all of it is one living rock and has wonderfully little earth.' It is little wonder that the early Colonial chronicles speak much of famines in Yucatán before the arrival of the Spaniards, and it might be that the province relied less upon plant husbandry than upon its famed production of honey, salt, and slaves.

It is now almost universally recognized, albeit unwillingly, that many tropical soils which are permanently deprived of their forest cover quickly decline in fertility and become quite unworkable as a layer of brick-like laterite develops on the surface. Tropical rainfall and a fierce sun, along with erosion, do their destructive work in a surprisingly brief span, and agricultural disaster results. On such soils about the only kind of farming possible is that practiced by the present-day lowland Maya – a shifting, slash-and-burn system under which the forest is permitted to regenerate at intervals. While seemingly simple, it requires great experience on the farmer's part. A patch of forest on well-drained land is chosen, and cut down in late fall or early winter. The felled wood and brush are fired at the end of the dry season, and all over the Maya lowlands the sun becomes obscured by 4 the smoke and haze which cover the sky at that time. The maize seed is planted in holes poked through the ash with a dibble stick. Then the farmer must pray to the gods to bring the rain.

A cleared plot or *milpa* usually has a life of only 2 years, by which time decreasing yields no longer make it worthwhile to plant a third year. The Maya farmer must then shift to a new section of forest and begin again, leaving his old *milpa* fallow for periods which may be from 4 to 7 years in the Petén, and from 15 to 20 years in Yucatán. In inhabited regions, the forest

4 Burning a lowland *milpa* or maize field at Uaxactún, Petén, Guatemala.

seen from the air looks like some great patchwork quilt of varying shades of green, a veritable mosaic of regenerating plots and new clearings.

The long-held notion that shifting cultivation was the *only* system of food production practiced by the ancient Maya has now been discarded. In 1972, the geographer Alfred Siemens and the late Dennis Puleston reported their discovery from the air of extensive areas of raised fields in southern Campeche; these are narrow, rectangular plots elevated above the low-lying, seasonally inundated land bordering rivers or in *bajos*, and are remarkably similar to the *chinampas* on which Aztec agriculture was based in central Mexico. Ancient raised fields have since been found over a wide area in northern Belize and in adjacent Quintana Roo, where water levels vary little through the annual cycle of dry and wet seasons.

Recent research suggests that at least some of the raised field systems of the southern lowlands may have been initiated in swampy areas as far back as the Late Preclassic (prior to AD 250), thus providing the subsistence base for the remarkably precocious increase in population which we know for that period.

Stone-walled terraces which probably acted as silt traps are common in various localities in the lowlands, especially in western Belize and the Río Bec region of southern Campeche. Both these and the raised fields show that in favorable areas, perhaps in response to population pressure, the Maya turned to intensive, highly productive, fixed-field systems. At the same time, it should be remembered that the artificial aquatic environment created by raised field agriculture would have harbored abundant edible fish and crocodilians.

And yet the claims that the Classic Maya were almost totally dependent upon the techniques of intensive maize agriculture are probably exaggerated through the understandable enthusiasm created by new finds. Much of the Maya lowland area is and was unsuitable for raised fields or for terracing, and it remains a certainty that most of the maize eaten by the pre-Conquest lowland Maya was grown in *milpa* plots by the still-used methods of shifting cultivation.

Puleston, tragically struck down in 1978 by a bolt of lightning on the Castillo of Chichén Itzá, was a provocative champion not only of the raised-field theory, but also of the idea that the lowland Classic Maya may well have relied as much upon the cultivation of the breadnut or *ramón* tree (*Brosimum alicastrum*) as upon maize, since the breadnut fruit stores well and the tree itself is remarkably common around old Maya ruins. Stimulating though the idea was, recent research suggests that the breadnut was never much more

5 Prehistoric Maya raised fields in the Río Hondo area, northern Belize. Rectangular plots can be seen extending out from the *terra firma* side of the floodplain.

than a famine food for the Maya, and that the frequency of its distribution near Maya sites is largely due to edaphic, or soil, factors and has little to do with human intervention.

Nevertheless, plants other than maize, particularly root crops, may have played an important role in the Maya diet, as was first suggested by Bennett Bronson. Sweet manioc, for instance, does very well in the lowlands, is easy to propagate, and requires very little attention.

What all this means is that the lowlands could have been far more densely occupied by the Classic Maya than we would have estimated under the old *milpa* hypothesis. This conclusion is reinforced by a recent aerial survey and mapping of ancient ruins in northern Yucatán, which revealed virtually continuous occupation from one end of the survey area to the other, implying a pre-Conquest population far higher than today's. Perhaps we should be talking of eight to ten million people in the lowlands at about AD 800. These new facts and hypotheses also bear upon the question of what proportion of this population would have been released from their agricultural pursuits to engage as full-time participants in the making of Maya civilization; they may also bear upon the question of why it collapsed (Chapter 6).

Natural resources

From the time of their initial contact with the Maya, the Spaniards learned to their bitter disappointment that there were no sources of gold and silver in the Maya lowlands, and the foreign colonizers soon came to look upon the region as a hardship post. Yet the native inhabitants, to whom the yellow metal was of little value and in fact unknown until about AD 800, had abundant resources which were of far greater importance to them in their daily life, in their rituals, and in their trade.

Construction materials in the form of easily quarried limestone occurred almost everywhere; since it only hardens after prolonged exposure to the air, it was easily worked with their stone-age technology. In some of the limestone beds of the southern lowlands, the Maya found deposits of flint and chert, from which they chipped the axes that were absolutely essential for slash-and-burn farming. Even in very early times, flint-working communities sprang up to exploit this resource, the great workshop at Colhá in northern Belize, for example, having been founded far back in the Preclassic period.

But rock harder than limestone was necessary for the production of the *manos* and *metates* used in grinding maize dough; trading networks brought vast quantities of these objects down from the volcanic regions of Guatemala, and from the granitic outcrops of the Maya Mountains in Belize.

As archaeologist Robert Cobean has noted, obsidian – a natural volcanic glass – was to ancient Mesoamerica what steel is to modern civilization. It was turned into knives, lance and dart points, prismatic blades for woodworking and shaving, and a host of other tools. For the Maya, the sources necessarily lay in the volcanic highlands, above all the great pumice and obsidian exposure at El Chayal, northeast of Guatemala City.

It is a human universal that the body demands a constant concentration of sodium in the blood, as this element is lost by excretion. Meats are rich in sodium, so that a primarily hunting people such as the Inuit (Eskimo) do not need to take in salt, but tropical farmers like the Maya require about 8 grams of salt a day to maintain their sodium balance. Anthony Andrews calculates that a great Classic city like Tikal, with a population conservatively estimated at 45,000, would have had to import over 131 tons of salt each year.

Happily, the greatest salt sources in all Mesoamerica lie within the Maya area. The major one consisted of the salt beds along the lagoons of Yucatán's north coast. There, grids of shallow, rectilinear pans (still in use) allowed the lagoon water to evaporate during the dry season. Once a thick layer of salt had hardened, it was raked up and transported in baskets. On the eve of the Conquest, these beds were controlled by Yucatán's most powerful kingdoms, and their product was traded to places as distant as the Río Pánuco in northern Veracruz. Similar conditions existed along the Pacific Coast, but there and at important, inland, mineral-spring sources such as Bolontehuitz on the Río Chixoy, the brine was cooked down rather than sun-evaporated. Regardless of method, access to salt sources or to salt trade networks was critical to the growth and security of Maya states.

The Maya elite had their special needs, above all jade and quetzal feathers. Apple-green jade was obtained along the middle reaches of the Río Motagua, where it occurs as pebbles and boulders in the river deposits. The highly prized tail feathers of the quetzal, which flash blue, green, and gold in dazzling iridescence, were obtained from the bird's natural habitat, the cloud forests of Alta Verapaz in Guatemala, Chiapas in southeastern Mexico, and Honduras. Many thousands of such feathers saw their way into the gorgeous costumes of Maya rulers and their retinues, so that the quetzal may well have been near extinction by the time Maya civilization collapsed in the ninth century AD.

Areas

The Maya occupied three separate areas, which is hardly surprising considering the great environmental contrasts within the Maya realm: Southern, Central, and Northern, the latter two entirely within the lowlands.

The Southern Area includes the highlands of Guatemala and adjacent Chiapas, together with the torrid coastal plain along the Pacific and the western half of El Salvador. In general, the Southern Area is somewhat aberrant (many books on the Maya ignore it altogether), almost surely because of the Mexican influence which has been powerful here over a very long time. Some of the most characteristically 'Maya' traits are missing: the corbel vault in architecture and, except in Late Preclassic times, the Maya Long Count and the stela-altar complex. We must admit that in many ways the Southern Area hardly seems Maya at all from a purely archaeological standpoint, while some of it, such as the central and eastern Chiapas highlands, was only occupied by Maya-speakers at a relatively late date.

In the Central Area, on the other hand, Maya civilization soared to its greatest heights. Focused upon what is now the Department of Petén in northern Guatemala, it reaches from Tabasco and southern Campeche across the densely forested southern lowlands to include Belize, the Río Motagua of Guatemala, and a narrow portion of westernmost Honduras. All the most typically 'Maya' traits are present – architectural features such as the corbel vault and roof comb, the fully developed Long Count with all its complexities, hieroglyphic writing, the stela-altar complex, and many others. These triumphs, however, were registered during the Classic period. Since the opening decades of the tenth century AD, most of the area has been a green wilderness.

As one would expect, the Northern and Central Areas have much in common, since there are virtually no natural barriers to cultural exchange or to movements of peoples between the two. There is, none the less, a good deal of individuality to the Northern Area. In part this may be due to the fact that agricultural potentialities in much of Yucatán are poorer, and that places where people may live in large concentrations (cities and towns) are often dictated by the distribution of *cenotes*; but it may also partly be the result of Mexican influences which are almost as strong here as in the Southern Area. In contrast with the situation in the southern lowlands, there was no mass abandonment of the Northern Area (although many of the cities were depopulated), and overall native population figures remain high even today.

Periods

The discovery of the ancient Maya civilization was a piecemeal process. Following the imposition of Spanish power in the Yucatán Peninsula, various persons such as the great Bishop Landa, or Fray Antonio de Ciudad Real who visited the famous site of Uxmal in 1588, wondered at the age of the mighty ruins which lay scattered across the land, but they could discover little from the natives. Real interest in Maya remains only began after the publication, in a London edition of 1822, of the pioneering explorations and excavations which Antonio del Río, a Spanish captain of dragoons, had made at the site of Palenque in the late eighteenth century. Modern Maya archaeology, however, stems from the epic journeys undertaken between 1839 and 1842 by the American diplomat and lawyer, John Lloyd Stephens, and his companion, the English topographical artist Frederick Catherwood, which revealed the full splendor of a vanished tropical civilization to the world.

Stephens and Catherwood were the first since Bishop Landa to assign the ruined 'cities' which they encountered to the actual inhabitants of the country – to the Maya Indians rather than to the peripatetic Israelites, Welshmen, Tartars, and so forth favored by other 'authorities' – but they had no way of even roughly guessing at their age. It was not until the Maya calendrical script had been studied by Ernst Förstemann, the State Librarian of Saxony, and others, and the Maya inscriptions magnificently published by the Englishman Alfred P. Maudslay at the close of the nineteenth century, that a real breakthrough was achieved in Maya chronology. In addition, large-scale excavations in Maya sites were begun at this time by the Peabody Museum of Harvard, to be followed by the Carnegie Institution of Washington, Tulane University, the University of Pennsylvania, and the Institute of Anthropology and History in Mexico.

The dating of the ancient Maya civilization now rests on four lines of evidence: 'dirt' archaeology itself, particularly the stratification of cultural materials like pottery; radiocarbon dating, in use since 1950; native historical traditions passed on to us by post-Conquest writers but bearing on the late pre-Conquest period; and the correct correlation of the Maya and Christian calendars.

The correlation problem is an unbelievably complex and still controversial topic which demands a few words of explanation. The Maya Long Count, which will be explained in greater detail in Chapters 3 and 9, is an absolute, day-to-day calendar which has run like some great clock from a point in the mythical past. Long Count dates began to be inscribed in 36 BC on present evidence and subsequently, during the Classic period, all over the ancient cities of the Central and Northern Areas. By the time of the Conquest, however, they were expressed in a very abbreviated and somewhat equivocal form. Now, it is explicitly stated in the native chronicles (the so-called Books of Chilam Balam) that the Spanish foundation of Mérida, capital city of Yucatán, which in our calendar took place in January 1542, also fell shortly after the close of a specified period of the truncated Long Count. Bishop Landa, an impeccable source, tells us that a certain date in a more primitive Maya system, the 52-year Calendar Round, fell on 16 July 1553 in the Julian calendar. All attempts to fit the Maya calendar to the Christian must take these two statements into account.

It so happens that there are only two correlations which meet these requirements as well as those of 'dirt' archaeology. These are the 11.16 or Thompson correlation, and the 12.9 or Spinden correlation, which would make all Maya dates 260 years earlier than does the former. Which of these is correct? The ancient Maya spanned the doorways of their temples with sapodilla wood beams, and these have not only survived but can be dated by 66 the radiocarbon process. A very long series of such samples has been run by the University of Pennsylvania, giving overwhelming support to the Thompson correlation. Most Mayanists have given sighs of relief, for any other chronology would play havoc with what we now think we know about the development of Maya culture over two millennia. Even further, any displacement in the dating of the Maya Classic period would disrupt the entire field of Mesoamerican research, for ultimately all archaeological chronologies in this part of the world are cross-tied with the Maya Long Count. Further details on the Maya-Christian correlation will be given in Chapter 9, for it bears directly on what we now know about ancient Maya astronomy.

As it now stands, the cultural sequence in the Maya area runs something like this. The earliest occupation of both highlands and lowlands was during the Early Hunters period, beginning by at least 13,000 years ago, and ending with the close of the Pleistocene, or Ice Age, about 7500 BC. Before 2000 BC there were simple horticulturalists, hunters, and farmers following a way of life called 'Archaic,' far better known for the upland peoples of Mexico. During the Preclassic (or Formative) period, between 2000 BC and AD 250, village-farming became firmly established in all three areas, marking the first really intensive settlement of the Maya land. More advanced cultural traits like pyramid-building, the construction of cities, and the inscribing of stone monuments are found by the terminal centuries of the Preclassic, and some have even wondered why this early florescence should not be included in the Classic which it presages. The spectacular Classic period, lasting from AD 250 to 900, is defined as that interval during which the lowland Maya were erecting stone monuments dated in the Long Count. A great and as yet unexplained cataclysm shook the lowlands during the ninth century, by the end of which the Classic cities had been largely abandoned, while the Northern and Southern Areas seem to have received the impact of invasions either by Mexicans, or more likely, by Mexicanized Maya. Thus was inaugurated the Post-Classic, which endured until the arrival of the bearded adventurers from across the seas.

Peoples and languages

While the cohesion of the Maya-speaking peoples is quite extraordinary for any time or place, the linguistic family called 'Mayan' contains a number of closely related but mutually unintelligible languages, the result of a long period of internal divergence. A Maya from Yucatán would have the same trouble understanding an Indian from highland Chiapas as an Englishman would a Dutchman. There have been several attempts to correlate the various Mayan tongues in larger groups; the most recent one by the linguists Terence Kaufman and Lyle Campbell is the one we adopt here. An ingenious method of vocabulary comparison developed by the late Maurice Swadesh has enabled linguists to suggest approximate dates for the splitting-off of these from the ancestral Mayan language and from each other. It should be stressed, however, that there are many uncertainties built into this methodology, above all the assumption that the rate of change or divergence in 'basic' vocabularies is constant throughout time and space. Nevertheless, even if these dates prove to be wrong in absolute terms, they would still be valid for the relative sequence of events.

Prior to 2000 BC, near the end of the Archaic period, there was a single Mayan language, Proto-Mayan, perhaps located in the western Guatemalan highlands. About this time, according to the linguistic scenario, Huaxtecan and Yucatecan split off from the parent body, with Huaxtec migrating up the Gulf Coast to northern Veracruz and Tamaulipas in Mexico, and Yucatecan occupying the Yucatán Peninsula. Of the Yucatecan languages, Yucatec today is the dominant tongue, spoken by townspeople and rural farmers alike, while Lacandón is represented by only a few hundred remaining natives – isolated Maya who wear their hair long and still make bows and arrows (now entirely directed at the tourist trade) – inhabiting the Chiapas rain forest, or what is left of it, southwest of the Usumacinta. The Lacandón

Key:
- **Huastecan**
- **Cholan**
- **Tzeltalan**
- **Chujean**
- **Kanjobalan**
- **Motozintlec**
- **Mamean**
- **Quichean**
- **Kekchian**
- **Yucatecan**

YUCATEC

NAHUATL

CHONTAL

CHOL

ZOQUE

TZELTAL

LACANDON

ITZA

TZOTZIL

MOPAN

TOJOLABAL

CHUJ

JACALTEC KANJOBAL

MOTOZINTLEC

IXIL

KEKCHI

CHICOMUCELTEC

AGUATEPEC

MAM

USPANTEC

QUICHE

POKONCHI

JICAQUE

TAPACHULTEPEC

PIPIL

CHORTI

UXHIQUEL

POKOMAM

LENCA

TZUTUHIL

PIPIL

XINCA

PIPIL

LENCA

6 Present-day distribution of languages in the Maya area.

appear to be pathetic survivors of a larger group which began diverging from Yucatec after the Classic Maya collapse, but which was probably always marginal to the more major tribes.

The parent body then split into two groups, a Western and an Eastern Division. In the Western group, the ancestral Cholan-Tzeltalan moved down into the Central Area, where they split into Cholan and Tzeltalan about AD 0. The subsequent history of the Tzeltalans is fairly well known from linguistics and archaeology, for they seem to have left the Central Area by AD 400 and returned to the highlands, pioneering the settlement of the mountain valleys around San Cristóbal de las Casas, Chiapas. There many thousands of their descendants, the Tzotzil and Tzeltal, maintain unchanged the old Maya patterns of life. Of the Cholans, who played a major role in the Maya story, we will see more later. Other Western language groups include the little known Kanjobal, Tojolabal, Motozintlec, and Chuj, which stayed close to the parental homeland and which seem to have had little to do with the main developmental line of Preclassic and Classic Maya civilization.

The Eastern Division includes the Mamean group of languages; Mam itself is a rather archaic tongue which has spilled down to the Pacific coastal plain in relatively late times. Another Mamean language is spoken by the Ixil, a very conservative Maya group centered on the ancient town of Nebaj; they have been the principal target of a particularly bloody repression within the past decade or more. Much of the late pre-Conquest history of the Southern Area concerns the powerful Quiché and Cakchiquel of the Eastern Division. They and their relatives, the Tzutuhil, who live in villages along the shores of the volcano-girt Lake Atitlán, speak languages which only 1,000 years ago were one, Quichean. Since the Spanish Conquest, a more dominant role has been taken by the Kekchi, who have expanded from a center in the Alta Verapaz of Guatemala to colonize southern Belize and the once Cholan-speaking lowlands around Lake Izabal, Guatemala.

What, then, was the language recorded by the ancient Maya inscriptions and books? A glance at the linguistic map will show that the Yucatán Peninsula is occupied by Yucatec to the exclusion of all others, and there can be no quibbling that this was the speech of the Maya scribes of the Northern Area, including those who produced three of the four surviving codices. Yucatecan was probably spoken over much of Belize during the Classic, for Mopán in the southern part of the country belongs to this group, and phonetic writing on the walls of Naj Tunich cave, not far from the Belize border in Guatemala, is a sure indication of Yucatecan in use there during the Late Classic.

But much of the Central Area appears as a blank on the map, with the exception of those lands occupied by the Lacandón, by the surely recent Kekchi, and by the Yucatecan Itzá, who are known to have moved into the Petén from the north no earlier than the thirteenth century AD and probably a good deal later. The idea that the language of most of the inscriptions of the Central Area was Yucatecan has little to recommend it.

Some years ago the late Sir Eric Thompson proposed that the Central Area was inhabited by Cholan-speakers during the Classic period. From its

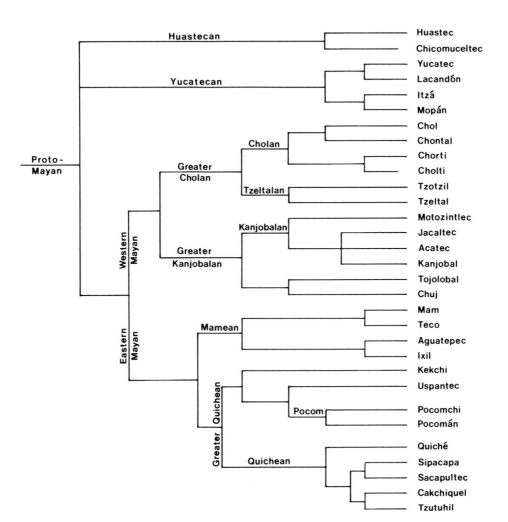

7 Classification and time depth of the Mayan languages.

present distribution alone – with Chontal and Chol in the low hills and plains in the northwest, and Chorti in the southeast – it seems certain that Cholan once predominated across a great arc extending right through the Central Area, at least to the Belize border, and we have some Spanish documents which confirm this point. It can hardly be coincidental that Chol is still spoken around the great Classic site of Palenque, and Chorti in the vicinity of Copán; phonetic readings of the Classic texts support this fact. Regardless of exactly where the boundary between Yucatecan and Cholan may have been, in cities which were adjacent to it there seems to have been a certain amount of bilingualism among royal scribes, with names and other words sometimes spelled in either language.

It seems inescapable, therefore, that much of the great civilization of the Central Area was the creation of the Cholan Maya, although during the Early Classic some Tzeltalans may have played a part, and the Yucatecans may well have dominated the land to the east of northern Petén. At any rate, hieroglyphic writing on stone appears on present evidence to have been in use only among Cholan and Yucatecan speakers.

Languages other than Mayan were found in isolated pockets, indicating either intrusions of peoples from foreign lands or remnant populations engulfed by the expansion of the Mayan tongues. The somewhat shadowy Pipil, whose speech is very close to Nahuatl, the official language of the Aztec Empire, were concentrated in western El Salvador, but there were other Pipil communities on the Pacific coast and in the Motagua valley of Guatemala. Some authorities think that they invaded the Maya country from Mexico during the Toltec disruptions of the Early Post-Classic, an idea which is not out of line with the lexicostatistic evidence on them, but they could have come earlier. Tiny populations of Zoquean speakers near the Pacific Coast in the Chiapas-Guatemala border region were probably vestiges of a once more-widespread distribution of the Mixe-Zoquean language family. Xincan, with no known affiliations, seems to have extended over all the eastern part of the Pacific coastal plain before the arrival of Mayan and Pipil, but the Xincan territory is an archaeological and ethnological blank. Nahuatl itself, as a great trading *lingua franca*, was spoken at the time of the Conquest at the port of Xicallanco on the Laguna de los Términos in southern Campeche.

Loan words from other languages do appear in Mayan, testifying to early contacts and cultural contributions. Those from the Mixe-Zoquean family of the Isthmus of Tehuantepec (locus of the very early Olmec civilization) include high-culture words such as *may, 'to count or divine', and *pom, 'copal incense,' and it has been suggested that Mixe-Zoquean was the tongue of the Olmec, of whom we shall speak more in the next chapter. The Zapotec of Oaxaca, who probably invented the essentials of the Mesoamerican calendar and who were surely the first to use hieroglyphic writing, contributed several names for the days in the 260-day count so fundamental to Maya thought. And in late times, during the Post-Classic epoch, many words, names, and titles were introduced into the Maya area from Nahua speech by Mexican or Mexicanized warlords.

2·The Earliest Maya

The Popol Vuh, the great epic of the Quiché Maya, recounts that the forefather gods, Tepeu and Gucumatz, brought forth the earth from a watery void, and endowed it with animals and plants. Anxious for praise and veneration after the creation, the divine progenitors fashioned man-like creatures from mud, but to mud they returned. Next a race of wooden figures appeared, but the mindless manikins were destroyed by the gods, to be replaced by men made from flesh. These, however, turned to wickedness and were annihilated as black rains fell and a great flood swept the earth. Finally true men, the ancestors of the Quiché, were created from maize dough.

Neither tradition nor archaeology have thrown much light on Maya origins. Tribal memories are weak, and a combination of luxuriant vegetation and unfavorable geological conditions has made the search for really early remains difficult. There are few caves and rock-shelters suitable for habitation by primitive hunters and gatherers, and open sites are virtually 8 impossible to detect, especially in the monsoon forests.

Early hunters

In spite of over six decades of research, there is little agreement among archaeologists as to when the first settlement of the New World took place. Some geologists have held that the initial colonization of this hemisphere must have been made by Siberian peoples crossing over the Bering Strait land bridge at about 14,000 years ago, during the last maximum of the Pleistocene when sea level was far lower than it is today. Yet long before this, boats must have been available to the peoples of Eurasia, for recent evidence shows that Australia, which was never connected to Asia by a land bridge, was settled as far back as 50,000 years ago. The presence or absence of a land bridge from Siberia to Alaska is thus not necessarily relevant to the problem, for the first Americans may well have taken a maritime route.

While radiocarbon dates from human occupations in Pennsylvania, the Valley of Mexico, the Andean highlands of Peru, and most recently Brazil suggest to some scholars that American Indians had colonized both North and South America by at least 20,000 years ago, many authorities still do not accept these dates as valid, preferring a post-14,000 year arrival. By the ninth millennium BC, the first Indians were already camped on the wind-swept Straits of Magellan, at the southern tip of South America, and so we may assume that primitive hunters had by then occupied all that part of the Americas that was worth inhabiting. Large areas of both continents were

8 Sites of the Early Hunters, Archaic, and Early and Middle Preclassic periods.

9,10 (*left*) A fluted point of obsidian of the Early Hunters period from San Rafael. L. $2\frac{1}{4}$ in. (5.7 cm). (*right*) Early Hunters period stone tools from Los Tapiales, Totonicapan, Guatemala. *1*, burin; *2*, scraper; *3*, obsidian uniface.

grassland over which roamed great herds of herbivores – mammoths, horses, camels, and giant bison.

In the western United States, Canada, and Alaska, where a number of camps belonging to this ancient epoch have been located, the earliest culture which has stood up to archaeological scrutiny is called Clovis, well dated to about 11,500–11,000 years ago. If we can rely upon the remains in several slaughtering sites in the American Southwest, the Clovis people lived mainly off mammoth-hunting, although in lean times they must have been content with more humble foods. These great elephants were killed with darts hurled from spear-throwers, fitted with finely chipped and 'fluted' points from the bases of which long channel flakes had been removed on one or both faces. Clovis points are widely distributed, from Alaska to Nova Scotia, down through Mexico and into Central America. They have even been found in Costa Rica and Panama.

One of the earliest known artifacts from Maya country is a small projectile point of obsidian, found by a picnicking schoolboy at San Rafael, in the pine-clad hills just west of Guatemala City. Even a neophyte would recognize this as a Clovis: fluting has been carried out on one side, the edges are ground down where the object was to be lashed to a dart or spear shaft. It is remarkably similar in outline to several such points which have been collected in Mexico, and to the smaller Clovis points of the United States.

9,10

In 1969 the archaeologists Ruth Gruhn and Alan Bryan discovered the highland Guatemalan site of Los Tapiales, which they excavated in 1973; it lies in an open meadow on the Continental Divide, in a cold, rainy, foggy environment, and probably represents a small, temporary camp of hunters located on an important pass. The stone tool industry is mainly basalt, and includes the base of a fluted point, bifaces, burins (for slotting bone), gravers, scrapers, and blades. Unfortunately no bone material has survived, but the site did produce radiocarbon dates extending back to 8760 BC.

The kind of game that these ancient people may have hunted may be revealed by a butchering site on the outskirts of the highland town of Huehuetenango, first investigated in 1977 by Herbert Alexander. This was located on or near the edge of a large, Pleistocene lake. Limited excavations have turned up the bones of at least three mastodons and one or more horses. Butchering marks are frequent on the bones, and four stone tools used in the process were found *in situ*, comprising a granite chopper and three unifacially worked tools.

The difficulties of prospecting for stone tools of the Early Hunters period in the Maya lowlands have already been mentioned. One of the few areas favorable for this kind of search is northern Belize, where there are extensive inland areas of low, eroded, sandy ridges with widely scattered pine cover. There, the Belize Archaic Archaeological Project directed by Dr Richard S. MacNeish found four different sites of what he calls the Lowe-Ha Phase, perhaps to be dated on typological grounds to 9000–7500 BC. These were the campsites of nomadic microbands; although little bone has survived in this acid environment, projectile points similar to fluted examples from Panama and Ecuador show that they hunted, and snub-nosed scrapers and sidescrapers testify to skin-working. Bifacial stone choppers found at Lowe-Ha sites may have been used in butchering and general food preparation.

Further north, in Yucatán, a Mexican project has discovered an Early Hunters period occupation with bones from extinct animals including wild horses in a corner of Loltún Cave, an enormous cavern complex utilized by the Maya for millennia.

Archaic collectors and cultivators

By about 7000 BC, the ice sheets which had covered much of North America in the higher latitudes were in full retreat, and during the next 5,500 years the climate of the world was everywhere warmer than it is today. In Europe, this interval has been called the 'Climatic Optimum,' but in many parts of the New World conditions were by no means so favorable, least of all for hunters. A fatal combination of hot, dry weather, which turned grasslands into desert, and over-hunting by man had finished off the big game. In upland Mexico, the Indians were diverted to another way of life, based on an intensified collection of the seeds and roots of wild plants, and upon the killing of smaller, more solitary animals. In their economy, in their semi-nomadic pattern of settlement, and even in the details of their tool-kits, the Mexican Indians of the Archaic period were only part of the 'Desert Culture,' extending at that time all the way from southern Oregon, through the Great Basin of the United States (where it survived into the nineteenth century), and down into southeastern Mexico.

It was in Mexico, however, and in this 'Desert Culture' context, that all the important plant foods of Mesoamerica – maize, beans, squashes, chile peppers, and many others – were first domesticated. It seems likely that the practice of plant cultivation must have reached the Maya area at some time during the Archaic period.

An earlier generation of scholars, particularly Sylvanus G. Morley, firmly believed that the Maya themselves had been the first to domesticate Indian corn (*Zea mays*). This idea was rooted on the often-revived premise that the wild progenitor of maize was *teosinte*, a common weed in cornfields of the western Guatemalan highlands. Whether this premise is correct is still a subject of acrimonious dispute among botanists. One school of thought, led by the late Paul C. Mangelsdorf, contended that *teosinte* was not the ancestor of maize but its offspring through hybridization with another grass, *Tripsacum*, and that the real progenitor was a tiny-cobbed wild species of corn with small, hard kernels that could be popped. Cobs of this sort have been found by MacNeish and his colleagues in dry caves in the Tehuacán Valley of Puebla, Mexico, in levels dating to about 5000 BC. According to Mangelsdorf, they represent ancestral maize; according to his opponents, they are probably *teosinte*. This complex problem has not yet been resolved.

Even if *teosinte*, which admittedly is extremely close botanically to maize, should prove to be the antecedent of domestic maize, this does not necessarily mean the domestication process took place in Guatemala, for it is widespread in southern and western Mexico as well. Nevertheless, Guatemala (which is no larger than the state of Ohio) has more distinct varieties of maize than can be found in all the United States put together, which suggests that this must have been a very old center for the evolution of this plant under the tutelage of man. Quite probably all the uplands, from southern Mexico through Chiapas and highland Guatemala, were involved in the processes leading to the modern races of this most productive of all food plants.

It will be recalled that, according to a linguistic method of dating called lexicostatistics, the Proto-Mayan language was already present in the highlands of western Guatemala, and probably Chiapas too, before 2000 BC, well within the Archaic span and before the most ancient pottery-using cultures, and it may have been they who brought maize and other cultigens to our area. Beyond the western border of the Maya area, the rock-shelter of Santa Marta in Chiapas may record traces of this *ur*-Maya group. Unfortunately, somewhat wetter conditions than those in the Tehuacán Valley have destroyed any perishables which may have been left by the ancient inhabitants of the shelter, but nut-cracking stones with pecked depressions, and pebble *manos* and *metates* tell us that seeds and other plant foods were well exploited. Other artifacts of the Santa Marta Complex, including chipped projectile points, choppers, and scrapers, strongly resemble those of the Tehuacán and Tamaulipas caves, and the whole assemblage, which is estimated to last from 7000 to 3500 BC, obviously belongs with the Mexican Archaic and more generally with the 'Desert Culture.'

Evidence for the Archaic period is generally poor in the highlands, but it is

8

II

11 Milling stones from Archaic sites in northern Belize.

improving in the Maya lowlands. We have some idea of what the Petén looked like then, based on analysis of windblown pollen recovered from a long core drilled into the bottom of Lake Petenxil, in the heart of the Central Area. It used to be thought that the savannahs which punctuate the tropical forest had resulted from an over-use of their fields by the Classic Maya, with a consequent invasion of unwanted grasses. This notion has now been turned upside-down. At 2000 BC, the Petén was like a parkland, with broad savannahs surrounded by copses of oak, the tropical forest being considerably more restricted than at present. The strong dominance of forest over grasslands has been shown to have begun only with the opening of the Classic period at about AD 250, reaching peak intensity after the Maya had fairly deserted the Petén.

The same pollen core has also provided an unexpected bit of information, namely that by 2000 BC a little maize was being grown near the margins of the lake, a good 1,000 years before the first pottery-using farmers are known for the region. Who were these people? If we accept the word of the linguists, they could have been the Yucatec on their trek north to Yucatán from the Maya homeland, but since their sites have not been located this is mere speculation. While some African peoples raise their crops in tropical grasslands, it is unlikely that the pioneer Maya, lacking metal tools, could have tilled the savannahs. More plausibly, they would have colonized patches of tropical forest which offered good soils and the possibility of clearing by the slash-and-burn method, avoiding the open country as assiduously as did the early Neolithic farmers of Europe.

In 1980, Richard S. MacNeish of the R. S. Peabody Foundation began a three-year investigation of the Archaic or Preceramic occupation of Belize. With his long experience in uncovering the early, incipient agricultural prehistory of highland and northeast Mexico, MacNeish was in a good position to recognize similar sequences in the Maya lowlands, unlike the usual Maya archaeologist more familiar with Classic pyramids than with humble, chipped-stone artifacts. The result has been the establishment of a tentative Archaic sequence running from about 7500 BC until after 2000 BC, with a slowly increasing number of grinding tools related to the processing of seeds and other vegetal materials, and gradually expanding and perhaps seasonal dependence upon marine resources. Unfortunately, preservation of plant materials and faunal remains is poor in his Belize sites, so that the data on the introduction and use of domesticated plants are virtually non-existent. Nevertheless, the question of whether native populations, ancestral Maya or not, had occupied the lowlands prior to the beginning of the Preclassic has now been answered in the affirmative.

Early Preclassic villages

Really effective farming, in the sense that densely inhabited villages were to be found throughout the Maya area, was an innovation of the Preclassic period, which lasted from about 1800 BC to about AD 250. What brought it about? Although some scholars favor the theory that it was a major improvement in the productivity of the maize plant, the adoption of the *nixtamal* process, which enormously increased the nutritional value of corn, may have been of more significance. Whatever the underlying cause, villages made up of thatched-roof houses, in no way very different from those in use among the modern Maya peasantry, now dotted the land.

Still, the evidence shows that the advance to Preclassic life did not take place everywhere at the same time. As will be seen, the Maya lowlands were remarkably backward in this respect, for reasons that are as yet unclear. The crucial area for an understanding of the Early Preclassic in southeastern Mesoamerica is not the Petén or the Yucatán Peninsula, or even the Maya highlands, but the hot, humid Pacific littoral of Chiapas, Guatemala, and westernmost El Salvador, a region of winding rivers, fertile soils, and an extensive lagoon-estuary system just in back of the barrier beaches.

Research in this zone has focussed on the old Aztec province of Xoconochco (modern Soconusco), covering part of the coastal plain of Chiapas and adjacent Guatemala. There, sedentary villages were fore-shadowed by the Late Archaic Chantuto phase, radiocarbon-dated to 3000–2000 BC. Numerous shell middens located in the mangrove-lined estuaries seem to represent seasonal occupation by somewhat mobile, non-farming band groups which largely subsisted upon hunting, fishing, the netting of shrimp, and mollusks.

10 cm

The Early Preclassic begins in Soconusco about 1800 BC, and is marked by profound changes in settlement pattern, subsistence, technology, and even society. During this period, which lasted until about 1000 BC, settlements were located further inland, and consisted of real villages, occupied throughout the year. Significantly, they were placed next to a series of *bajos* – old stream channels or oxbow lakes – which flooded during the rainy season. As they dried up, fish became concentrated in these and could be easily taken; at the height of the dry season, as archaeologists John Clark and Michael Blake have noted, the *bajos* could have served as sunken fields for agriculture, as they retained enough moisture for a third corn crop to be raised in addition to the two that are normal for the Soconusco plain.

What crop or crops were being grown to support these developments? Maize cobs are found in Soconusco sites beginning about 1700 BC, but these are from small and not very productive ears; further, carbon pathway analysis of human skeletal material has shown that maize was not very important in the diet of these Early Preclassic villagers. Gareth Lowe, of the New World Archaeological Foundation, and myself once speculated that they might have been relying on manioc or cassava, an ancient root crop of the New World tropics, rather than maize, but the evidence for this remains elusive, and the case is unproven.

From a technological point of view, the most significant innovation was the invention or introduction of pottery, which appears at the beginning of the Barra phase at about 1800 BC. Although Barra ceramics may well be the oldest in Mesoamerica, they are of remarkable sophistication and beauty. They largely consist of thin-walled, neckless jars (called *tecomates* by archaeologists), the remainder comprising deep bowls. Vessel surfaces include monochromes, bichromes, and trichromes, and have been manipulated by the potter by grooving, incising, and modeling.

12

12 (*left*) Reconstructed Barra phase pottery, Pacific Coast of Chiapas, Mexico.

13 (*right*) Early Locona phase hollow figurine head, from San Carlos, coastal Chiapas. Ht 3½ in. (9 cm).

As Clark and Blake make clear, these are not mere cooking vessels; based on forms and decoration of gourd prototypes, they were more likely containers for liquids and foods used during rituals. Then how did they cook? Quantities of fire-cracked rock indicate that the technique was stone-boiling: rocks were heated, then dropped into water contained in water-proofed baskets.

Barra also marks the beginning of fired clay figurines in Mesoamerica, a tradition that was to continue throughout the Preclassic. These objects, generally female, were made by the thousands in many later Preclassic villages of both Mexico and the Maya area, and while nobody is exactly sure of their meaning, it is generally thought that they had something to do with the fertility of crops, in much the same way as did the Mother Goddess figurines of Neolithic and Bronze Age Europe.

Pottery becomes even more complex in the succeeding Locona phase (1700–1500 BC), with the addition of rocker-stamping (carried out with the edge of a shell, by 'walking' the edge of the shell in zigzags across the wet clay), and of striping with a pinkish-iridescent slip; and true cooking vessels make their first appearance. But more significant than these is the evidence for the first ranked societies in this part of the New World. Clusters of villages and communities were organized under a single polity, dominated by a large 'capital' village, which could have contained over 1,000 people. At one such 'capital,' excavators found the clay foundations of a very large, long house with apsidal ends; the floor area covered by its once-thatched roof would have been 122 sq. m (1313 sq. ft). This surely was a chiefly residence where public rituals were carried out, and perhaps occupied over several generations.

Social differentiation in Locona is also suggested by the burial of a child who had been covered with red pigment and who had a mica mirror on his forehead, and by figurines depicting enormously fat men, perhaps shaman-chiefs, seated on stools and wearing chest mirrors and sometimes animal masks.

The subsequent Ocós phase (1500–1400 BC), discovered by my wife and me in 1958, is in most respects a continuation of Locona, with the addition of a pottery decoration known as cord-marking, made by impressing the wet surface of the clay with a paddle wrapped in fine cotton twine – a technique unique in Mesoamerica, but common on the most ancient ceramics of east Asia and North America. Ocós figurines are highly sophisticated, many appearing to be almost human caricatures out of the imagination of Da Vinci, but some being anatomically perfect (but armless) representations of beautiful young women. After Ocós, the Soconusco story is one of powerful influence from the Early Preclassic Olmec civilization of the Mexican Gulf Coast, but that is another story.

Now, Early Preclassic sites with materials and settlement pattern very similar to the Soconusco cultures have been located all along the Pacific littoral of Guatemala as far as El Carmen in El Salvador. In stark contrast, in spite of decades of intensive search and excavation, no pottery-using, village culture on this time level has yet been uncovered anywhere in the Central and Northern Maya area, or, for that matter, on the level of the earliest known Olmec civilization of the Gulf Coast. This is one of the unexplained mysteries of Mesoamerican archaeology.

The Middle Preclassic expansion

If conditions before 1000 BC were less than optimum for the spread of effective village farming except for the Pacific littoral, in the following centuries the reverse must have been true. Heavy populations, all with pottery and probably most of them Maya-speaking, began to establish themselves in both highlands and lowlands during the Middle Preclassic period, which lasted until about 300 BC. In only one instance (Nakbé) do we have remains suggesting that these were anything more than simple peasants: there was no writing, little that could be called architecture, and hardly any development of art. In fact, nothing but a rapidly mounting population would make us think that the Maya in this period were much different from their immediate ancestors.

There was, however, something very different that had been taking place in Mexico, in the hot coastal plain of southern Veracruz and adjacent Tabasco. This was the developing Olmec civilization, which began in the Early Preclassic, reached its peak toward the end of the Middle Preclassic, and then collapsed as suddenly as did the Maya at a much later time. So far, the oldest known Olmec site is San Lorenzo, lying near a branch of the Coatzacoalcos River in Veracruz. Excavated by a Yale expedition between 1966 and 1969, fully developed Olmec culture, represented typically by gigantic basalt sculptures fashioned in a distinctive style, proved to date back

14

14 (*opposite*) Monument 52 at San Lorenzo, Veracruz, an Olmec were-jaguar deity of the San Lorenzo phase (1200–900 BC). Early Preclassic period.

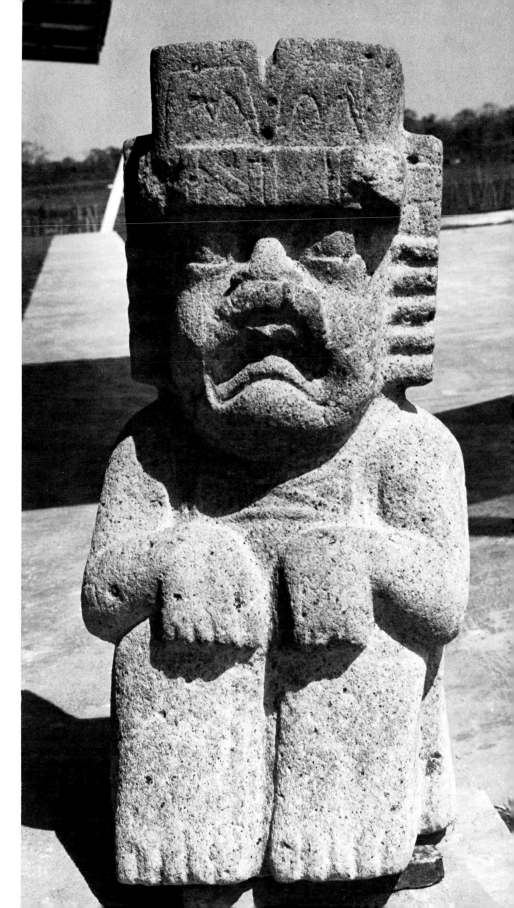

to 1400 BC. By 1000 BC, San Lorenzo had been destroyed by an unknown hand, but during the four centuries of its *floruit*, Olmec influence emanating from this area was to be found throughout Mesoamerica, with the curious exception of the Maya domain – perhaps because there were few Maya populations at that time sufficiently large to have interested the expanding Olmec.

During the Middle Preclassic, following the demise of San Lorenzo, the great Olmec center was La Venta, situated on an island in the midst of the swampy wastes of the lower Tonalá River, and dominated by a 100-ft-high (30 m) mound of clay. Elaborate tombs and spectacular offerings of jade and serpentine figurines were concealed by various constructions, both there and at other Olmec sites. The Olmec art style was centered upon the representations of creatures which combined the features of a snarling jaguar with those of a weeping human infant; among these were-jaguars almost surely was a rain god, one of the first recognizable deities of the Mesoamerican pantheon. From the unity of the art style, from the size and beauty of the sculptured monuments, and from the massive scale of the public architecture, there can be no doubt that there was a powerful Olmec state on the Gulf Coast which even at this early time was able to command enormous resources both in manpower and in materials.

More important to the study of the Maya, there are also good reasons to believe that it was the Olmec who devised the elaborate Long Count calendar, and the Olmec – or, more likely, the Zapotec of Oaxaca – who invented writing. Whether or not one thinks of the Olmec as the 'mother culture' of Mesoamerica, the fact is that many other civilizations, including the Maya, were ultimately dependent on the Olmec achievement. This is especially true during the Middle Preclassic, when lesser peasant cultures away from the Gulf Coast were acquiring traits which had filtered to them from their more advanced neighbors, just as in ancient Europe barbarian peoples in the west and north eventually had the benefits of the achievements of the contemporaneous Bronze Age civilizations of the Near East.

One of the greatest of all archaeological sites in the New World is Kaminaljuyú, on the western margins of Guatemala City in a broad, fertile valley lying athwart the Continental Divide. Although it consisted of several hundred great temple mounds in Maudslay's day, all but a handful have been swallowed up by the rapidly expanding slums and real estate developments of the capital. Rescue operations by the Carnegie Institution of Washington and Pennsylvania State University have shown that whereas part of the site was constructed during the Early Classic, the great majority of the mounds were definitely Preclassic. The loss to science through the depredations of brickyards and bulldozers has been incalculable.

It has been no easy task, under these circumstances, to work out an archaeological succession for Kaminaljuyú, but the oldest culture is probably Arévalo, for which we have little more than some sherds from *tecomates* and red-slipped bowls. This is followed by Las Charcas, which marks a major occupation of the Valley of Guatemala, for Las Charcas remains are scattered widely. Its stratigraphic position underneath deposits of the Late Preclassic,

15 (*opposite*) A Middle Preclassic pottery figurine of a seated woman, from the Las Charcas culture site of Copolchí. Ht *c.* 4 in. (10 cm).

16 Pottery vessels of the Las Charcas culture (Middle Preclassic period). *a*, *c*, interiors of red-on-white bowls; *b*, grey-brown bowl with modeled decoration. *a*, 12 in. (30.5 cm) diam.; *b*, *c*, to scale.

backed up by a number of slightly contradictory radiocarbon dates, suggests that this village culture falls toward the end of the Middle Preclassic, around the fifth or fourth century BC.

The best-preserved Las Charcas remains come from a series of bottle-shaped pits which had been cut in ancient times down through the topsoil into the underlying volcanic ash. No one has a firm idea of the purpose of these excavations. Perhaps some may have been cooking pits, and it is entirely possible that, as among the historic Hidatsa Indians of the Great Plains, others may have been for the storage of maize and beans, but surely their final use was as refuse containers. In them have been found carbonized avocado seeds, maize cobs, and remnants of textiles, basketry and probably mats, and rope fragments. The magnificent Las Charcas white ware, manufactured from a kaolin-like clay, is extremely sophisticated, with designs in red showing spider monkeys with upraised arms, grotesque dragon masks, and other more abstract motifs. Las Charcas figurines are predominantly female, but with a liveliness of concept seldom found elsewhere.

In the Maya lowlands, both in the Central and in the Northern Areas, we now have for the first time substantial evidence for a Maya population. Presumably, prior to that time, the lowland forests and savannahs contained only small groups of preceramic hunters and gathers of unknown tongue, but in lieu of solid archaeological evidence, that is pure speculation.

One of the oldest Middle Preclassic cultures in the lowlands is the little-known Xe phase of the western Petén, which appears in deep levels at the site of Altar de Sacrificios and at Seibal, and may represent some kind of intrusion from the highlands via the Lacantún drainage system. While on the one hand Xe ceramics are related to coeval hard, white pottery of Chiapas, there are ties with the Olmec of the Gulf Coast, for at Seibal Professor Gordon Willey and his Harvard group found a cache of jade celts and a jade perforating instrument of probable La Venta manufacture.

The spread of Maya-speakers in the Petén, Belize, and the Northern Maya area is almost surely to be associated with the adoption of red and mottled orange ceramics, the earliest manifestation of which seems to be in the Swasey/Bladen phase, at the site of Cuello in northern Belize; its excavator, Professor Norman Hammond, once assigned it to the Early Preclassic, but recent radiocarbon evidence places it at about 1000–700 BC. In Swasey deposits there have been preserved tiny cobs of pop corn, and root crops such as native yam (*Dioscorea*), cocoyam (*Xanthosoma*), and possibly manioc. There is also some evidence of architectural beginnings, with plastered platforms which once supported perishable superstructures.

Swasey/Bladen leads directly into the Mamóm culture, dated from 700 to about 400 BC. Mamóm is spread over almost of the Maya lowlands, and looks like a simple village culture, since until recently there were no real examples of public architecture on the scale of La Venta, for instance. However, the special conditions of excavation in the Petén must be considered. The lowland Maya almost always built their temples over older ones, so that in the course of centuries the earliest constructions would eventually come to be deeply buried within the towering accretions of Classic period rubble and plaster. Consequently, to prospect for Mamóm temples in one of the larger sites would be extremely costly in time and labor.

The recent discoveries by Richard Hansen of the University of California, Los Angeles, at the northern Petén site of Nakbé (to be further considered in the next chapter) have drastically changed our minds about Mamóm temple architecture. At first no more than a large Middle Preclassic village, by 750 BC, Nakbé had begun to look like a city, with buildings and platforms as high as 59 ft (18 m) covering up the old village structures. While these lack the spectacular mask-panels that were to be a hallmark of this and other cities in the Late Preclassic, the Nakbé temples testify that the lowland Maya had begun to emerge at even this early date from simple peasant life to a more complex society.

Mamóm pottery is quite simple when compared with Las Charcas to which it seems related. The commonest wares are red and orange-red monochromes, with polychrome decoration absent. Usually the only embellishment is simple incising on the inside of bowls, or daubing of necked jars with red blobs. The figurine cult, if such it may be called, is present in Mamóm, with a wide range of stylistic treatment carried out by punching and with applied strips of clay. At Tikal, a cache of Mamóm ceramics was discovered in a sealed *chultun*. This is a bottle-shaped chamber below the plaza floor, quite comparable in shape and perhaps in use to those of Las

Charcas. *Chultunob* are ubiquitous in sites of the Central and Northern Areas, cut down into the limestone marl from the surface. We know that by the Classic, they were used as cisterns in the Puuc region, and in the Central Area for burials and perhaps sweat baths. Initially, they could have been utilized as sources of the fine *sascab* lime employed in construction by Maya architects, but their use as storage pits (perhaps for the fruit of the breadnut tree, as suggested by Dennis Puleston) should not be overlooked. However, they are often so damp that stored food may have rotted. Whatever the answer to the '*chultun* mystery,' they are as old as the Mamóm phase.

In the southeastern corner of the Central Area, the pioneers who first settled in the rich valley surrounding the ancient city of Copán had other roots. Towards the end of the Early Preclassic, village cultures all along the Pacific littoral as far as El Salvador had become 'Olmec-ized,' a tradition that was to continue into the Middle Preclassic, and that was to be manifested in carved ceramics of Olmec type and even in Olmec stone monuments. This Olmec-like wave even penetrated the Copán Valley, during the Middle Preclassic Uir phase (900–400 BC), with the sudden appearance of pottery bowls incised and carved with such Olmec motifs as the paw-wing and the so-called 'flame eyebrows.' In a deep layer of an outlying suburb of the Classic city, Professor William Fash discovered a Uir phase burial accompanied by Olmecoid ceramics, 9 polished stone celts, and over 300 drilled jade objects. Although the rest of the Maya lowlands seems to have been of little interest to the Olmec peoples, the Copán area definitely was.

There is still a great deal to understand about the Middle Preclassic, the base on which the flowering of Maya culture took place. Certainly it was during this period when the Maya area became truly 'Maya.' But Maya civilization as we know it – the vaulted masonry architecture, the naturalistic painting and relief style, the Long Count calendar and writing – had not even begun to germinate during this epoch.

3·The Rise of Maya Civilization

It is a long step from the village cultures that we have thus far been considering to the awe-inspiring achievements of the Classic Maya, but by no means an impossible one. The all-important questions are, what happened during the intervening time covered by the Late Preclassic period, and how did those traits that are considered as typical of the Classic Maya actually develop?

There have been a number of contradictory theories to account for the rise of Maya civilization. One of the most persistent holds that the previously undistinguished Maya came under the influence of travelers from shores as distant as the China coast; as a matter of interest to the lay public, it should be categorically emphasized that *no* objects manufactured in any part of the Old World have been identified in any Maya site, and that ever since the days of Stephens and Catherwood few theories involving trans-Pacific or trans-Atlantic contact have survived scientific scrutiny.

The possibility of some trans-Pacific influence on Mesoamerican cultures cannot, however, be so easily dismissed. Its most consistent proponent has been Professor David Kelley of the University of Calgary, who has long pointed out that within the twenty named days of the 260-day calendar so fundamental to Mesoamericans (see below) is a sequence of animals that can be matched in similar sequence within the lunar zodiacs of many East and Southeast-Asian civilizations. To Kelley, this resemblance is far too close to be merely coincidental. Furthermore, Asian and Mesoamerican cosmological systems, which emphasize a quadripartite universe of four cardinal points associated with specific colors, plants, animals, and even gods, are amazingly similar. Both Asian and Mesoamerican religions see a rabbit on the face of the full moon (whereas we see a 'Man in the Moon'), and they also associate this luminary with a woman weaving at a loom.

Even more extraordinary, as the historian of science Dr Joseph Needham reminds us, Chinese astronomers of the Han Dynasty as well as the ancient Maya used exactly the same complex calculations to give warning about the likelihood of lunar and solar eclipses. These data would suggest that there was direct contact across the Pacific. As oriental seafaring was always on a far higher technological plane than anything ever known in the prehispanic New World, it is possible that Asian intellectuals may have established some sort of contact with their Mesoamerican counterparts by the end of the Preclassic.

Lest this be thought to be idle speculation along the lines of the lunatic fringe books so common in this field, let me point out one further piece of

17 Sites of the Late Preclassic period. Underlined sites have giant architectural masks.

evidence. Dr Paul Tolstoy of the University of Montreal has made a meticulous study of the occurrence of the techniques and tools utilized in the manufacture of bark paper around the Pacific basin. It is his well-founded conclusion that this technology, known in ancient China, Southeast Asia and Indonesia, as well as in Mesoamerica, was diffused from eastern Indonesia to Mesoamerica at a very early date. The main use of such paper in Mesoamerica was in the production of screen fold books to record ritual, calendrical, and astronomical information. It is not unreasonable to suppose that it was through the medium of such books, which are still in use by Indonesian people like the Batak, that an intellectual exchange took place.

This by no means implies that the Maya – or any other Mesoamerican civilization – were merely derivative from Old World prototypes. What it does suggest is that at a few times in their early history, the Maya may have been receptive to some important ideas originating in the Eastern Hemisphere.

Another school of thought holds that, because of the supposedly low agricultural potential of the Petén and Yucatán, civilization was introduced to the lowlands from an outside area with a more favorable ecology. There are others who claim that this potential has been gravely underrated, and that Maya culture as it is known for the Classic period is completely *sui generis*, with no trace of outside influence. Needless to say, both of these points of view are overstated, and both are at least partly wrong. The fact is that the Maya of both highlands and lowlands have never been isolated from the rest of Mesoamerica, and that Mexican influences have sporadically guided the course of Maya cultural history since very early times, as we shall see in this and subsequent chapters. It is also increasingly apparent that the reverse was also the case: strong Maya influence can be detected in central Mexico and the Gulf Coast of Veracruz, particularly during the last phase of the Classic.

How are we to define the word 'civilization'? How do the civilized differ from the barbaric? Archaeologists have usually dodged this question by offering lists of traits which they think to be important. Cities are one criterion. The late V. G. Childe thought that writing should be another, but the obviously advanced Inca of Peru were completely illiterate. Civilization, in fact, is different in degree rather than in kind from what precedes it, but has certainly been achieved by the time that state institutions, large-scale public works, temple buildings, and widespread, unified art styles have appeared. With few exceptions, the complex state apparatus demands some form of records, and writing has usually been the answer: so has the invention of a more-or-less accurate means of keeping time.

Yet all civilizations are in themselves unique. The Classic Maya of the lowlands had a very elaborate calendar; writing; temple-pyramids and palaces of limestone masonry with vaulted rooms; architectural layouts emphasizing buildings arranged around plazas with rows of stone stelae lined up before some; polychrome pottery; and a very sophisticated art style expressed in bas-reliefs and in wall paintings. These traits are now known to have been developed in the Late Preclassic (300 BC–AD 250) period.

18 Schematic representation of the 260-day count.

The birth of the calendar

Some system of recording time is essential to all higher cultures – to fix critical events in the lives of the persons ruling the state, to guide the agricultural and ceremonial year, and to record celestial motions. The Calendar Round of 52 years was present among all the Mesoamericans, including the Maya, and is presumably of very great age. It consists of two permutating cycles. One is of 260 days, representing the intermeshing of a sequence of the numbers 1 through 13 with twenty named days. Among the Maya, the 260-day count (sometimes called by the *ersatz* term *tzolkin*) began with 1 Imix, followed 2 Ik, 3 Akbal, 4 Kan, until 13 Ben had been reached; the day following was Ix, with the coefficient 1 again, leading to 2 Men, and so on. The last day of the 260-day cycle would be 13 Ahau, and it would repeat once again commencing with 1 Imix. How such a period of time even came into being remains an enigma, but the use to which it was put is clear. Every single day had its own omens and associations, and the inexorable march of the twenty days acted as a kind of perpetual fortune-telling machine guiding the destinies of the Maya and of all the peoples of Mexico. It still survives in unchanged form among some indigenous peoples in southern Mexico and the Maya highlands, under the care of calendar priests.

Meshing with the 260-day count is a 'Vague Year' of 365 days, so called because the *actual* length of the solar year is about a quarter-day more, a circumstance that leads us to intercalate one day every four years to keep our calendar in march with the sun, but which was ignored by the Maya. Within

POP	UO	ZIP	ZOTZ	TZEC
XUL	YAXKIN	MOL	CHEN	YAX
ZAC	CEH	MAC	KANKIN	MUAN
PAX	KAYAB	CUMKU		UAYEB

19 Signs for the months in the 365-day count.

it, there were eighteen named 'months' of twenty days each, with a much-dreaded interval of five unlucky days added at the end. The Maya New Year started with 1 Pop, the next day being 2 Pop, etc. The final day of the month, however, carried not the coefficient 20, but a sign indicating the 'seating' of the month to follow, in line with the Maya philosophy that the influence of any particular span of time is felt *before* it actually begins and persists somewhat beyond its apparent termination.

20

From this it follows that a particular day in the 260-day count, such as 1 Kan, also had a position in the Vague Year, for instance 2 Pop. A day designated as 1 Kan 2 Pop could not return until 52 Vague Years (18,980 days) had passed. This is the Calendar Round, and it is the only annual time count possessed by the highland peoples of Mexico, one that obviously has its disadvantages where events taking place over a span of more than 52 years are concerned.

Although it is usually assumed to be 'Maya,' the Long Count was widely distributed in Classic and earlier times in the lowland country of Mesoamerica; but it was carried to its highest degree of refinement by the Maya of the Central Area. This is really another kind of permutation count, except that the cycles used are so large that, unlike the Calendar Round, any event within the span of historical time could be fixed without fear of ambiguity. Instead of taking the Vague Year as the basis for the Long Count, the Maya and other peoples employed the *tun*, a period of 360 days. The Long Count cycles are:

144

20 kins	1 uinal or 20 days
18 uinals	1 tun or 360 days
20 tuns	1 katun or 7,200 days
20 katuns	1 baktun or 144,000 days.

Long Count dates inscribed by the Maya on their monuments consist of the above cycles listed from top to bottom in descending order of magnitude, each with its numerical coefficient, and all to be added up so as to express the number of days elapsed since the end of the last Great Cycle, a period of 13 baktuns whose ending fell on the date 4 Ahau 8 Cumku. The starting point of the present Great Cycle corresponds, in the Thompson correlation, to 13 August 3114 BC (Gregorian calendar). Thus, a Long Count date conventionally written as 9.10.19.5.11 10 Chuen 4 Cumku would be:

9 baktuns	1,296,000 days
10 katuns	72,000 days
19 tuns	6,840 days
5 uinals	100 days
11 kins	11 days

c.f.143

or 1,374,951 days since the close of the last Great Cycle, reaching the Calendar Round position 10 Chuen 4 Cumku.

Something should also be said about the coefficients themselves. The Maya, along with a few other groups of the lowlands and the Zapotec and Mixtec of Oaxaca, had a number system of great simplicity, employing only two symbols: a dot with the value of 'one' and a horizontal bar for 'five.' Numerals up to four were expressed by dots only, six was a bar with a dot above, and ten two bars. Nineteen, the highest coefficient in calendrical use, took the form of four dots above three bars. The treatment of higher numbers, for which the 'nought' symbol (a stylized shell) was essential, will be discussed in Chapter 9.

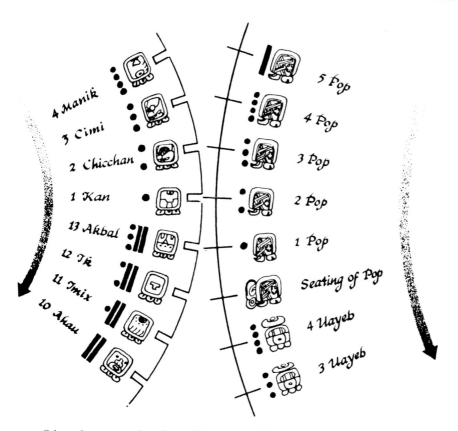

4 Manik

3 Cimi

2 Chicchan

1 Kan

13 Akbal

12 Ik

11 Imix

10 Ahau

5 Pop

4 Pop

3 Pop

2 Pop

1 Pop

Seating of Pop

4 Uayeb

3 Uayeb

20 Schematic representation of part of the 52-year Calendar Round.

It is generally agreed that the Long Count must have been set in motion long after the inception of the Calendar Round, but by just how many centuries or millennia is uncertain. Be that as it may, the oldest recorded Long Count dates fall within Baktun 7, and appear on monuments which lie *outside* the Maya area. At present, the most ancient seems to be Stela 2 at Chiapa de Corzo, a major ceremonial center which had been in existence since Early Preclassic times in the dry Grijalva Valley of central Chiapas: in a vertical column are carved the numerical coefficients [7.16.]3.2.13, followed by the day 6 Ben, the 'month' of the Vague Year being suppressed as in all these early inscriptions. This would correspond to 7 December 36 BC. Five years later, the famous Stela C at the Olmec site of Tres Zapotes in Veracruz was inscribed with the date 7.16.6.16.18 6 Eznab. On the Chiapa de Corzo monument, the initial coefficients are missing but reconstructable.

Now, the 16th katun of Baktun 7 would fall within the Late Preclassic, and we can be sure that unless these dates are to be counted forward from some base *other* than 13.0.0.0.0 4 Ahau 8 Cumku (as the end of the last Great Cycle is sometimes recorded), which seems improbable, then the 'Maya' calendar

17

had reached what was pretty much its final form by the first century BC among peoples who were under powerful Olmec influence and who may not even have been Maya.

Who might they have been? It will be remembered from Chapter 1 that the most likely candidate for the language of the Olmec was an early form of Mixe-Zoquean; languages belonging to this group are still spoken on the Isthmus of Tehuanatepec and in western Chiapas. Many scholars are now willing to ascribe the earliest Long Count monuments outside the Maya area proper to Mixe-Zoquean as well, and a recent discovery in southern Veracruz may provide confirmation. This is Stela 1 from La Mojarra, a magnificent monument inscribed with two Baktun 8 dates corresponding respectively to AD 143 and 156. These are accompanied by a text of about 400 signs, in a script which is now called 'Isthmian' (the famous 'Tuxtla Statuette,' also found in southern Veracruz, is in the same system, and dates to AD 162). While Isthmian writing is far from deciphered, it also appears to be Mixe-Zoquean.

From the Mixe-Zoqueans, then, writing and the calendar were spread along the Pacific Coast of Guatemala and into the Maya highlands, eventually reaching the developing states of the Petén forests and Yucatán.

Izapa and the Pacific Coast

Crucial to the problem of how higher culture came about among the Maya is the Izapan civilization, for it occupies a middle ground in time and in space between the Middle Preclassic Olmec and the Early Classic Maya. Its hallmark is an elaborate art style, found on monuments scattered over a wide zone from Tres Zapotes on the Veracruz coast, to the Pacific plain of Chiapas and Guatemala, and up into the Guatemala City area.

Izapa itself is a very large site made up of over eighty temple mounds of earthen construction faced with river cobbles, just east of Tapachula, Chiapas, in the moist, slightly hilly country about 20 miles inland from the Pacific shore. Whether it belongs with Mexico, culturally speaking, or with the Maya area is debatable, but the tongue anciently spoken here was not Maya but Tapachulteco, a vestigial member of the once more widespread Mixe-Zoquean group. While Izapa was founded as a ceremonial center as far back as Early Preclassic times and continued in use until the Early Classic, the bulk of the constructions and probably all of the many carved monuments belong to the Late Preclassic era. The Izapan art style consists in the main of large, ambitiously conceived but somewhat cluttered scenes carried out in bas-relief. Many of the activities shown are profane, such as a richly attired person decapitating a vanquished foe, but there are deities as well. One of these is a 'Long-lipped God,' part human and part fish (most likely shark), who apparently is the prototype of God GI of Palenque and thus the ancestral form of Chac, the ubiquitous Maya patron of lightning and rain. Another supernatural being present at Izapa has one leg ending in a serpent's body and head, and is thus the earliest known representation of God K, in Classic times the presiding deity of Maya ruling houses. But by far the leading figure in the crystallizing Maya pantheon as seen in Izapan monumental art, extending to the giant stucco masks of Late Preclassic temples in the Petén and Belize, is the monstrous form of Vucub Caquix, an anthropomorphic vulture who shows up in the Popol Vuh as the arrogant 'sun' of the creation preceding this one.

Certain recurrent elements must represent well-understood iconographic motifs, such as a U-shaped form between diagonal bars above the principal scene, perhaps an early occurrence of the sky-band so ubiquitous in Classic Maya art; the 'U' itself is most likely the prototype of the Maya glyph for the moon, and is found repeated many times on the same relief.   145*d*

Izapa, then, is a major center with some of the features which we consider more typical of the lowland Maya already in full flower – the stela-altar complex, the Long-lipped God who becomes transformed into the Maya rain god Chac, and a highly painterly, two-dimensional art style which emphasizes historical and mythic scenography with great attention to plumage and other costume details. Writing and the calendar are absent, but as one moves along the Pacific slopes east into Guatemala, one finds sites with inscriptions and Baktun 7 dates.

One of these Guatemalan stations is Abaj Takalik, situated in a lush, well-watered piedmont zone that in the days of the Conquest was a great producer of chocolate, and is now devoted to coffee. Like Izapa, it is made up of earthern mounds scattered about the site with little attention to formal arrangement. That the Olmec had once intruded here is apparent from a large boulder located less than a mile from the main group of mounds, carved in relief with a bearded were-jaguar in the purest Olmec style. Stela 1 from the site is purely Izapan but dateless. On the other hand, Stela 2, now somewhat damaged, bore on its carved face two richly attired Izapan figures with tall, plumed headdresses, facing each other across a vertical row of glyphs, below a cloud-like mass of volutes from which peers the face of a sky god. The topmost sign in the column is beyond doubt a very early form of the Introductory Glyph which in later Classic inscriptions stands at the head of a Long Count date. Just beneath is the baktun coefficient, which is pretty clearly the number 7. In recent decades, a University of California expedition has found a number of significant new monuments at Abaj Takalik, including a stela with two Baktun 8 dates, so that this site may have equaled Izapa in importance.

A more complete Baktun 7 inscription appears on Stela 1, the 'Herrera   21
Stela,' from El Baúl, a coffee plantation considerably to the southeast of Abaj Takalik in a region studded with Early Classic centers of the Cotzumalhuapa culture. This object has attracted fairly hot debate ever since it was found in 1923, some refusing to believe it even as old as the Classic period, and its very discoverer claiming it as Aztec! On the right, a profile figure is stiffly posed with spear in hand below a cloud-scroll; over the lower part of his face is some sort of covering, while to his headdress is attached a chin strap, a feature known to be extremely early in the Maya lowlands. In front of him are two vertical columns of glyphs, the right-hand of which consists of little more than empty cartouches which were probably meant to be painted. Let us,

21 Stela 1 from El Baúl, the earliest dated monument (AD 37) in the Maya area proper. On the right a figure in profile stands stiffly posed beneath a cloud-scroll.

however, consider the row on the extreme left, for this is almost surely the earliest dated monument in the Maya area proper. At the top is the coefficient 12 above a fleshless jaw, a Mexican form of the day sign Eb. Then there are four indecipherable signs, followed by a series of Long Count numbers which can be reconstructed as 7.19.15.7.12, reaching the Calendar Round position 12 Eb; in terms of our own calendar, this would be in the year AD 36, some 256 years prior to the first such date in the Maya lowlands, but significantly later than the precocious inscriptions of Chiapas and the Veracruz coast.

We cannot leave the Pacific coastal zone without mentioning a second sculptural tradition which reaches some degree of popularity both there and at Kaminaljuyú. This is expressed in large, crude, pot-bellied statues with puffy faces and lower jaws so inflated that they have been compared with the late Il Duce of Italy. At Monte Alto, not far from El Baúl, a group of these monstrous forms is placed in a row along with a colossal head carried out in the same style, and some believe that the entire pot-bellied complex is connected with the Olmec culture and precedes the Izapan. However, since Monte Alto is strewn with Late Preclassic pottery sherds, it is most likely that this was a subsidiary cult that coexisted with the Izapan Rain God, just as Egyptian and Graeco-Roman religious art flourished side-by-side in ancient Alexandria. But a cult to what deity? A fairly good case can be made out for this being none other than the Fat God, without known functions but ubiquitous among the peoples of Mexico and the Northern Maya Area in Classic times.

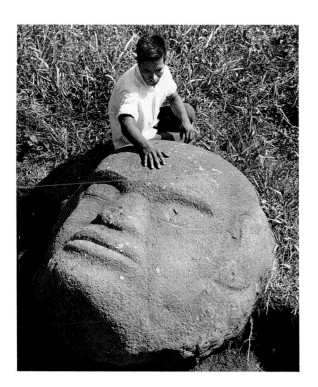

22 Monument 1 at Monte Alto, a site of the Late Preclassic period. Ht 4 ft 8 in. (1.42 m).

Kaminaljuyú and the Maya highlands

A Late Preclassic rival to Izapa in size and number of temple mounds and in the splendor of its carved monuments was Kaminaljuyú during the Miraflores phase. This, it will be recalled, was once a major ceremonial site on the western outskirts of Guatemala City. The majority of the approximately 200 mounds once to be found there were probably constructed by the Miraflores people, whose rulers must have possessed a formidable economic and political power over much of the Maya highlands at this time.

The excavation of two Miraflores tombs has thrown much light on the luxury to which these rulers were accustomed. Mound E-III-3 at Kaminaljuyú consists of several superimposed temple platforms, each a flat-topped, stepped pyramid fronted by a broad stairway; in its final form it reaches a height of more than 60 ft (18 m). In lieu of easily worked building stone, which was unavailable in the vicinity, these platforms were built from ordinary clay and basketloads of earth and household rubbish. Almost certainly the temples themselves were thatched-roof affairs supported by upright timbers. Apparently each successive building operation took place to house the remains of an exalted person, whose tomb was cut down from the top in a series of stepped rectangles of decreasing size into the earlier temple platform, and then covered over with a new floor of clay. The function of Maya pyramids as funerary monuments thus harks back to Preclassic times.

The corpse was wrapped in finery and covered from head to toe with

23

24

23 View of Kaminaljuyú, looking west, from a photograph taken by A. P. Maudslay. Most of the earthen mounds are temple substructures of the Miraflores culture.

cinnabar pigment, then laid on a wooden litter and lowered into the tomb. Both sacrificed adults and children accompanied the illustrious dead, together with offerings of an astonishing richness and profusion. In one tomb, over 300 objects of the most beautiful workmanship were placed with the body or above the timber roof, but ancient grave-robbers, probably acting after noticing the slump in the temple floor caused by the collapse of the underlying tomb, had filched from the corpse the jades which once covered the chest and head. Among the finery recovered were the remains of a mask or headdress of jade plaques perhaps once fixed to a background of wood, jade flares which once adorned the ear lobes of the honored dead, 25–27 bowls carved from chlorite-schist engraved with Miraflores scroll designs, and little carved bottles of soapstone and fuchsite.

Miraflores pottery vessels from E-III-3 and elsewhere belong to a ceramic tradition prevalent throughout southeastern Mesoamerica during the Late Preclassic horizon, from Izapa to El Salvador, and up into the Central and Northern Maya area, but are set off from this in their refinement and sophistication. Shapes have now become exuberant, with re-curved outlines, elaborate flanges on rims and bodies, and the appearance of vessel feet. Some of the most amusing examples of the potter's art are effigy vessels, a few of which show smiling old men. Painted stucco is often used to achieve effects in colors such as pink and green, unobtainable in fired slips. Most bowls and jars are embellished with engraved and carved scroll designs. A more peculiar

24 Plan of Tomb II, mound E-III-3, a burial of the Miraflores culture at Kaminaljuyú. *1*, jade beads; *2*, obsidian flake-blades; *3*, mica sheets; *4*, jade mosaic element; *5*, stuccoed gourds; *6*, pebbles; *7*, basalt implements; *8*, human teeth; *9*, jade mosaic mask or headdress; *10*, obsidian stones; *11*, pyrite-incrusted sherd; *12*, soapstone implement; *13*, bone objects, fish teeth, and quartz crystals; *14*, sting-ray spines; *15*, spatulate bone object. All other circular objects are pottery vessels.

Kaminaljuyú

25 A Late Preclassic effigy of grey-green chlorite schist from Tomb I, Mound E-III-3 (Miraflores culture) at Kaminaljuyú. Overall length $8\frac{1}{4}$ in. (21 cm).

26 A grey soapstone jar from Tomb I, Mound E-III-3 at Kaminaljuyú. Ht $3\frac{1}{2}$ in. (9.2 cm).

27 A fine-line incised bowl from Tomb I, Mound E-III-3 at Kaminaljuyú. W. 12 in. (30.5 cm).

28 A man wearing masks of Vucub Caquix is carved on this granite stela from Kaminaljuyú. Ht 6 ft (1.8 m).

kind of decoration which is virtually a marker for the Late Preclassic period in the Maya area is Usulután, believed to originate in El Salvador where it attains great popularity. On this widely traded ware, a resistant substance such as wax or thin clay was applied to bowls with a multiple-brush applicator; after smudging or darkening in a reducing fire, the material was removed to leave a design of wavy, parallel, yellowish lines on a darker orange or brown background.

As for stone carving on a large scale, it was once believed that the Miraflores people made only 'mushroom stones.' These peculiar objects, one of which was found in an E-III-3 tomb, are of unknown use. Some see vaguely phallic associations. Others, such as the late Stephan de Borhegyi, connect them with the cult of the hallucinogenic mushrooms still to this day prevalent in the Mexican highlands, and it is claimed that the mortars and pestles with which the stones are so often associated were used in the preparatory rites.

But we have much more to go by than that, thanks to the devastation of Kaminaljuyú by modern real-estate entrepreneurs. It now appears that there were Miraflores artists capable of creating sculpture on a large scale, in an Izapan style that can only be called the forerunner of the Classic Maya. Moreover, the elite of this valley were fully literate at a time when other Maya were perhaps just learning that writing existed. Two of these monuments were encountered by accident in a drainage ditch. One is a tall, granite stela
28 embellished with a striding figure wearing a series of grotesque masks of Izapan gods (the one over his face is the head of the bird-monster Vucub Caquix), and carrying a chipped flint of eccentric form in one hand. On either side of him are spiked clay incense burners exactly like those found in Miraflores excavations. The other is even more extraordinary. It must have
29 been of gigantic proportions before its deliberate breakage; the surviving fragments show that there were several Izapan gods, one bearded, surrounding a human figure with downpointing tridents in place of eyes, probably a precursor of a god who later appears at Tikal; he too, wields an eccentric flint. The glyphs associated with these figures may be their calendric names, for in ancient Mesoamerica, both gods and men were identified by the days on which they were born. A much longer text in several columns is incised below in a script which is otherwise unknown but which, in the opinion of Tatiana Proskouriakoff and others, may foreshadow Classic Maya writing, since there are strong similarities in form if not in specific characters. It cannot, however, yet be read.

Not only were stelae of major size carved by the Miraflores artisans, but also tenoned figures called 'silhouette sculptures,' which were perhaps originally meant to be stuck upright into temple and plaza floors; frog- or toad-effigy figures of all sizes; and many other forms. Once more, the pot-bellied figures are ubiquitous: did they represent a cult of the people, separate from the more aristocratic religion of the rulers? Or do they, as some believe, belong to an earlier horizon? Archaeology has unfortunately arrived on the scene too late to answer this.

The astonishing wealth of the Miraflores people, their artistic and

29 Broken Miraflores stela from Kaminaljuyú depicting Izapan gods (top) and a human figure in profile.

architectural capabilities, their obvious relation to the Classic Maya in matters of style, iconography, and script – all these things lead one to believe that the Izapan culture of the highlands must have had a good deal to do with the adoption of civilized life in the Central and Northern Areas. While the pre-eminence of Kaminaljuyú during the Late Preclassic period is plain to see, its star began to sink by the second and third centuries AD, and most of it was left in ruin at the close of the Late Preclassic. It was not until the Mexican invasions of the Early Classic that this great center regained its former splendor.

Elsewhere in the Guatemalan highlands, the French archaeologist Alain Ichon has excavated the mound site of La Lagunita, located in the Chixoy drainage some 25 miles northeast of the Quiché center of Chichicastenango. There he encountered a number of relief sculptures in a terminal Late Preclassic style related to the Izapan culture, but somewhat aberrant, including one representation of Vucub Caquix. There were four stone sarcophagi, one containing two superimposed human skeletons with a wealth of offerings, including jade, variously colored obsidian, and white flint, along with a pottery effigy of a terrifying deity with long nose and gaping mouth revealing a lolling tongue and huge fangs.

The Petén and the Maya lowlands

While the Maya highlands and Pacific Coast were experiencing an extraordinary cultural efflorescence in the Late Preclassic, the Central and Northern Areas were hardly slumbering. Within the boundless forests, the agricultural economy and society had advanced to such a degree that massive temple centers were already rising in jungle clearings. But it is clear that from the very beginning the people of the lowlands were taking a somewhat different course from that of their kinsmen to the south, and it is their unique qualities which so distinguish them in the Classic period which was soon to be inaugurated.

Although there are minor differences from region to region, a single widespread culture, Chicanel, dominated the Central and Northern Areas at this time. Usulután ware and vessels with widely everted lips, elaborate rim flanges, or complex outline are, as in the Southern Area, hallmarks for the period. Most pottery is legless, and confined to a simple black or red monochrome, with thick glossy slips that feel waxy to the touch. It is strange that in most known Chicanel sites, figurines are not found, from which it may be supposed that there was a change in popular cults.

The most unusual feature of Chicanel culture, however, is the high elaboration of architecture. It must be remembered that the Petén-Yucatán shelf is blessed with an inexhaustible supply of easily cut limestone, and with abundant flint for tools with which to work it. Moreover, the Maya of the lowlands had discovered as far back as Mamóm times that if limestone

30

30 Usulután ware bowl from Burial 85, Tikal (Chicanel culture). Diam. *c.* 7¾ in. (20 cm).

31 The north side of Pyramid E-VII-sub, Uaxactún, a Late Preclassic site belonging to the Chicanel culture. On top of this stucco-faced pyramid had once been a pole-and-thatch temple. Ht 26 ft 4 in. (8 m).

fragments were burnt, and the resulting powder mixed with water, a white plaster of great durability was obtained. And finally, they quickly realized the structural value of a concrete-like fill made from limestone rubble and marl.

With these resources at hand, the Maya temple architect was able to create some massive constructions at a very early date. At the great Petén sites of Uaxactún, Tikal, El Mirador, and Nakbé, deep excavations have shown that major pyramids, platforms, and courts were already taking shape by Chicanel times. There is general agreement, for instance, that the E-VII-sub pyramid 31 at Uaxactún, excavated by the Carnegie Institution of Washington in the 1930s, was built in the Chicanel phase; beautifully preserved by the overlay of later structures, this truncated temple platform is faced by brilliantly white plaster and rises in several tiers, each having the apron moldings which are so distinctive a feature of Maya architecture in the lowlands. On all four sides are centrally placed, inset stairways flanked by great monster masks which apparently represent the Jaguar God of the Underworld (the night sun), as well as sky-serpents. Postholes sunk into the floor show that the super-structure was a building of pole and thatch.

Although Group H at Uaxactún was discovered by Carnegie as long ago as 1935, it was only in 1985 that excavations under Juan Antonio Valdés of Guatemala's Institute of Anthropology and History revealed that its major constructions were almost entirely Late Preclassic, with hardly any Classic period overburden. The South Plaza, the focus of Valdés' research, is essentially a great platform supporting on the east a high, truncated pyramid (H-sub-3) with a central stairway; flanking it are two buildings with rooms which were once spanned by the corbel vault, or so-called 'false arch,' while three other buildings faced it on the west, all of them enclosing a small plaza.

Most of the South Plaza structures have huge, perfectly preserved masks and friezes formed of stucco over a stone core, and these were polychromed. On each side of the central stairway of H-sub-3 are two superimposed masks, each 8.7 ft (2.65 m) high. The iconography of the South Plaza is complex, with several deities represented, some of them with quite Olmecoid characteristics.

Even more advanced temples have been uncovered at Tikal, which lies only a half-day's walk south of Uaxactún. Two late Chicanel structures, for instance, had superstructures with masonry walls, and it is possible, though certainly not proved, that the rooms were corbel-vaulted. Some quite extraordinary paintings embellished the outer walls of one of these temples, showing human figures standing in a background of cloud-like scrolls, carried out by a sure hand in black, yellow, red, and pink. Another set of murals, this time in black on a red background, was found inside a late Chicanel burial chamber at Tikal. The subject matter comprises six richly attired figures, probably both human and divine. The two sets, which are thought to date from the last half of the first century BC, are pretty clearly in the Izapan style characteristic of Kaminaljuyú.

Some of the Late Preclassic tombs at Tikal prove that the Chicanel elite did not lag behind the nobles of Miraflores in wealth and honor. Burial 85, for instance, like all the others enclosed by platform substructures and covered by a primitive corbel vault, contained a single skeleton. Surprisingly, this individual lacked head and thigh bones, but from the richness of the goods placed with him it may be guessed that he must have perished in battle and been despoiled by his enemies, his mutilated body being later recovered by his subjects. The remains were carefully wrapped-up in textiles, and the bundle placed in an upright position. A small, greenstone mask with shell-inlaid eyes and teeth seems to have been sewn to the bundle to represent the head. A sting-ray spine, the symbol of self-sacrifice among the Maya, and a spondylus shell were added to the gruesome contents. Packed around the burial chamber were no less than twenty-six vessels of the late Chicanel period, one of which contained pine-wood charcoal dated by the radiocarbon process to AD 16 ± 131.

The towering achievements of the Classic Maya in building and maintaining their enormous centers have blinded us to the equally remarkable florescence of Late Preclassic Maya culture. Two sites in Belize have provided exciting new data shedding light on this phenomenon. The first is Cerros, a relatively compact site located on a small, narrow peninsula near the mouth of the New River, on the southern edge of Chetumal Bay. Excavations and mapping carried out by David A. Freidel of Southern Methodist University have shown that this Late Preclassic center, with four

32 A greenstone mask, with shell-inlaid teeth and eyes, from Burial 85, Tikal. Ht 5 in. (12.7 cm).

primary pyramidal structures along with a host of other buildings, was surrounded by a moat-like canal which may have been connected with raised agricultural fields. One such pyramid was a two-tiered temple platform; its central stairway was flanked by four elaborate plaster-sculpture masks. Freidel interprets this as an elaborate cosmological diagram involving four important gods, and its relationship to the huge platform masks found at Uaxactún and on early buildings at Tikal is obvious.

Far up the New River, a considerable distance to the southwest of Cerros, is the important site of Lamanai (known as 'Indian Church' on older maps of Belize), which has been excavated by David M. Pendergast of the Royal Ontario Museum during a series of field seasons beginning in 1974. Lamanai lies on a long lake formed by the river, and its 718 mapped structures are stretched out in strip form along its shore. There is even an ancient harbor in the northern part of the site, testifying to its entrepreneurial importance in the regulation of ancient Maya trade. While it was occupied from earliest

33 A reconstruction of the impressive Late Preclassic architecture at El Mirador, Guatemala.

times right into the post-Conquest period, much of its importance lies in the large, imposing, Late Preclassic temple-pyramids which usually underlie Early Classic constructions, including one with a plaster-work mask closely resembling those from Cerros.

But the full scope of this Late Preclassic achievement in the southern Maya lowlands has only come to light at the sites of Nakbé and El Mirador, located in the northernmost Petén in a region with extensive swamps or *bajos*. We have already seen that Nakbé had a precocious development of monumental architecture during the Mamóm phase of the Middle Preclassic. El Mirador, some 8 miles northwest of Nakbé and connected to it by a causeway which crosses the intervening *bajos*, has turned out to be the oldest Maya capital city, far in advance of Tikal, which it dwarfs by its size and lessens by its antiquity. The investigations and mapping carried out initially by Professors Bruce Dahlin and Ray Matheny, and later by Dr Richard Hansen, have shown that El Mirador is almost entirely of Late Preclassic (Chicanel) date; it was abandoned throughout the Early Classic, but there is a shoddy, Late Classic reoccupation which had little importance.

There are two groups of monumental construction, connected by a causeway, and in fact a whole network of causeways radiates out from El

Mirador across the surrounding swampy landscape. The East Group is dominated by the Danta pyramid and its associated platforms, which cover an area of 18 hectares; the pyramid and the structure upon which it sits reach a height of 230 ft (70 m), and thus with its smaller superstructures must comprise an overall bulk which may be the largest in Mesoamerica, if not the New World. The Tigre pyramid in the West Group is no less than 180 ft (55 m) high, with an estimated volume of 380,000 cubic meters.

As at Cerros, Lamanai, Uaxactún, and Tikal, gigantic stucco masks of deities flanked stairways at El Mirador; one excavated structure has huge masks of Vucub Caquix, the great bird deity typical of the Late Preclassic. Typical also of this intriguing period in Maya culture history is the 'triadic' pattern of architecture found here and at other similarly early lowland sites: this consists of a principal pyramid, plus two other ones which face each other, with all stairs leading from a central plaza. Richard Hansen suggests a mythological basis for the pattern, perhaps a triad of gods such as we find much later at the Classic city of Palenque.

The largest buildings at Nakbé were erected at the beginning of the Late Preclassic (*c.* 300 BC) over Middle Preclassic platforms. Thus far, Dr Hansen has uncovered no less than nine monumental architectural masks and panels,

34   including the largest yet known for the Maya – situated at the base of Structure 1, a vast relief of the Vucub Caquix bird over 16 ft (4.9 m) high and 36 ft (11 m) wide, completely polychromed. Nakbé also has a stela, reconstructed by the archaeologists from many fragments, which shows two important personages facing each other; details of costume link this relief in time and style to the Miraflores granite stela from Kaminaljuyú, which must have been exerting a potent influence on the lowlands during this era of nascent Maya civilization.

Such Late Preclassic splendor is found throughout the Petén-Yucatán peninsula wherever the spade has gone deep enough. Even in the seemingly less-favorable Northern Area, there are enormous constructions datable to this period, such as the great high mound at Yaxuná, a temple substructure having a ground plan of 197 by 427 ft (60 by 130 m). At the site of Edzná in north-central Campeche, research carried out by Ray Matheny has shown that the Late Preclassic occupants had constructed a massive hydraulic system, consisting of 13.75 miles (22 km) of canals radiating out in all directions from the city's center, and even a moat surrounding a kind of 'fortress'. The moat is obviously defensive, but Professor Matheny speculates that the canals could have been used to drain good agricultural land, to transport goods and people to the urban center, and to provide a habitat for game birds, fish, mollusks, and other food animals.

By the terminal Late Preclassic of the second and third centuries AD we are on the threshold of Classic Maya civilization. Temples arranged around plazas, construction with limestone and plaster, apron moldings and frontal stairways on pyramids, tomb building, and frescoes with naturalistic subjects – all had already taken shape by the end of the Late Preclassic. This brief epoch sees the intrusion of new ceramic traits which seem to have been first elaborated in El Salvador and later in Belize, the most important of these being the addition of hollow, breast-shaped supports to bowls, hour-glass-shaped pot-stands, and polychrome. Maya polychrome is distinguished by a brilliant range of colors applied over a glossy, translucent orange underslip, but wherever it was first invented it certainly was not native of the Petén region. Corbeling of rooms must have evolved from methods employed in the construction of tombs, and by AD 250 began to be in universal use at Petén
c.f. 56,76   sites. The principle is simple: above the springline of the walls, successive courses of stones were set in overlapping rows up to the vault summit, which was capped by flat stones. However, there is an inherent structural weakness, and the great thrust from above is taken up in Maya buildings by massive walls and by the strength of the rubble-cement fill. Nevertheless, once adopted it became the badge of Maya architecture in the lowlands, as opposed to the thatched or flat-beam roofs of Mexico.

The list is impressive, and one would think on the face of it that Maya civilization had emerged independently here in the lowlands, several centuries before the opening of the Classic era. But two items are missing or exceedingly rare: monuments with Long Count dates, and writing. These we know were present among the coeval Izapan centers of the highlands and Pacific Coast, and it is probable that they were derived from the even older

34 Giant stucco mask, Nakbé, Guatemala.

Olmec civilization of the Gulf Coast. The Izapan style was spread from outside into the Central and Northern areas – a broken carving from a terminal Late Preclassic level of the Tikal acropolis, the early Tikal frescoes, the Nakbé stela, and a human figure in relief on the walls of Loltún cave in Yucatán all testify to this – but literacy and a concern with recording dates did not become prevalent in the lowlands until the eve of the Classic period.

It is entirely possible that this apparent lack of interest in written and dated records in the lowlands persisted because the Late Preclassic cities of the area were basically 'acephalous', that is, they might not have been headed by a hereditary elite as they were to be in Classic times; we do know that the adoption of writing and the calendar in Mesoamerica goes hand in hand with the rise of elites. In this vein, it may be significant that archaeologists have thus far failed to find royal tombs or elite burials at El Mirador and Nakbé – or really outstanding ones at any other lowland site of the period, for that matter.

But towards the close of the Late Preclassic, writing had begun to appear sporadically, and it definitely celebrated the doings of great personages. A good example of this would be the greenstone pectoral at Dumbarton Oaks, said to be from Quintana Roo. A were-jaguar face on one side indicates that the object was originally Olmec; during the Late Preclassic, the reverse was delicately incised with the seated figure of a richly garbed ruler, facing four vertical columns of hieroglyphs. Next to the personage's shoulder is inscribed his name, almost surely to be read *Chan Muan*, 'Sky Owl.' The same glyph combination appears twice in the text, once following a sign now known to be a very early form of the verb 'to be seated.' Epigraphers conclude

35

35 Incised greenstone pendant, Collection Dumbarton Oaks, Washington, DC. Late Preclassic period.

that the pectoral reverse records the 'seating,' or accession to power, of the ruler in question.

By the time the Long Count calendar made its debut in the lowlands, at the opening of the Early Classic about AD 250, the life and times of the royal house had come to be the major preoccupation of the Maya state, and full Maya civilization had begun.

4·Classic Splendor: the Early Period

During a span of six centuries, from about AD 250 to 900, the Maya, particularly those of the Central Area, reached intellectual and artistic heights which no others in the New World, and few in the Old, could match at that time. The Classic period was a kind of Golden Age, not only for them but for the rest of the Mesoamerican peoples. Large populations, a flourishing economy, and widespread trade were typical of the Classic, but although it was once thought to have been a period of relative peace and tranquillity in comparison with what followed, that notion has in the main been disproved. It is an equally unfounded assumption that the Classic peoples were ruled by priests. On the contrary, we shall see that the ancient Maya were just as warlike and had as thoroughly secular a government as the supposedly more bloodthirsty states of the Post-Classic.

The Classic in fact can only be defined accurately as that span during which the lowland Maya were using the Long Count calendar on their monuments. In 1864, workmen engaged in digging a canal near Puerto Barrios, on the steamy Caribbean coast of Guatemala, came across a jade plaque which subsequently found its way to Leiden, Holland. The Leiden Plate, generally agreed to have been made at Tikal, has engraved on one face a richly bedecked Maya lord at his accession, trampling underfoot a sorry-looking captive, a theme repeated on so many Maya stelae of later times. On the other side is inscribed the Long Count date 8.14.3.1.12, corresponding to 17 September AD 320. The style of the glyphs and the costume and pose of the person depicted call to mind the Late Preclassic monuments of the highlands and Pacific Coast, but in this case the date is preceded by the typical Maya Introductory Glyph, and the bar-and-dot numbers are followed by the signs for baktun and lesser periods. Until recently the Leiden Plate was considered the most ancient object dated in Maya fashion, but now we have Stela 29 from Tikal, erected in 8.12.14.8.15 (AD 292).

The possibility that even earlier objects dated in the Maya system will some day be found in the Maya lowlands should be kept open, especially in the light of the Hauberg Stela, a miniature monument in a Seattle, Washington, private collection. This depicts a masked Maya lord in the act of a mystic blood-letting rite, and its very aberrant date (probably because of its antiquity) has been interpreted by the art historian Dr Linda Schele and the linguist John Justeson as a day in the year AD 199. This important relief would thus be intermediate in time between dated inscriptions of the Izapan culture and the dawn of Classic Maya civilization.

Thus, the lowland Maya had definitely received the Long Count by the

36 Sites of the Classic period.

37 The Leiden Plate, a jade plaque found in 1864, shows a Maya lord trampling a captive underfoot and, on the reverse side, carries the Long Count date 8.14.3.1.12, corresponding to a day in the year AD 320. Ht 8½ in. (21.6 cm).

close of the third century AD. From this event until the Classic downfall, we have a very closely dated archaeological sequence governed by the carving of stelae and other monuments, which themselves have been tied at Uaxactún and other sites with the construction of floors, building stages, and tombs. The Classic very conveniently divides itself into an Early and a Late period at about AD 600; however, this division is not merely an invention of the archaeologist, for not only did a profound upheaval take place in the Central Area at that time, but there are considerable cultural differences between the two halves.

Two things set off the Early from the Late Classic: firstly, the strong Izapan element still discernible in Maya culture, and secondly, the appearance in the middle part of the Early Classic of powerful waves of influence from the site of Teotihuacan in central Mexico. This city was founded at about the time of Christ in a small but fertile valley opening onto the northeast side of the Valley of Mexico itself. On the eve of its destruction at the hands of unknown peoples, at the end of the sixth century AD, it covered an area of over 8 square miles. Teotihuacan is noted for the regularity of its great avenues, for its Pyramids of the Sun and Moon, and for the delicacy and sophistication of the wall paintings which graced the walls of its luxurious palaces. So mighty was the city that it held dominion over most of Mexico in the Early Classic, as the center of a military and commercial empire which may well have been greater than that of the much later Aztec. From what economic base such political and cultural power derived is unclear, but it may have been linked to adoption of the unique and incredibly productive system of *chinampa* cultivation carried out by draining and cultivating the swampy margins of the Great Lake which then filled the Valley of Mexico. This was the city which interfered in such a significant way with the course of Maya history.

The Esperanza culture

The disintegration of Maya culture in the highlands began with the close of the Miraflores period, when building activity slackened at major sites. In fact, by the end of the Preclassic, the great ceremonial center of Kaminaljuyú, focal point of Maya cultural and political affairs in the Southern Area, appears to have been a virtual ruin.

Shortly after AD 400, the highlands fell under Teotihuacan domination. An intrusive group of central Mexicans from that city seized Kaminaljuyú and built for themselves a miniature version of their capital. An elite class ruling over a captive population of Maya descent, they were swayed by native cultural tastes and traditions and became 'Mayanized' to the extent that they imported from the Central Area pottery and other wares with which to stock their tombs. The Esperanza culture which arose at Kaminaljuyú during the Early Classic, then, is a kind of hybrid.

There are several complexes of Esperanza architecture at Kaminaljuyú, all built on a plan which is not in the least bit Maya. Essentially these are stepped
38 temple platforms with the typical Teotihuacan *talud-tablero* motif, in which a rectangular panel with inset (*tablero*) is placed over a sloping batter (*talud*). The good building stone which is so abundant in the Mexican highlands is missing at Kaminaljuyú, so that the architect, almost certainly a Teotihuacano himself, had to be content with clay faced with red-painted stucco. A single stairway fronted each stage of the platform, while on top a temple sanctuary was roofed either with thatch or with the more usual flat-beam-and-mortar construction of Teotihuacan.

The foreign lords of the Esperanza phase chose the temple platforms themselves as their final resting-places. As with the earlier Miraflores people, each platform was actually built to enclose the ruler's tomb, a log-roofed chamber usually placed beneath the frontal staircase, successive burials and their platforms being placed over older ones. The honored deceased was buried in a seated posture upon a wooden bier and was accompanied to the other world not only by rich offerings of pottery and other artifacts, but also by one to three persons sacrificed for the occasion, generally children or

38 Structure A-7 at Kaminaljuyú, a temple-pyramid of the Esperanza culture.

adolescents. Surrounding him were rich funerary vessels, undoubtedly containing food and drink for his own use, as well as implements such as *metates* and *manos* needed to prepare them.

Jade ornaments, some in the process of manufacture, were recovered in quantity from the Esperanza tombs: beads, complex ear ornaments in the form of flared spools, pendants, and spangles are ubiquitous. Underneath one staircase was found a 200-lb (90-kg) boulder of jade from which V-shaped slices had been sawn, indicating that the Esperanza elite had access to a major source of this substance so precious to all the peoples of Mesoamerica.

Few of the pottery vessels from the Esperanza tombs are represented in the rubbish strewn around Kaminaljuyú, from which it is clear that they were intended for the use of the invading class alone. Some of these were actually imported from Teotihuacan itself, probably carried laboriously over the intervening 800 or 900 miles on back racks such as those still used by native traders in the Maya highlands. The ceramic hallmarks of the Teotihuacan civilization are the cylindrical vessel with three slab feet and cover; a little jug with open spout and handle; the '*florero*,' so called from its resemblance to a small flower-vase; and Thin Orange ware, made to Teotihuacan taste in northern Puebla. All are present in Esperanza, but so are polychrome bowls from the Petén, with their peculiar 'basal flanges.'

Certain of the tripod vessels have been stuccoed and painted in brilliant colors with feather-bedecked Teotihuacan lords, or seated Maya personages

39

40

41

and both Maya and Teotihuacan deities, including the Butterfly Goddess so popular in Mexico. One Petén Maya polychrome bowl had even been overpainted with processional figures in Teotihuacan style, speech scrolls curling from their mouths.

All sorts of other valuables were placed with the dead. That Esperanza pomp, perhaps the funeral itself, was accompanied by music is shown by shell trumpets and by large turtle carapaces used with deer-antler beaters as percussive instruments. On a large effigy incense burner from one grave, a seated person strikes a two-toned slit drum. Besides jade, the corpse was ornamented with pearls, cut-out pieces of mica, and rich textiles which have long since rotted away. Included in several tombs were pairs of jaguar paws, symbols of royal power among the highland Maya. The highest technical achievement is seen in the mirrors made up of pyrite plates cut into polygonal shapes and fitted to each other over a circular disk of slate. These are in all likelihood another import from Teotihuacan, but the back of one proved to have remarkable carving in an elaborate scrollwork style that is associated with the Classic Veracruz civilization then developing on the Gulf Coast of Mexico. The ability of the Esperanza rulers to amass luxurious objects from the most distant parts must have been considerable.

The Esperanza culture may have its spectacular side, but almost as striking are omissions. The Long Count calendar had disappeared from the Southern Maya area for good, which is strange considering its ancient roots here. The figurine cult had utterly disappeared. Nor is there any sure indication of stone sculpture on any scale in Esperanza Kaminaljuyú. The evolution of Maya culture in the Southern Area, especially in the highlands, had come to a very abrupt end with the establishment of Teotihuacan hegemony, and apart from the imports of Petén products, Maya ways of doing things were replaced with Mexican from the Early Classic on. Were these intruders warriors or traders? They may well have been both. By Aztec times in central Mexico there was a special caste of armed merchants called *pochteca*, who journeyed into distant countries in search of rare manufactures and raw materials not available in the homeland, all of which were destined for the king. From representations of the *pochteca* god at Teotihuacan, we know that the institution is at least as old as the Early Classic. Thus, Kaminaljuyú may have been a southeasterly outpost of long-distance traders from that great city, established for the purpose of exporting Maya riches for the Teotihuacan throne. As will be seen, the presence of this foreign group was felt through the Petén and as far north as Yucatán itself.

As for the vanquished Maya of the Guatemalan highlands, they must have continued on as before, rendering tribute to Mexican rather than native overlords, tillers of the land and laborers on public construction projects. The great public ceremonials of Kaminaljuyú may even have been forbidden to them. But one cult in which they were certainly allowed to participate was centered upon Lake Amatitlán, not far south of the Esperanza capital, where hot springs and fumaroles along the southern shore must have attracted annual processions rendering homage to the gods of water and fire. Skindivers have brought up many hundreds of blackened vessels from the hot

The Esperanza Culture

39 (*above left*) A long jade bead carved with a human figure, from Tomb A-VI, Kaminaljuyú (Esperanza culture). L. 6 in. (15.6 cm).

40 (*above*) Restored Thin Orange ware vessel in the form of a seated man, from Tomb X, Kaminaljuyú (Esperanza culture). This ware was manufactured in Teotihuacan taste in northern Puebla, and appears wherever the Teotihuacan people had penetrated. Ht of vessel *c.* 11¾ in. (30 cm).

41 (*left*) An Esperanza culture tripod vessel with cover, from Tomb B–II, Kaminaljuyú. The exterior had been stuccoed and painted in buff, red and light green. The figures on the vessel are Maya, while the glyphs on the lid are Teotihuacanoid. Ht 12½ in. (32 cm).

42 Pottery incense burner with heads of the Death God and Xipe Totec, Mexican god of the springtime, from the Zarzal underwater site, Lake Amatitlán, Guatemala. Ht 9½ in. (24 cm).

42   mud of the lake bottom, ranging from extraordinary incense burners to the pots and pans of the peasant household, all cast by devotees into the steaming waters.

In 1969 farm tractors plowing the fields in the Tiquisate region of the Pacific coastal plain of Guatemala, an area located south-southwest of Lake Atitlán that is covered with ancient (and untested) mounds, unearthed rich tombs and caches which contained a total of over 1,000 ceramic objects. These have been examined by Nicholas Hellmuth of the Foundation for Latin American Archaeological Research, and proved to consist of two-piece censers, slab-legged tripod cylinders, hollow moldmade figures, and other objects, all in the Teotihuacan style. Numerous finds of fired clay molds suggest that these were mass-produced from Teotihuacan prototypes by military-merchant groups intrusive from central Mexico during the last half of the Early Classic.

Tzakol culture in the Central Area

Early Classic remains in the Central Area are burdened with towering constructions of Late Classic date, and it has only been quite recently that the elaboration of Maya civilization during this period has been fully realized. The Tzakol culture, as the civilization of the Petén and surrounding regions is called, endures until about 9.8.0.0.0, or to round it off in Christian years, until AD 600.

Already Maya civilization is in full flower, with enormous ceremonial centers crowded with masonry temples and 'palaces' facing onto spacious plazas covered with white stucco. Stelae and altars are carved with dates and embellished with the figures of men and perhaps gods. Polychrome pottery, the finest examples of which were sealed up in the tombs of honored personages, emphasizes stylized polychrome designs of cranes, flying parrots, or men, often on bowls with a kind of apron or basal flange encircling the lower part. Along with these purely Maya ceramics are vessels which show the imprint of distant Teotihuacan: again, the cylindrical vase supported by three slab legs, the small, spouted jug, and the *florero*.   c.f. 53

Dynastic rule among the lowland Maya clearly has its deepest roots at Tikal. Later historical annals have retrospective reference to a putative founder of the dynasty, one Yax-Moch-Xoc, who may have lived in the third century AD. Uaxactún, less than a day's march north of Tikal, is only slightly younger; in spite of early independence, its fortunes became tied to the destiny of its giant neighbor, as the Early Classic records show. The 9th successor to the Tikal throne, known to epigraphers as 'Great Jaguar-Paw,' opened hostilities against Uaxactún, under the command of his brother and war-leader 'Smoking-Frog.' Uaxactún fell on 16 January AD 378, and

43 Pottery of the Tzakol phase at Uaxactún (Early Classic period). *a, b,* polychrome basal-flange bowls; *c,* spouted jug; *d, e,* tripod cylindrical vessels. *a,* 9⅜ in. (23.8 cm) wide; *b–e,* to scale.

44 Polychrome two-part ceramic effigy from Burial 10, Tikal (Tzakol culture). This may represent an old god receiving a severed head as an offering. Ht 14 in. (36 cm).

'Smoking-Frog' was installed as king or *ahau* of the defeated city, a post which he occupied for many years.

This great conquest was celebrated at Tikal by several monuments, perhaps most significantly by a very non-Maya structure erected just south of the 'Lost World' compound. This is an altar-platform in the purest Teotihuacan style, complete with *talud-tablero*; placed atop was a Teotihuacan ball court marker – a thin cylinder surmounted by a doughnut-shaped stone, which in turn was topped by an upright ring. Around the cylinder is a Maya inscription commemorating the fall of Uaxactún. Now, while this and other monuments and artifacts are ample testimony to the strong Teotihuacan element throughout the Petén in Tzakol times, the exact nature of this presence is still under debate. Had a real force of Teotihuacanos penetrated the heart of the Petén? Or was the military and religious prestige of Teotihuacan so awesome that local Maya dynasts were eager to emulate the rites and symbols of that far-off metropolis?

Maya archaeologists are currently inclined to accept the latter explanation. For instance, early in the fifth century, a powerful ruler with the modern nickname 'Stormy Sky' (epigraphers cannot yet read his name glyph), the son of 'Curl-Nose' and grandson of 'Great Jaguar-Paw,' ascended the throne of Tikal. In AD 415 he erected a monument (Stela 31) in his own honor; the main hieroglyphic text, according to Dr Peter Mathews, is largely concerned with the historical annals of Tikal, leading from a time anterior to the accession recorded on the Leiden Plate, up to the day when 'Stormy Sky' marked the end of his first katun of power at the great city. 'Stormy Sky' is depicted on the front as a great Maya *ahau*, holding aloft his royal headdress;

in the crook of his left arm he carries the head of a god wearing in *its* headdress the Tikal 'Emblem Glyph' (see Chapter 9). On either side of the ruler is a figure garbed as a Teotihuacan warrior, complete with war-serpent headgear, feathered *atlatl* (spearthrower), and rectangular shield bearing the visage of the central Mexican god Tlaloc, patron of rain and war. Although at first glance these flanking figures might seem to be foreigners at the Tikal court, the glyphic texts above them make it clear that they are two views of the same man, and a Maya at that: this is 'Curl-Nose,' father of 'Stormy Sky,' present on the stela to give legitimacy to his son. Even though dead, the late ruler remained a force through his identification with the Teotihuacan war cult. Such use of the military symbols of central Mexico was to remain a feature among lowland dynasties for many centuries thereafter.

Burials of great richness have been uncovered beneath the Tzakol temples of Tikal's North Acropolis. Among the most striking is Burial 48, now generally accepted as the final resting place of 'Stormy Sky,' following the suggestion by art-historian Clemency Coggins. The tomb chamber was cut from the soft underlying bedrock, and contained three interments: 'Stormy Sky' himself and two adolescent victims sacrificed to accompany the dead king. The white, stuccoed walls had been covered with glyphs applied in black paint by a sure hand, including the Long Count date 9.1.1.10.10 (21 March AD 457), probably the date of 'Stormy Sky's death or of his funeral.

During the 1960s and early 1970s, a period which saw the apogee (or nadir) of Maya tomb robbery in the southern lowlands, the modestly sized site of

45

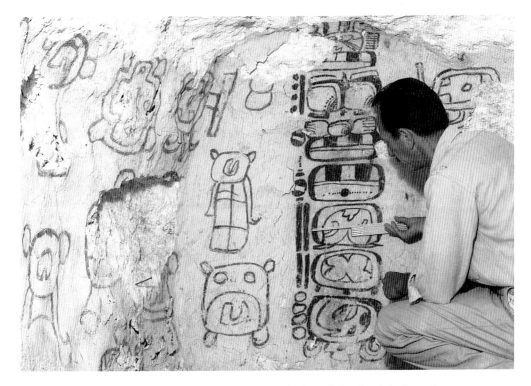

45 The tomb chamber of Burial 48, Tikal (Tzakol culture). On its walls is painted the Long Count date 9.1.1.10.10 4 Oc (21 March AD 457), together with other glyphs of probably stellar significance.

Tikal and Teotihuacan

46 Fragmentary stela in Teotihuacan style from Tikal showing a large Tlaloc face exactly like that upon the shield in Stela 31 (ill. 48).

47 Lid of a stuccoed bowl from Burial 10, Tikal (Tzakol culture). The head and hands painted here in Teotihuacan style belong to Xipe Totec, the Mexican god of the springtime.

48 (*opposite*) Side view of Stela 31 at Tikal, with a warrior shown in relief in Teotihuacan costume. In one hand he carries an *atlatl* or spear-thrower, and in the other a shield with the face of Tlaloc, the Mexican Rain God.

Río Azul in the northeasternmost Petén was heavily looted, and produced for the international market an extraordinary variety of élite objects of the utmost beauty, mainly but not entirely of Early Classic date. Three of these emptied tombs had Tzakol culture murals painted in red and black on the bare walls, including glyphic texts of dynastic nature, and a scene depicting the undulating surface of the Underwater world, a theme linked by Dr Hellmuth with Xibalbá, the Maya realm of the dead. In the last several years, a project led by Dr R. E. W. Adams has uncovered an intact tomb with further murals and Early Classic offerings, although not on the scale or magnificence of those already stripped of their finery.

If, as some scholars believe, Teotihuacanos were present in the Petén cities, might they have tried to impose the worship of their own gods upon the Petén Maya, substituting their own rain god for the native Chac? To this the upper part of a shattered stela from Tikal, showing a large Tlaloc face exactly like that upon the shield of Stela 31, is testimony. On finely stuccoed and 46,48 painted vessels from the Tikal tombs is the blue-faced Tlaloc again, together 47 with the Mexican god of spring, Xipe Totec, recognized by the open mouth and the pairs of vertical lines which pass through the eyes across the cheeks. Some of these vessels are Thin Orange ware manufactured in the Mexican highlands, another comes from the Tiquisate region on the Pacific Coast of Guatemala, while others represent hybrids in shape and decoration between Maya and Teotihuacan traditions.

There almost certainly was trade between the Petén and the Valley of Mexico. Tzakol sherds from basal flange bowls have been found at Teotihuacan, and green obsidian blades from central Mexico were placed with the Tikal dead. However, of all the perishable products which must have traveled the same routes – textiles, quetzal feathers, jaguar pelts, wooden objects, and so forth – nothing at all remains.

The wonderful Maya mural art has its roots in the Chicanel wallpaintings of Tikal, but by Tzakol times it had reached a very high degree of elaboration. Now mutilated by local vandals, the lovely Early Classic wall paintings of Temple B-XIII at Uaxactún were executed in muted tones of red, brown, tan, and black. The scene is one from real life: before a palace building sheltering three Maya ladies, two male figures, one painted a warlike black, are in conversation (which is undoubtedly recorded in several columns of indecipherable glyphs). At one side are two horizontal rows of figures, probably meant to be standing on two levels of a stepped platform, painted with a strong feeling for individual caricature; a few are chattering in excited discourse. Some are singers shaking rattles, while a small boy beats time on a skin-covered drum.

Not only in the northern Petén, but at many other places in the Central Area, major Maya centers were well established by the fifth century AD and even earlier. At these, Teotihuacan domination is less easy, or even impossible, to demonstrate, and one can suppose that this was restricted to the Tikal-Uaxactún area alone. None the less, Yaxhá, a small Maya city located southeast of Tikal, has a stela in pure Teotihuacan style apparently depicting a warrior-goddess with Tlaloc mask, and a city plan which

49 Early Classic jade plaque of the bird-monster god Vucub Caquix, from Copán, Honduras. Ht 4¼ in. (10.7 cm).

50 A jade object shaped like an ear flare from Pomona, Belize (early Tzakol culture). The four glyphs refer to gods. Diam. 7 in. (17.8 cm).

combines the amorphous Maya pattern with formal 'streets' laid out in the central Mexican fashion. Whatever might be the nature of Teotihuacan influence on the affairs, both political and cultural, of the Petén Maya, in the last half of the sixth century a serious crisis shook the Central Area. No more stelae were erected, and there are signs of widespread and purposeful mutilation of public monuments. It is not clear what all this means, but although none of the Petén sites actually seems to have been abandoned near the close of the Early Classic, there might have been fierce internecine warfare or perhaps even a popular revolt.

c.f. 46–48

When the smoke clears, in the first decades of the seventh century, Classic Maya life is seen to have been reconstituted much as before, possibly with new rulers and new dynasties. But Teotihuacan is no longer a factor in Maya civilization. In some great even of which we have no written record, that city was destroyed, and the empire of which it was the capital came to an end. This took place by AD 600, and probably was the decisive factor resulting in the Maya disturbances in the closing decades of the Early Classic. However, the release from a foreign yoke which was economic and probably also political enabled the lowland Maya of the Central Area to reach unparalleled heights in the Late Classic period.

Copán in the Early Classic

Perhaps because of its isolation in a remote valley on the southeastern perimeter of the Central Area, Copán escaped both the heavy cultural grip of Teotihuacan and the disruptions that marked the transition from Early to Late Classic in the Petén. According to later inscriptions, the Copán dynasty was founded in the early fifth century AD by Yax Kuk Mo' ('Green Quetzal-Macaw'); this royal line was to persist essentially unbroken until the death of the sixteenth ruler in AD 820. Yet there must have been earlier chiefs or even kings who failed to be recorded in the annals of the Late Classic.

In the summer of 1992, the long-term project directed by Professor William Fash of Northern Illinois University encountered what appears to be Copán's oldest monument, in a deep, exploratory tunnel underneath the famous Hieroglyphic Stairway. This seems to be a marker set into a floor some time in the fourth century AD (long before Yax Kuk Mo' made his debut), and depicts two males facing each other across a central pair of glyph columns. Are these twin gods (we shall come across such later)? or are they co-rulers of the Copán polity? The answer will have to wait until the text is fully deciphered.

Previous tunneling into the mass supporting the Hieroglyphic Stairway has disclosed a fifth-century temple which may be contemporary with Yax Kuk Mo'; while much destroyed by later building activities, enough has remained of the upper façade to see that it was covered with an enormous crocodile in stucco relief. At about the same time, Copán's first ball court was constructed, out in the open plaza to the northwest of the earlier one; this was to be the first of three successively built on the same spot, and already it had

51 (*opposite*) The finest Maya wood carving known, this seated figure from Tabasco, Mexico, represents a moustachioed lord with folded arms; traces of hematite pigment remain on the piece. Ht 14 in. (35.5 cm). Cf. frontispiece illustration.

52 Elevation of the west side of the Rosalila Structure, Copán, showing the stucco façade sculpture uncovered in 1991.

stone macaw heads as boundary markers, as in the final one seen by modern tourists.

One of the more spectacular discoveries at Copán in recent years was made by Honduran archaeologist Ricardo Agurcia. Dubbed the Rosalila Structure, this is a temple dating to the close of the Early Classic which had been buried almost intact by later building, and gives Mayanists a good idea of what the splendid exterior of an intact stuccoed and polychromed temple looked like before time and the elements have done their work of destruction. Even part of the roof crest is preserved. On the front (facing west) is the Principal Bird Deity, Vucub Caquix in all his glory. His huge head with Sun God eyes is on the second story, and his serpent-bird wings are spread out on the upper façade of the lower one. An archaeological bonus was the find of sacred objects left on the floor of Rosalila, including nine eccentric flints which had been wrapped in blue cloth, some of which still adhered to the flints.

As has been said, there is no real break, no 'hiatus,' at Copán between the Early and Late Classic: the eleventh ruler, 'Budz Chan,' spans the gap, dying peacefully in the year AD 628. Although war was eventually to bring temporary reverse to Copán's fortunes, being on the periphery of great civilizations sometimes has its rewards.

The Northern Area

There is abundant pictorial and glyphic evidence for warfare across the Maya area during the Early Classic, but proof of warfare is remarkably difficult to derive from 'dirt' archaeology. A vivid exception to this rule is provided by Becán in the Chenes region just north of the Petén, which was completely surrounded by massive defensive earthworks some time between the second and fourth centuries BC. These consist of a ditch and inner rampart, with a total height of 38 ft (11.6 m), and would have been formidable, according to David Webster of Pennsylvania State University, if the rampart had been surmounted by a palisade. It would be tempting to see this as a consequence of a putative Teotihuacan invasion of the Chenes, but it is a purely Maya matter as the earthwork was built before the appearance of strong Teotihuacan influence at Becán.

A good deal less is known about the Early Classic in the stony land of Yucatán and Campeche than in the south. In both ceramics and architecture, these Maya closely adhered to Petén standards. One of the earliest centers is   53 Oxkintok in the scrubby plain of western Yucatán, with a stone lintel carved in the fifth century AD, and some contemporary but aesthetically inferior reliefs.

53 A double-chambered vessel of the Tzakol culture, possibly from Campeche, Mexico. On the two lids one of the Hero Twin gods faces Vucub Caquix. Ht 11⅞ in. (30.3 cm).

54 The stuccoed figure of a jaguar or puma, a speech scroll issuing from its mouth, is shown in Teotihuacan style on the upper façade of an Early Classic building at Acanceh, Mexico.

A more interesting site is Acanceh, southeast of Mérida, the present-day capital of Yucatán. On the one hand, there is a stepped pyramid-platform with inset stairway of apron moldings of straightforward Petén Maya type. On the other, there is an extraordinary platform with a *talud-tablero* façade, stuccoed with relief figures in Teotihuacan style: anthropomorphic bats, birds of prey, a squirrel, and a representation of the central deity of Teotihuacan, known as the Feathered Serpent or Quetzalcoatl. There is nothing Maya about this building. On the contrary, it may be evidence that the dynamic people of Teotihuacan had established outposts not only in the Southern and Central Areas, but also here in the Northern Area, foreshadowing the great Mexican invasions that were to take place in Yucatán five centuries later.

54

5·Classic Splendor:
the Late Period

The great culture of the Maya lowlands during the Late Classic period is one of the 'lost' civilizations of the world, its hundreds of cities and towns often buried under an almost unbroken canopy of tropical forest. At one time it could be said that we did not know who lived in these now-decayed centers, and how the Maya realm was then governed. It was even thought that the major sites which are often called 'cities' were nothing of the sort.

Large masonry buildings are easy to map, but, curiously enough, so are the simple huts of the common people, for the ancient Maya conveniently raised their houses on low, rectangular mounds of earth and stone to avoid the summer floods. Topographic surveys of large Maya sites like Tikal and Seibal in the Petén, or Dzibilchaltún in northern Yucatán, reveal a very amorphous pattern of structures ranging from great temple-pyramids and so-called 'palaces' down to individual house mounds arranged around tiny plazas (these were probably family compounds). This pattern is a far cry from the neat gridiron layout of Teotihuacan in central Mexico, which conforms far more to our idea of what a city should be. An earlier generation of archaeologists considered the great sites to be nothing more than relatively empty ceremonial centers, staffed only by the putative priest-rulers and their retinues, and bustling with populace only during great rituals and times of corvée labor.

The intellectual tide has changed in the light of new data and new concepts. While it is true that, with the exception of the Teotihuacan-influenced Yaxhá in the Petén, there are no streets to be discerned in lowland sites during the Classic, these nevertheless functioned as cities, since they were the administrative and ritual centers for city-states and had populations as large as many post-Roman cities of the Old World. In early, pre-industrial cities and towns of the Eastern Hemisphere, we are used to seeing city walls, but these are not found at Classic Maya sites. Because of the seemingly unplanned nature of the settlement pattern, the boundaries of Maya cities are difficult to determine. Becán in the Río Bec region is surrounded by a moat, the Petexbatún site of Punta de Chimino is isolated on its peninsula by a deep moat, and Uaxactún and Tikal are separated by a defensive earthwork, but these are exceptions to the rule. When city walls are found, as at Dos Pilas and Uxmal, they seem to date to the Terminal Classic, when Maya civilization was generally on the decline.

The late Sylvanus G. Morley once classified all known Maya centers, both Classic and Post-Classic, according to their supposed degrees of relative importance, ranging from Class 1 giants like Tikal and Copán down to Class

55 Plan of the central part of Tikal (the area covered is slightly over 1 sq. mile). *1–5* Temples I–V; *6* Temple of Inscriptions; *7* Great Plaza; *8–14* Reservoirs: *8* Bejucal, *9* Causeway, *10* Temple, *11* Palace, *12* Hidden, *13* Madeira, *14* Perdido.

4 centers such as Bonampak and Acanceh. In 1946 he listed a total of 116 sites in the Northern and Central Areas, but explorations since then suggest that the figure could probably be doubled.

How large were the great cities in terms of size and population? Tikal and Calakmul are the largest of all Maya sites and have been completely mapped down to the last house mound, although in view of the difficulty of drawing boundaries around any settlement of the lowlands it is hard to say exactly where they end. At Tikal, within a little over 6 square miles, there are about 3,000 structures, ranging from lofty temple-pyramids and massive palaces to tiny household units of thatch-roofed huts. Estimates of the total Tikal population in Late Classic times vary all the way from 10,000 to 90,000 persons. If one accepted the latter figure, which many Mayanists think is the most likely, this would mean a density higher than that of an average city in modern Europe or America. A glance at the Tikal layout will show that this is a concentration of a basically dispersed population, with a slight increase in frequency and size of houses as one moves closer to the heart of the site itself, where the dwellings of aristocrats and bureaucrats alike would have been more splendid.

The same somewhat 'colloidal' appearance is typical of all other known Classic centers, which in the northeast Petén were always placed on low ridges so that they could be easily seen for several miles, if the trees around them were cut. They look, in fact, rather like artificial mountains. Water was scarce in the Petén, and at huge centers like Tikal there are several artificial reservoirs of some size, surrounded by embankments, which provided sufficient water to the inhabitants over the winter dry season.

Classic sites in the Central Area

A Classic Maya center typically consists of a series of stepped platforms topped by masonry superstructures, arranged around broad plazas or courtyards. In the really large sites such as Tikal there may be a number of building complexes interconnected by causeways. Towering above all are the mighty temple-pyramids built from limestone blocks over a rubble core. Although the temples themselves contain one or more corbeled and plaster-covered rooms, these are so narrow that they could only have been used on the occasion of ceremonies meant to be kept from plebeian eyes. Tall they are, but the Maya architects were not content and almost always added a further extension to the upper temple, a so-called roof comb, which along with the temple façade was highly embellished with painted stucco reliefs.

The bulk of the construction at a Maya site, however, is taken up by the palaces, single-storied structures built on similar principles to the temple-pyramids but on much lower platforms and containing more plastered rooms, sometimes up to several dozen in the same building. Occasionally, there may be one or two interior courtyards within the palaces. There is little agreement on just what a 'palace' was used for. Did the rulers and other members of the elite live in these? They seem singularly uncomfortable (and bat-infested) to those archaeologists forced by circumstances to camp in

55

56

93

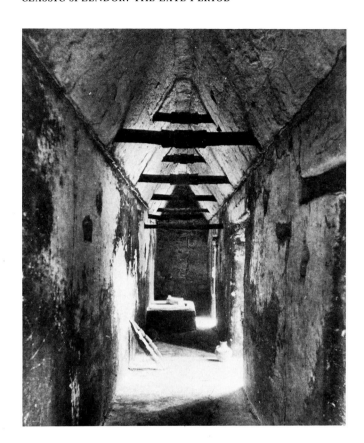

56 A room in the Five-Story Palace at Tikal, from a photograph taken by Teobert Maler. The use to which these 'palaces' were put remains uncertain. As seen here, there are usually one or more plastered benches along the back wall of the rooms.

them, and it seems more likely that the royal household was sheltered in perishable buildings which have not survived the lowland climate. It has also been suggested on the evidence of their cell-like rooms that they might have been monasteries or quarters for the priesthood, but it is entirely uncertain whether there were ecclesiastical or monastic orders in Classic times. The 'palace' mystery has only been compounded by recent epigraphic evidence which names these structures as 'sleeping places.'

In any Classic center in the Central Area with a claim to importance, standing stelae were placed in the stucco floors of the plazas, usually fronting certain important temples but sometimes palaces as well. At times the stelae appear on platforms supporting temple-pyramids, but the rule seems to have been that certain stelae were always associated with specific structures, for reasons which until recently were something of a mystery. Generally a stela will have a low, round, flat-topped 'altar' standing before it. The subject-matter of the relief carvings on one or both stela faces seems always the same: a richly attired Maya ruler, generally a male, carrying peculiar emblems such 57 as the so-called ceremonial bar or manikin scepter, or else a similarly garbed person with spear and shield, trampling a captive underfoot. We shall examine these reliefs and the Long Count dates and glyphs which are inscribed on them in Chapter 9, for the story that they tell is now unfolding.

57 Stela 4, Machaquilá,
Guatemala (Late Classic period).
The figure holds a 'Manikin
Scepter' (God K), the symbol of
rulership.

Ball courts seem to be present at many sites in the Central Area, but they
are more frequent and better made in the southeast, at sites like Copán.   59
These courts are of stucco-faced masonry, and have sloping playing surfaces.
At Copán, three stone markers were placed on each side, and three set into
the floor of the court, but the exact method of scoring in the game is obscure.
Toward the western part of the Central Area, in centers along the
Usumacinta River, sweat baths are known, possibly adopted from Mexico
where such structures can still be found in many highland towns.

Awe-inspiring though the great Maya 'cities' are, there is little overt
indication of any overall planning in their arrangement. Rather, the typical
center seems to have grown by accretion as temples, palaces, and entire
complexes were rebuilt over and over again through the centuries. There was
a gradual accumulation of architectural features that seem to have had social
and political functions of a special (but still largely undetermined) nature.
Nothing could be more alien to the Maya center than the kind of grid plan
seen in some of the great urban sites of Mexico, such as Teotihuacan.

Copán and Quiriguá
Certainly one of the loveliest of all Classic Maya ruins is Copán, situated   58
above a tributary of the Río Motagua in a section of western Honduras famed

58 A restoration drawing of the site of Copán, Honduras, by Tatiana Proskouriakoff. To the right is the Acropolis, to the left the Great Plaza. The bulk of the construction shown here is of the Late Classic period.

59 The Ball Court at Copán from the south (Late Classic period).

60 Monkey-man scribal god, from Copán.

61 Stone head and torso of the Young Maize God, from Copán, one of the wonderfully baroque carvings at this site. Ht 28 in. (71 cm).

The glories of Copán

62 Stela D and its 'altar,' north side of the Great Plaza at Copán, from a lithograph published by Frederick Catherwood in 1844. The 'altar' represents the Death God with fleshless jaws. On the stela is the *tun* ending date 9.15.5.0.0 (26 July AD 736 in the Gregorian calendar). Ht of stela 11 ft 9 in. (3.6 m).

for its tobacco. Stephens, who explored the site in 1839 (and bought it for 50 dollars!) called it 'a valley of romance and wonder, where . . . the genii who attended on King Solomon seem to have been the artists.' The principal temple-pyramids rest on an artificial acropolis which has been partly carried away by the Copán River, but many of the structures remain intact. Among them is the Temple of the Hieroglyphic Stairway, completed in the eighth century AD, with a staircase every one of whose sixty-three steps is embellished on the risers with an immensely long text of about 2,500 glyphs. The ball court at Copán is the most perfect known for the Classic Maya, with tenon sculptures in the shape of macaw heads as its markers. But it is the wonderfully baroque qualities of its carving in the round which distinguish this site from all others, for the Copán artists worked in a greenish volcanic tuff superior to the limestone in use among the Petén centers. Not only were doorways, jambs, and façades of the major temples ornamented with stone figures of the Rain God, young Maize God, and other deities, but no fewer than twenty stelae were carved and erected in Early and Late Classic times, together with fourteen 'altars.' It appears that the majority of the stelae were placed on the north end of the site, in a broad court bounded by narrow stepped platforms from which the populace could gaze upon the spectacles involved with the stela cult.

60,61

62

In recent years, Copán has been the focus of a large-scale international archaeological project that has thrown much light on the most important Maya site in the southeast lowlands. Apparently founded by Olmec who had come to this region to exploit the apple-green jade native to the nearby Motagua valley, this remained one of the great regional city-states until the Classic collapse. Excavations and the analysis of dynastic records preserved on stelae, 'altars' (such as Altar Q, which pictures sixteen successive kings), and the Hieroglyphic Stairway have thrown considerable light on the history of the city.

The thirteenth ruler of Copán was the man usually known as '18 Rabbit' (his real name has been shown by epigrapher David Stuart to be 18 *Ubah Kauil*, '18 Gopher-Provider'), a great but ultimately unfortunate monarch, who took power on 9 July AD 695. During his reign, the Acropolis and ceremonial precinct began to take on its present form; and to him may be attributed the marvellous Temple 22, probably dedicated to the Young Maize God whose sculptured busts once adorned it. Like all Classic kings, '18 Rabbit' was something of an egoist, and the Great Plaza is crowded with his monuments, including the curious Stela H which depicts him in women's costume. On the fateful day 9.15.6.4.16 6 Cimi 4 Tzec (3 May AD 738), shortly after he had dedicated the final version of the ball court, '18 Rabbit' was ignominiously captured and beheaded by 'Cauac Sky' of Quiriguá, a nearby city (see below) which had largely been under Copán's thumb in past centuries.

This sudden downturn in Copán's fortunes, however, was short-lived, and the fourteenth successor, 'Smoke-Monkey,' took office the following month. This man was responsible for a remarkable building recently identified by artist-archaeologist Barbara Fash as a *Popol Na* ('Mat House'), the council chamber of the city. On its upper façade, both front and back, are cut-stone mats; interspersed with them are eight figures seated crosslegged over hieroglyphs, most probably names of places within the Copán polity. In apparent corroboration of William Fash's suggestion that the building functioned as a meeting chamber for local chiefs, a nearby midden seems to hold the remains of banquets held within it.

Copán's final well-attested ruler was the sixteenth, 'Yax Pac,' seemingly a weak and ineffective lord who allowed the nobility to expand in number and in power; David Stuart has found that one of these even had the temerity to style himself a *ch'ul ahau*, 'holy king.' This state of affairs may explain the splendor of the suburban palace complex known austerely as Structure 9N-82, dedicated in AD 781. Devoted to the Monkey-Man Scribes of the Classic Maya, this palace may well have been inhabited by a high-ranking noble scribe and his family (see Chapter 9).

Quiriguá lies only 30 miles north of Copán; it is a far humbler Classic center which seems on the testimony of the inscriptions to have been one of the latter's suzerainties, at least at certain times of its history. Situated not far from the western bank of the Río Motagua, in its lush lower reaches, Quiriguá contains a few architectural groups of no great distinction. Its enormous sandstone stelae and carved zoomorphic stones, however, are quite another matter; indeed Stela E, erected late in the eighth century, might claim to be the greatest stone monument of the New World, its shaft measuring 35 ft (10.7 m) in height. On the front face it is carved with the figure of a bearded ruler holding a small hand shield and a 'manikin scepter' in either hand, while the sides are covered with texts containing several Long Count dates. The great skill of the Quiriguá sculptors can be seen in the grotesque full figures which take the place of cycle glyphs in the inscriptions of several other stelae, in the stone 'zoomorphs' representing crouching earth monsters or sky deities with humans seated among their snake-like coils, and in the richly embellished boulders ('altars') associated with them.

63

64

Tikal

It is more than likely that the ruins of Tikal, in the very heart of the Petén, were first encountered by the brave Father Avendaño and his companions in 1695. Lost and starving among the swampy *bajos* and thorny forests of northern Guatemala, they came across a 'variety of old buildings, excepting some in which I recognized apartments, and though they were very high and my strength was little, I climbed up them (though with trouble).' Tikal, now partly restored by the University of Pennsylvania and the Guatemalan government, is a giant among Maya centers; it is one of the largest Classic sites in the Maya area, and one of the greatest in the New World. Particularly impressive are its six temple-pyramids, veritable skyscrapers among buildings of their class. From the level of the plaza floor to the top of its roof comb, Temple IV, the mightiest of all, measures 229 ft (70 m) in height. The core of Tikal must be its great plaza, flanked on west and east by two of these temple-pyramids, and on the north by the acropolis already mentioned in connection with its Late Preclassic and Early Classic tombs. Some of the

63 (*opposite*) Stela D at Quiriguá, Guatemala, from a photograph taken by A. P. Maudslay in 1885. This monument was erected on 9.16.15.0.0, or 18 February AD 766. Ht 19 ft 6 in. (5.9 m).

64 Altar of Zoomorph O at Quiriguá. On the left of this enormous monument, which was dedicated on the *katun* ending 9.18.0.0.0 (11 October AD 790), is the figure of the rain god dancing in the coils of a serpent. L. 12 ft 4 in. (3.8 m).

major architectural groups are connected to the Great Plaza and with each other by broad causeways, over which many splendid processions must have passed in the days of Tikal's glory. The 'palaces' are also impressive, their plastered rooms often still retaining in their vaults the sapodilla-wood spanner beams which had only a decorative function.

Tikal is not particularly noteworthy for its stone sculptures. Among the many limestone stelae lined up in the Great Plaza before the acropolis, the best are of the Early Classic period. None the less, there were great artists in the service of Tikal's rulers, for the fortunately preserved wooden lintels 66 above the doorways of the temple-pyramids are covered with lovely reliefs of Maya rulers in various poses accompanied by lengthy glyphic texts. Artistry of a different sort can be seen in the remarkable offerings accompanying the splendid tomb underneath Temple I, discovered in 1962 by Aubrey Trik of 67 the University of Pennsylvania. In it, a very great ruler named *Hasau Chan Kauil* (*Hasau* 'Heavenly Provider') had been laid to rest with his riches – his ornaments of jade and shell – and with vessels filled with food and drink, then a mighty pyramid built over his remains. But what was really unusual was a large collection of bone tubes and strips which had been delicately incised 65,68 with scenes of gods and men carried out with the most extreme

65 Two incised bones from the Temple I tomb, Tikal. *Top*, three Chacs (Rain Gods) are catching fish. *Above*, seven Maya deities travel in a canoe into the Underworld. In the middle is the Maize God.

66 A carved wooden lintel from Temple IV at Tikal. Beneath the body of a double-headed serpent is seated a Maya king upon a throne, with spear in one hand and shield in the other. The terraced platform below is apparently a sort of palanquin. Probably dedicated in AD 747. L. in greatest dimension 6 ft 9 in. (2.1 m).

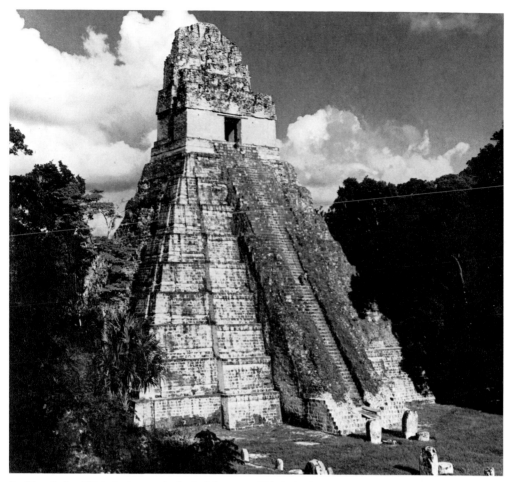

67 Temple I at Tikal, the largest site in the Maya area. This is the funerary pyramid of Ruler A (*Hasan Chan Kauil*).

sophistication. The fine drawing and calligraphy give us some idea of what a Classic Maya codex may have looked like, none of these bark-paper books having survived except in the most fragmentary form in tombs at sites like Altun Ha and Uaxactún.

There are ten reservoirs at Tikal from which the Maya obtained their drinking water, one of which was perforce refurbished by the modern archaeologists in lieu of any other potable source. These are often surrounded by artificial earthen levees, and contain sufficient water throughout the dry season. Some of them no doubt began as quarries, although the latter are known in many other places around the site, where outcrops and half-worked blocks of limestone still bear the marks of the crudely chipped tools with which they were hewn by the stone-masons of over one thousand years ago.

68 (*right*) Incised bone of the Late Classic period from the tomb beneath Temple I, Tikal. A hand holding a brush pen appears from the jaws of Itzamná, inventor of writing, in his serpent form.

Yaxchilán, Piedras Negras, and Bonampak

The many dozens of Classic Maya centers scattered over the Petén and Belize – such as Uaxactún, Nakum, Naranjo, Xunantunich, and Altun Ha – are witnesses to the importance of this region before its abandonment. Maya sites are as numerous along the banks of the Usumacinta and its tributaries, in the southwestern part of the Central Area. Yaxchilán is a major center strung out along a terrace of the Usumacinta, with some of its components perched on the hills above. While its temple-pyramids reach no great height, their upper façades and roof combs were beautifully ornamented with figures in stucco and stone. Yaxchilán is famous for its many stone lintels, carved in relief with scenes of conquest and ceremonial life, with which are associated dates and glyphic texts providing clues to the real meaning of the Classic Maya inscriptions. All this must wait, however, until Chapter 9. Further downstream is Piedras Negras, which has also produced similar data. This site is more extensive than Yaxchilán, and has a large number of particularly fine stelae set in place before its temples, as well as eight sweat baths, complete with stone-built hearths lined with potsherds, masonry benches for the bathers, and drains to carry off water used in the bath.

Few discoveries in the Maya area can rank with that of Bonampak, an otherwise insignificant Late Classic center clearly under the cultural and political thumb of Yaxchilán. Bonampak, which lies not far from the Río Lacanhá, a tributary of the Usumacinta system, was first stumbled across in February 1946 by two American adventurers who were taken there by Lacandón Indians among whom they had been living. Three months later, the photographer Giles Healey was led by a group of Lacandón to the same ruins, and he was the first non-Maya to gaze at the stupendous paintings which covered the walls of three rooms in one of the structures.

The Bonampak murals, which can be dated to shortly before AD 800 on the basis of Long Count texts and stylistic considerations, obviously relate a single narrative, a story of a battle, its aftermath, and the victory celebrations. Against a background of stylized jungle foliage, a skirmish takes place among magnificently arrayed Maya warriors, while musicians blow long war trumpets of wood or bark. The scene shifts to a stepped platform in Bonampak itself; the miserable prisoners have been stripped, and are having the nails torn from their fingers. An important captive sprawls on the steps, perhaps tortured to exhaustion, and a severed head lies nearby on a bed of leaves. A naked figure seated on the platform summit pleads for his life to the central figure, the great lord Chaan-muan, king of Bonampak, clad in jaguar-skin battle-jacket surrounded by his subordinates in gorgeous costume. Among the noble spectators is a lady in a white robe, holding a folding-screen fan in one hand. Chaan-muan's principal wife, she is identified by the glyphic text as coming from Yaxchilán. One of the final ceremonies includes a group of mummers fantastically disguised as water gods, accompanied by an orchestra of rattles, drums, turtle carapaces (struck with antlers), and long trumpets. Perhaps the culminating scene is the great sacrificial dance performed to the sound of trumpets by lords wearing towering headdresses of quetzal plumes; in preparation for it, white-robed Maya ladies seated on a

69 Stela 14, from Piedras Negras, Guatemala. The monument marks the accession to the throne in AD 761 of the young lord seated in the niche. At the foot of the platform stands a middle-aged woman, perhaps the new king's mother. Ht 9 ft 3 in. (2.8 m).

70 (*right*) A detail of one of the remarkable wall paintings in Room 1 at Bonampak, dating to *c*. AD 790. Musicians sing and beat time, while to the left a group of mummers perform masked as water gods.

71 (*below*) A Maya lord is seated on a dais above three lesser figures on this engraved stone from Bonampak, Mexico. Dedicated AD 692. Ht 38½ in. (98 cm).

Lords of Bonampak and Yaxchilán

72 (*above*) A wall painting in Room 2 at Bonampak, *c.* AD 790. On a terraced platform stands the ruler of Bonampak and his subordinates. Below, captives taken in a jungle skirmish are being tortured by having their finger-nails removed.

73 (*right*) A richly robed woman, Lady Xoc, kneels before the Yaxchilán ruler 'Shield Jaguar,' and draws blood by passing a rope with thorns through her tongue. This relief from Yaxchilán, Mexico, was dedicated AD 709, not long after 'Shield Jaguar' had captured his enemy 'Death.' Ht 3 ft 7 in. (1.1 m).

throne draw blood from their tongues, and a strange, pot-bellied, dwarf-like figure standing on a palanquin is carried on-stage.

A more profound and subtle meaning than mere Maya saber-rattling has been ascribed to these murals by the art historian Mary Miller, who tells us that the three rooms 'record a splendid pageant of rulership.' At different times in its history, which goes back to the Early Classic, Bonampak was both an ally and enemy of Yaxchilán (a recently discovered causeway goes off in the direction of the latter). In 790, relations between the two powers were close: the real theme of the paintings is the presentation and consecration of a little male heir who may also have been heir to the Yaxchilán throne. His father Chaan-muan took his troops into battle to secure prisoners for the celebrations in honor of the heir apparent; the great occasion was eventually solemnized by the torture and decapitation of these captives, and by the ritual shedding of their own blood by great lords and ladies.

No verbal description could do justice to the beautiful colors and to the skill of the hand (or hands) which executed these paintings. Suffice it to say Bonampak has thrown an entirely new light on the warlike interests of the Maya leaders, upon social organization and stratification in a Maya center, and upon the magnificence of Late Classic Maya culture in general, before time destroyed most of its creations. Bonampak was abandoned before the murals were finished, and the artists dispersed. The heir apparent probably never ascended this or any other throne, as Maya civilization went into eclipse.

Dos Pilas, Toniná, and Palenque

A Vanderbilt University project under the direction of Arthur Demarest has recently been investigating a particularly important group of sites, all located atop an escarpment overlooking the shallow Lake Petexbatún, south of the Río Pasión which forms one of the main branches of the Usumacinta. These are Tamarandito, Arroyo de Piedra, Aguateca, and Dos Pilas; the last-named city seems to have dominated the rest, and, in fact, to have begun putting together a large-scale state as early as the seventh century AD. So powerful had Dos Pilas become that, on 3 December AD 735, its ruler had the audacity to attack Seibal, a far larger and more ancient city located on a bluff above the Pasión; the next day, Mo'l Balam ('Claw-Jaguar') fell captive to Dos Pilas, and was beheaded on the day following.

As with Copán on the southeast Maya frontier, the cities of the far southwestern lowlands often display considerable innovation in art and architecture, as compared with the more staid central Petén sites. Comalcalco, for instance, out on the alluvial plains of Tabasco, is unique in the pre-Conquest New World for its use of fired brick in construction, an adaptation to a virtually stoneless environment, while Toniná specialized in sculpture-in-the-round to an extent not seen since the demise of the Olmec civilization. In 1991, Mexican archaeologists uncovered an extraordinary stucco relief at Toniná, in which the skeletalized Death God brandishes the severed head of an important captive; this city, in the hill country of central Chiapas, must have been a feared military power, for its ruler managed to capture 'Kan-Xul,' king of the great city of Palenque and second son of the renowned Palenque *ahau* Pacal.

The late Sylvanus Morley considered Palenque to be the most beautiful of all the Maya centers, albeit in comparison with a giant like Tikal it is of no great size. The setting is incomparable: Palenque lies at the foot of a chain of low hills covered with tall rain forest, just above the green flood plain of the Usumacinta. Parrots and macaws of brilliant plumage fly at tree-top level; on rainy days the strange roar of howler monkeys can be heard near the ruins. A small stream runs through the site and is carried underneath the principal complex, the Palace, by a corbel-vaulted aqueduct. A veritable labyrinth, the 74 Palace is about 300 ft long and 240 ft wide (91 by 73 m), and consists of a series of vaulted galleries and rooms arranged about interior courtyards or patios, dominated by a unique four-story square tower with an interior stairway. It has been suggested that the tower was used as an observatory, but it commands a wide view and could also have served as a watch-tower. Arranged along the sides of two of the patios are grotesque reliefs, almost

74 View from the southwest of the Late Classic Palace and Tower, Palenque. In the distance is the floodplain of the Río Usumacinta.

75 Decorated pier on the Palace, Palenque, from a photograph by A. P. Maudslay. In this Late Classic stucco relief, both figures grasp a fantastic serpent.

76 Cross-section of the Temple of the Cross at Palenque, showing construction of the roof comb, vaults, and inner sanctuary.

caricatures of prisoners showing submission by the usual means, one hand raised to the opposite shoulder, and it could have been in these courts that the captured enemies of Palenque were arraigned, tortured, and sacrificed.

The Palenque artists excelled in stucco work, and the exteriors of the pilasters ranged along the galleries of the Palace are marvelously embellished in that medium with Maya lords in relief, carrying the symbols of their authority, while lesser individuals sit cross-legged at their side. All these stuccoes were once painted, and the noted Palenque authority Merle Greene Robertson has found a definite color code: for instance, the exposed skin of humans was painted red, while that of gods was covered with blue.

Of the temple-pyramids of Palenque, three were constructed on more or less the same plan, and must have served somewhat the same function. These are the Temples of the Sun, the Cross, and the Foliated Cross, arranged about three sides of a plaza on the eastern side of the site. Each temple rests on a stepped platform with frontal stairway, each has a mansard roof with comb, and each has an outer and an inner vaulted room. Against the back wall of the latter is a 'sanctuary,' a miniature version of the larger temple; in its rear is set up a magnificent low relief tablet carved with long hieroglyphic texts and exhibiting the same motif, two Maya men, one taller than the other, facing each other on either side of a ceremonial object. In the case of the Temple of the Sun, the most perfect of all Maya buildings, this central object is the mask of the Jaguar God of the Underworld, the sun in its night aspect, before two

75

76,77

crossed spears. The two other temples have in its place a branching world-tree (which bears an astonishing resemblance to the Christian cross) surmounted by a monstrous quetzal bird. The exterior pilasters of the sanctuaries also bear stone reliefs of standing figures, the one on the right side of the Cross sanctuary unusual in that it shows God L, one of the aged Lords of the Underworld, smoking a cigar.

Thanks to some remarkable recent advances in our understanding of the Palenque inscriptions, we now know why these three temples are so similar: the tablets in their sanctuaries all record the accession in AD 683 of the king known as Sun Lord 'Chan-Bahlum' (or 'Snake-Jaguar'). He is the taller of the two figures on each tablet; the shorter is his great predecessor Sun Lord Pacal, of whom more below.

From time to time over the past 60 years that excavations have been carried out at Palenque, finds have been made of fairly well-stocked tombs that were intruded into temple platforms and into the Palaces itself. But these are nothing compared with the remarkable discovery made in June 1952 by the Mexican archaeologist Alberto Ruz. The Temple of the Inscriptions rests on a 65-ft-high (19.8-m) stepped pyramid approached by a noble frontal stairway. On the walls of its portico and central chamber are three panels containing a total of 620 hieroglyphs with many dates, the latest of which corresponds to AD 692. The floor of the temple itself is covered by large stone slabs, but Ruz was particularly curious about one which had a double row of holes provided with removable stone stoppers; on removing this it was clear that he had hit upon a vaulted stairway leading down into the interior of the pyramid, but intentionally choked with rubble. In four field seasons he had completely cleared the stairs, which changed direction half-way down, finally reaching a chamber on about the same level as the base of the pyramid. It too had been filled, but on its floor were encountered the skeletons of five or six young adults, probably all sacrifices. At its far end, the passage was blocked by a huge triangular slab which filled the entire vault.

It was on removing this slab that Ruz first looked into the great Funerary
79 Crypt, a discovery rivaling that of Bonampak in importance. The chamber is 30 ft long and 23 ft high (9 by 7 m), and its floor lies underneath the frontal stairway but below the level of the plaza, some 80 ft (24 m) down from the floor of the upper temple. Around its walls stride stucco relief figures of men in very archaic costume, perhaps the Nine Lords of the Night of Maya theology, but it is equally possible that they were meant to be distant ancestors of the deceased. A huge rectangular stone slab, $12\frac{1}{2}$ ft (3.8 m) long and covered with relief carvings, was found to overlie a monolithic sarcophagus within which an ancient Maya ruler had been put to rest. A treasure-trove of jade accompanied the corpse: a life-sized mosaic mask of
78 jade was placed over the face, jade and mother-of-pearl disks served him as ear spools, several necklaces of tubular jade beads festooned the chest, and jade rings adorned his fingers. A large jade was held in each hand and another was placed in the mouth, a practice documented for the late Yucatec Maya, for the Aztec, and for the Chinese. Two jade figures, and two sensitively modeled heads in stucco were placed on the floor of the funerary chamber.

77 (*opposite*) View from the northeast of the Temple of the Sun, Palenque, dating from the late seventh century AD.

Sun Lord Pacal
of Palenque

78 Life-sized jade mosaic mask of Lord Pacal, from the Funerary Crypt, Temple of the Inscriptions, Palenque, and dated to AD 683. The eyes are fashioned of shell and obsidian, and all the pieces were once affixed to a wooden backing, now rotted away.

79 Funerary Crypt in the Temple of the Inscriptions, Palenque, dated to AD 683. The sarcophagus of Sun Lord Pacal lies below and supports the great stone slab. Around the walls of the corbeled chamber are nine stuccoed figures.

Epigraphic detective work has revealed that the man in the Funerary Crypt was the mightiest of all of Palenque's rulers. Sun Lord Pacal (or 'Hand-shield'), who had ascended the throne when he was twelve years old and had died in AD 683 at the venerable age of eighty. It is immediately evident that this great man had the Crypt built to contain his own remains; further, that he might have had the entire temple-pyramid above it raised in his own lifetime. Thus it seems that the Temple of the Inscriptions was a funerary monument with exactly the same primary function as the Egyptian pyramids. And this, of course, leads one to look upon most Maya temple-pyramids as sepulchral monuments, dedicated to the worship of deceased kings.

Such a conclusion is backed up by many finds in the Central Area, and not just at the really large sites. Altun Ha, for example, is a relatively small center – perhaps qualifying only as a Maya town – in northern Belize, with an antiquity reaching back into Preclassic times. It has no stelae, and thus played no great role on the Classic political stage, but some fairly spectacular finds have been made there by David M. Pendergast of the Royal Ontario Museum. One of these was the famous 'Sun God's Tomb' constructed in a modestly sized funerary pyramid. Before the interment of the honored deceased (an adult male), virtually the entire crypt had been draped in cloth. The corpse had then been placed on a wooden platform, and accompanied by the skins of jaguars or pumas, by matting and cordage, and by necklaces and pendants of jade and *Spondylus* (thorny oyster) shell. The *pièce de résistance* was the largest carved jade ever found in Mesoamerica, a 14.9-cm-high effigy head of the monstrous bird-deity Vucub Caquix, according to the Popol Vuh epic the 'sun' of the era preceding our own.

Classic sites in the Northern Area: Río Bec, Chenes, and Cobá

The deserted forests of southern Campeche and Quintana Roo form the wildest part of the Maya region, but scattered through them are many ruined centers which have as yet been untouched by pick or spade. Our knowledge of these sites, as Tatiana Proskouriakoff pointed out, is owed 'to the gum-chewing habit of our sedentary city-dwellers,' for it is the chicle hunters who have come across them while searching for the sapodilla trees from which the gum is extracted. Several share in an aberrant architectural style named after the large site of Río Bec. Here showiness rather than function is what was apparently sought, for characteristic of this style of the Late Classic is the decoration of perfectly ordinary small 'palaces' with high towers imitating the fronts of temple-pyramids; these towers are solid, however, the steps being impossibly narrow and steep, and the 'doorway' at the summit leading to nothing. It is as though the Río Bec architects wished to imitate the great Tikal temples without going to any trouble. In the Río Bec sites, such as Xpuhil and Hormiguero, we begin to see on façades and roof combs the 80,81 elaborate ornamentation emphasizing masks of the sky-serpent and the *uitz* ('mountain') monster, which become of increasing concern to Maya architects as one moves further north into the Yucatán Peninsula. To today's 'functionalists,' the fakery of the Río Bec style is somewhat repellent, but no one could help but be awed by these mysterious sites crumbling in their jungle fastness.

Between the Río Bec area and the Puuc Hills of Yucatán is the Chenes, a well-populated zone of northern Campeche. Like those of Río Bec, with whom they must have been in close contact, the Chenes architects lavishly ornamented façades with sky-serpent masks and volutes, but the false towers of the former are missing. And, as at the Puuc sites to the north (see Chapter 6), the ornamentation consists of hundreds of small sculptural elements set into the buildings. One enters the front room through fantastic jaws, and is faced with tiers of masks, one over the other, on the corners.

While the two sub-areas that we have been discussing are clearly intermediate in space and style between the Petén and the terminal Late Classic Puuc styles, there are centers in the wild eastern half of the peninsula which are obviously direct extensions of central Petén ideas and perhaps peoples. One of these is Cobá, a name implying something like 'ruffled waters,' a fitting epithet since it was built among a small group of shallow,

80 North façade of Structure V at Hormiguero, Mexico (Río Bec culture), from a photograph taken by Karl Ruppert in 1933. The figure stands before the doorway of the one-room temple, entered through the jaws of a monstrous mask. On the west side are the remains of a false tower.

81 Palace at Xpuhil (Río Bec culture), from a reconstruction drawing by Tatiana Proskouriakoff. The three towers are completely solid and served no other function than decoration.

reedy lakes in northern Quintano Roo; until the middle of this century the zone was frequented only by Maya hunters who occasionally burned incense before the stelae scattered among its ruins. Cobá is not a single site but a whole group linked to a central complex by long, perfectly straight masonry causeways usually called by the Maya term *sacbe* ('white road'). There are more than sixteen of these, but what the idea was behind their construction we cannot even guess, for quite often a *sacbe* several miles in length will reach a ruin of very paltry dimensions. *Sacbe* No. 1 is the strangest of all, for it continues west from Cobá in a generally straight direction for no less than 62 miles, finally reaching the site of Yaxuná, some 12 miles southwest of Chichén Itzá. Some have claimed that the Maya *sacbe* were arteries of commerce, but a purely ceremonial function is far more plausible.

The buildings of Cobá are in a sorry state of preservation, but there appear to have been temple-pyramids and palaces like those of the Petén. It continued to be inhabited into Post-Classic times, for there are a few structures like those of Tulum (a very late town on the east coast of the peninsula), and there are references to Cobá in late Maya legends in which the center is associated with the Sun God.

Art of the Late Classic

Late Classic Maya art evolves directly out of that of the early half of the period, but excepting the demonstrably Terminal Classic sculpture of the Puuc, there is very little outside influence still to be seen. Maya artists now were free to go their own way, developing a remarkably sophisticated style as introspective as that of Asia and almost as 'naturalistic' as that of Europe and the Mediterranean. But the Maya were not always interested in three-dimensionality, although they could when they wished give depth to a scene by foreshortening, and to figures by backlighting. Their art is essentially a painterly one, narrative and baroque, tremendously involved with ornament and grotesques but preserving what Proskouriakoff has called 'order in complexity.' Finally, the Late Classic Maya were, with their predecessors the Olmec and their contemporaries the Moche of Peru, the only American Indians interested in rendering the uniqueness of individual characters through portraiture.

The Maya artists excelled in low relief carving, and that is what most Maya sculpture is, whether on stelae, lintels, or panels. By the eighth century AD, they had achieved a complete mastery of this medium, posing their figures in such a manner that in place of the rigid formality prevalent in earlier monuments, a kind of dynamic imbalance among the different parts of the composition was sought which leads the eye restlessly along. A lintel from 82 Kuná, a site only a few miles from Bonampak, provides a magnificent example of artistic contraposition, the goateed Maya resting on one leg and leaning forward clasping a ceremonial bar; but surely the perfection of relief 84 carving was attained on the Late Classic tablets from Palenque, particularly 83 the Tablet of the Slaves which shows Sun Lord Chac Zutz ('Great Bat')

82 Stone lintel from the Late Classic site of Kuná (Lacanhá), Mexico. The protagonist, a lord subordinate to the king of Bonampak, holds a 'ceremonial bar', a stylized, double-headed sky-serpent. In the text to the left is carved the *tun* ending 9.15.15.0.0. (4 June AD 746 in the Gregorian calendar). Ht 27¼ in. (68.8 cm).

83 Detail from the Tablet of the Slaves, Palenque, dated to AD 730. Shown here is the head of Sun Lord Chac Zutz, who sits cross-legged on the backs of two crouching captives. On either side of him are placed a man and woman carrying the symbols of rulership in their hands.

84 (*below*) Stone tablet incised with the head of Chac Xib Chac, from the Late Classic period at Palenque.

The potters' art

85 (*opposite*) Large pottery censer, probably from a cave in Chiapas or Tabasco, Mexico. The main face is that of the Jaguar God of the Underworld, the guise of the Sun on his nightly journey beneath the earth. Censers of this form were especially popular at Palenque. Ht 23¾ in. (60.3 cm).

86 (*right*) Pottery figurine of a woman sheltering a man, Jaina, Mexico. Ht 8 in. (20.3 cm).

87 Pottery figurine, probably from Jaina. The subject is the Fat God, wearing feathered war costume and carrying a shield. Ht 11½ in. (29.2 cm).

88 Pottery figurine from Jaina. A seated man holds an unidentified object, possibly a celt. Like all the finest pieces from Jaina, this figurine was made partly with a pottery mold and partly with the fingers, and was painted after firing. Ht 4½ in. (11.4 cm).

seated upon the backs of two barbaric-looking captives. Naturally, over such a wide area there were specializations, real schools of carvers at various sites. Copán, as has been mentioned, had a notable development of three-dimensional sculpture (as did Toniná in the Chiapas hills), while Palenque, at the other end of the Central Area, concentrated on reliefs carried out with extremely sophisticated use of carved and engraved lines.

Pottery objects of Late Classic manufacture run the gamut from crude, mold-made figurines and the ordinary pots and pans of everyday life to real works of art. Among the latter are the fantastic incense burners common at Palenque and in some of the caves of Chiapas and Tabasco, consisting of tall, hollow tubes modeled with the figures or heads of gods, particularly the Jaguar God of the Underworld, sometimes placed one on top of the other like Alaskan totem poles. Vertical flanges were placed on either side, and the whole painted in reds, ochers, blue, and white, after firing.

Jaina, a small limestone island just off the coast of Campeche and separated from the mainland by a tidal inlet, is one of the most enigmatic archaeological sites in the Maya area. For some reason known only to themselves, the ancients had used it as a necropolis, and it is close enough to the Puuc sites inland (Chapter 6) for it to have been their rulers and nobles who were buried there. Certainly the puniness of the temples constructed on the island is not in keeping with the great number of graves or with the magnificence of the offerings found in them. It is from these that archaeologists and looters have recovered the delicate, sophisticated figurines for which Jaina is famous. All objects are hollow and fitted with whistles at their backs; the faces were usually made in molds, but these and other details were embellished by the fingers of the artist. At one level of comprehension the emphasis is upon portraiture of real persons, perhaps the occupants of the graves: haughty nobles and armed warriors, some with tattooed or scarified faces, beautiful young women and fat old matrons. But at another level, these might also represent deities. For example, of two common, rather Freudian motifs, one depicts a mature woman sheltering a grown man as though he were her child, and might well be Ix Chel, the Mother Goddess; while the other, an ugly old man making advances to a handsome female must be an aged underworld divinity and his consort, Ix Chel, who is also the Moon Goddess. Another common supernatural in Jaina collections is the Fat God, who seems to have been popular among the Maya of Campeche.

Maya potters achieved chromatic effects of great brilliance in their vessels by firing them at low temperatures, sacrificing durability for aesthetic effect. Late Classic polychromes, generally deep bowls, cylindrical vessels, or footed dishes, are sometimes painted with the same narrative skill as the wall paintings exhibit. One vessel (ill. 89) is a 10-inch-high (25-cm) vase from an otherwise run-of-the-mill grave at Altar de Sacrificios in the Central Area. Justifiably described as 'a ceramic masterpiece,' six strange figures, all of them dead or wearing the attributes of death and darkness, are painted on its exterior along with glyphs including a Calendar Round date corresponding to AD 754. The figure of an old god with closed eyes apparently dancing with a sinister, grossly fat snake is so well done that it suggests the employment of

Ceramic masterpieces

89 Polychrome pottery vase of the Tepeu culture from Altar de Sacrificios, Guatemala. This side shows an old god, perhaps Itzamná, apparently dead, but dancing with a monstrous snake. Five other figures appear on the vase, all with death associations. In the text is a Calendar Round date probably corresponding to AD 754. Ht 10 in. (25.4 cm).

90 Black pottery jar, from Cholchá (southern Yucatán), Mexico. The vessel has been deeply carved with the figure of the rain deity, Chac Xib Chac, against a swirling background, and red pigment rubbed into the cut-away areas. Ht 5½ in. (14 cm).

91 Incised pottery bowl (Slate ware) from the Northern Area. The design, a modified step-and-fret pattern, is carried out in a negative smudging technique. Ht 4½ in. (11.4 cm).

92 This carved jade plaque from Nebaj, Guatemala, is emerald green with white clouding, and represents a Maya lord in conversation with a palace dwarf. W. 5¾ in. (14.6 cm).

93 Onyx bowl, said to be from the state of Campeche, Mexico. A row of incised glyphs encircles the rim. Below, on the fluted sides, are incised three seated profile figures, two men (one of whom is visible here) and a robed woman, with additional glyphs; each figure holds a symbolic object. Ht 4½ in. (11.4 cm).

Maya mastercarvers

94 The profiles of two gods can be seen facing left in this tour-de-force of the Tepeu flint chipper's art from Quiriguá, Guatemala. Ht 10 in. (25.4 cm).

95 Carved shell pendant, probably from Jaina. A young man with the flattened head so highly esteemed by the Maya appears above a fantastic fish, the body of which is covered with unreadable glyphs. The cut-away areas were once inlaid with jade. Ht $3\frac{1}{8}$ in. (7.9 cm).

96 Incised obsidians from an offering placed beneath a stela at Tikal (Tepeu culture). The flat side of a crude flake has in each instance been engraved with the figure of a deity or with a simplified mat design. L. of long piece $2\frac{3}{4}$ in. (7 cm).

artists of genius in decorating pottery. Vessels could also be carved when leather-hard, just before firing, some excellent vases in this style from

90   Yucatán depicting God GI (Chac Xib Chac), seated among swirling volutes.

It is natural that the Maya lavished upon jade, the most precious substance known to them, their full artistry. That these jades were traded over considerable distances is evident from late Classic Usumacinta-style pieces which were tossed into the Sacred Cenote at Chichén Itzá during the Post-Classic period, and some from the lowland Maya even found their way to Oaxaca and the Valley of Mexico. Most are very thin plaques with low relief carving on one face, probably executed by tubular drills of cane used with jade sand. A fine plaque from Nebaj in the Southern Area must be a product

92   of a Central Area artist, and shows a recurrent theme, a richly dressed noble seated upon a throne, leaning forward to chat with a dwarf, perhaps a court buffoon.

Not only jade, but marble as well was worked by the lowland Maya lapidaries; but it must have been a rare substance, for objects made from it are infrequent. A fluted vase of translucent onyx marble, with incising in Late

93   Classic style, is a fine example of the genre. It is somewhat doubtful if the well-known marble vessels from the Ulua region of western Honduras are to be considered as Maya at all, but fragments from them have been found in deposits assigned to the Terminal Classic in Belize and Petén sites. That the Maya could impose their artistic conventions on any medium is apparent in

94   the 'eccentric' flint blades chipped to include divine faces in profile, and small

96   blades of obsidian incised with the gods of the Maya pantheon; these were favorite objects for placing in caches under stelae or beneath temple floors in Central Area sites. Along the coast of Campeche, above all at Jaina, art in carved shell reached a high level, the Maya typically painting the lily by

95   inlaying these lovely objects with small pieces of apple-green jade.

It should always be borne in mind, however, that almost all Maya art which survived the vicissitudes of time is in imperishable materials. Classic murals and pictorial ceramics testify that the vast majority of it consisted not of stone, jade, and pottery, but of carved wood and woven and painted textiles. Virtually all of this has disappeared without a trace in the tropical environment. It is a certainty that there must have been many thousands of Classic Maya books written on bark-paper, but not a single one has come down to us (although unsalvageable traces are occasionally found in elite graves). All of this, and more, perished in the great cataclysm described in the next chapter.

6·The Terminal Classic

Maya civilization in the Central Area reached its full glory in the eighth century, but it must have contained the seeds of its own destruction, for in the hundred or more years that followed all of its magnificent cities had fallen into decline and ultimately suffered abandonment. This was surely one of the most profound social and demographic catastrophes of all human history. Yet ironically, during the terrible century that saw the Classic collapse in the southern lowlands, the Maya exerted an altogether unprecedented influence over the Gulf Coast and even the central highlands of Mexico. And it is clear that there was no similar decline in the Northern Area: quite the contrary, in the Puuc region and at Chichén Itzá, cities achieved a remarkable florescence – including some of the finest architecture ever seen in the pre-Conquest New World – that was only snuffed out by foreign invasion.

The Terminal Classic, from about AD 800 until 925, was therefore a time of tragedy and triumph, in which old thrones toppled in the south as a new political order took shape in the north, in which southern cities fell into the dust as northern ones flourished. It was an era marked by widespread movements of peoples, during which the destinies of central Mexico and the Maya area became as closely intertwined as they had been in the days of Teotihuacan's hegemony, and in which the stage was set for the rise of a new power in Mexico: the Toltec.

The collapse

Almost the only fact surely known about the collapse in the southern lowlands is that it really happened. Scholarly imaginations have run rife in coming up with explanations, and have included just about everything from epidemic diseases, invasion by foreigners from Mexico, social revolution (championed by Eric Thompson and still a plausible hypothesis), and even earthquakes and hurricanes. Unfortunately, the latest Classic inscriptions throw little light on the problem, since their parsimonious texts never deal with mundane matters as censuses or agricultural production figures.

Basing himself on the assumption that cessation of monument erection at a particular city means its abandonment, John W. G. Lowe has performed a systems simulation of the Classic collapse and the processes that might have induced it. As summarized by Robert Sharer, the basic scenario runs something like this. Between AD 672 and 751 (considered by many to mark the civilization's florescence), the number of communities carving new monuments continued to increase, but new construction took place only in already-established cities: Maya civilization had ceased to expand geographically. From 751 to about 790, long-standing alliances began to break down, interstate trade declined, and conflicts between neighboring city-states increased (the battle of 792 commemorated by the Bonampak murals illustrates this situation). From 790 to 830, the death rate of cities outstripped the birth rate, while after 830 construction stopped throughout the Central Area, with the exception of peripherally located sites like Lamanai. The katun ending date 10.3.0.0.0 (AD 889) was celebrated by inscriptions at only three sites. And the very last Long Count date to be recorded anywhere was the katun ending 10.4.0.0.0 (AD 909), incised on a jade from a site in southern Quintana Roo.

According to Lowe, this 'apocalypse' as he calls it, was brought about by the mutually enforcing interaction of several factors, set in motion by population growth, particularly among the elite, and by food shortages. Paradoxically, agricultural intensification (for instance, raised fields) would have led to declining per capita production through stress on the soil and through a labor shortage caused by the diversion of field hands to the elite centers to satisfy the cultural demands of the burgeoning upper class.

This explanation, although at present almost impossible to document archaeologically, is one that many Mayanists find plausible. It has found recent confirmation in research undertaken by Kevin Johnston at the site of Itzán, on a small tributary of the Río Pasión. Thanks to a long road bulldozed through a residential part of the site, Johnston has determined that about a half of all domestic house floors were *not* located on top of house mounds, and thus would have been invisible to the usual archaeological surface survey. What this means is that we may have to double our previous population estimates for the Central Area, which already run into the many millions.

One can only conclude that by the end of the eighth century, the Classic Maya population of the southern lowlands had probably increased beyond the carrying capacity of the land, no matter what system of agriculture was in use. There is mounting evidence for massive deforestation and erosion throughout the Central Area, only alleviated in a few favorable zones by dry slope terracing. In short, overpopulation and environmental degradation had advanced to a degree only matched by what is happening in many of the poorest tropical countries today. The Maya apocalypse, for such it was, surely had ecological roots.

It was not just the 'stela cult' – the inscribed glorification of royal lineages and their achievements – that disappeared with the collapse, but an entire world of esoteric knowledge, mythology, and ritual. Much of the elite cultural behavior to be described in Chapter 9, such as the complex Underworld mythology and iconography found on Classic Maya funerary ceramics, failed to re-emerge with the advent of the Post-Classic era, and one can only conclude that the royalty and nobility, including the scribes who were the repository of so much sacred and scientific knowledge, had 'gone with the wind.' They may well have been massacred by an enraged populace, and their screenfold books consumed in a holocaust similar to that carried out centuries later by Bishop Landa.

New investigations have shown that at least some of the Central Area population survived the debacle, for instance in the valleys of the Belize and New Rivers, finally to succumb to diseases introduced by the Spanish invaders of the sixteenth and seventeenth centuries. But these dwindling groups would have known little about the glories of the Classic past, and some would have been wanderers among the now-empty centers, camping out like savages, or archaeologists, in the rooms of forgotten palaces – peoples like the Lacandón, burning copal incense before the strange depictions of mortal men and women who had now become gods.

Seibal and the Putún Maya

The great city of Seibal on the Río Pasión apparently recovered from its defeat at the hands of the far smaller Dos Pilas, but during the Terminal Classic it seems to have come under the sway of warriors (or warrior-traders) from further afield. The evidence is to be found in the part of the site known as Group A; in its south plaza sits an unusual four-sided structure with four stairways. In front of each stairway is a stela, and a fifth stands inside the temple. All five record the katun ending 10.1.0.0.0 (1 December AD 849). Two of them show an obvious foreigner, with clipped moustache and page-boy haircut, but wearing Classic Maya regalia; since apparently different individuals are portrayed on the remaining stelae, we may be dealing with a kind of four-way joint rule, a kind of government which we will see at Chichén Itzá at the same time.

There are even more 'foreign'-looking stelae at Seibal which belong to this period, with non-Maya calendrical glyphs, and one figure wears the bird mask of the central Mexican wing god, Ehecatl, with a Mexican speech scroll curling from the beak.

Who were these people? We have much to learn about the ninth century in the southern Maya lowlands, but surely Eric Thompson was right in thinking that the Putún or Chontal Maya of the Tabasco and southern Campeche plains had begun taking over some of the more important sites in the southern Petén, such as Seibal, perhaps moving into a power vacuum. These somewhat Mexicanized merchant-warriors controlled the great entrepôt of Xicallanco where Mexican and Maya traders met, and were known to the later Aztecs as 'Olmeca-Xicallanca.' There is now incontrovertible evidence that the Putún had not only penetrated into the lowland Maya 'heartland,' they had reached the central highlands of Mexico. In recent years, excavations at the hilltop site of Cacaxtla, traditionally ascribed to the Olmeca-Xicallanca, have uncovered a ninth-century palace with brilliant polychrome murals in Maya style. Among other things, these show dignitaries in Maya costume bearing Maya 'ceremonial bars,' which are in the style of the Putún-influenced stelae of Seibal, and a great war going on between two contending factions, which immediately recalls the battle scene of Bonampak.

The question remains, what were these Olmeca-Xicallanca or Putún Maya doing there, almost 500 miles from their homeland? For that matter, why are there bas-reliefs showing seated figures in Maya style on the ninth-century Temple of the Feathered Serpent at Xochicalco in Morelos, just south of the Valley of Mexico? It is now evident that the ninth century was a time of turmoil over much of Mesoamerica, with the power of Teotihuacan long since gone, and the old order in the Maya lowlands breaking down. In this power vacuum, the Putún, seasoned businessmen with strong contacts ranging from central Mexico to the Caribbean coast of Honduras, must have played a very aggressive role in a time of troubles, and their presence in the Mexican highlands may have played a formative role in what was to become the Toltec state.

Terminal Classic sites in the Northern Area: the Puuc

'If Yucatán were to gain a name and reputation,' wrote Bishop Landa in 1566, 'from the multitude, the grandeur and the beauty of its buildings, as other regions of the Indies have obtained these by gold, silver and riches, its glory would spread like that of Peru and New Spain.' Landa was not exaggerating, for ruins there are by the hundreds. Sylvanus Morley saw this as evidence for what he called a 'New Empire' founded by refugees from the derelict civilization of the Central Area, his so-called 'Old Empire,' and he claimed to find references in the late Maya chronicles to a double-pronged migration from the south. However, ceramics recovered from excavations, along with a better reading of the ethnohistoric sources, led Eric Thompson and George Brainerd to the view that many of the Yucatecan sites were coeval with the Petén centers which were claimed to pre-date them. Modern scholarship has found that both schools were partly right and partly wrong: the great era of Yucatecan culture was the Terminal Classic, when many Petén cities had fallen into ruin, but there never was a real 'empire' among the Maya, as Morley had believed. And if there ever had been a movement of refugees streaming from the collapsed culture of the south into Yucatán, one would have expected to find enclaves of Cholan-speakers there at the time of the Conquest, which is definitely not the case.

It will be remembered that a group of very low hills, the Puuc, is to be found in southwestern Yucatán, a region, as Nicholas Dunning and Jeff Kowalski tell us, that has deep and fertile soils, in fact the best in the northern part of the peninsula. Perhaps by the Late Preclassic the Maya of the region had learned how to construct *chultuns* or bottle-shaped cisterns to provide scarce drinking water over the dry season, and populations began to expand. During the Late Classic itself, the Puuc was fragmented into many relatively small major centers controlling domains that included pockets of particularly productive soil.

It is in the Puuc that the dominant Terminal Classic style of the peninsula took form, by the end of the Late Classic. The problem of dating is acute, for some of these centers are mentioned in the chronicles by late upstart lineages who claimed to have founded them, but there are truncated Long Count dates painted on capstones in the late ninth and early tenth baktun; the very latest reads 10.3.17.12.1, or AD 905, but Thompson believed on excellent grounds that the Puuc style may have lasted until 10.8.0.0.0 (AD 987), when Toltec invaders usher in the Post-Classic.

Characteristic of Puuc buildings are facings of very thin squares of limestone veneer over the cement-and-rubble core; boot-shaped vault stones; decorated cornices; round columns in doorways; engaged or half-columns repeated in long rows; and the exuberant use of stone mosaics on upper façades, emphasizing the usual monster-masks with long, hook-shaped snouts, as well as frets and lattice-like designs of criss-crossed elements. In the perfection of architectural façades, the Puuc is far ahead of the more sloppy Petén style.

Uxmal is by far the largest Puuc site, and one of the triumphs of Maya civilization. Traditionally, this was the seat of the Xiu family, but this was a johnny-come-lately lineage of Mexican origin which could not possibly have built the site. The archaeological and epigraphic evidence testifies that Uxmal had emerged as the capital of a large, Terminal Classic state centered in the eastern Puuc between AD 850 and 925. Uxmal is dominated by two mighty temple-pyramids, the Great Pyramid and the House of the Magician, the upper temple of the latter entered through a monster-mask doorway like those of the Chenes. Next to the Magician is the imaginatively named Nunnery, actually a palace group made up of four separate rectangular buildings arranged around an interior court; although the group could be entered from the corners, the principal gateway with its corbel arch lies on the south side. The mosaic elements making up the masonry façades of the Nunnery Quadrangle are particularly interesting; they include miniature representations of the thatched-roof huts of the ordinary folk of the time.

A recent iconographic study by Professor Kowalski suggests a cosmological layout for the Nunnery. The higher placement of the North Building, with its 13 exterior doorways (reflecting the 13 layers of heaven), and the celestial serpents surmounting the huts identify it with the celestial sphere. The iconography of the West Building, with 7 exterior doorways (7 is the mystic number of the earth's surface), and figures of Pauahtun – the earth god as a turtle – indicate this to be the Middleworld, the place of the sun's descent into the Underworld. The East Building has mosaic elements reflecting the old war cult of Teotihuacan, where tradition had it that the sun was born; thus, this may also be Middleworld, the place of the rising sun. Finally, the South Building has 9 exterior doorways (the Underworld or Xibalbá had 9 layers), and has the lowest placement in the complex; it thus seems to be associated with death and the nether regions.

Below the Great Pyramid, on its own artificial terrace, is the House of the Governor, the finest structure at Uxmal and the culmination of the Puuc style. The upper façade or frieze of the three long interconnected structures of this building is covered by a fantastically elaborate mosaic of thousands of separate masonry elements set into the rubble core, a symphony of step-and-fret, lattice-work, and monster-mask motifs combined into a single harmonious whole.

There are only a handful of carved stelae at Uxmal; not only are they sloppily executed, but they are in a sorry state of preservation. Nevertheless,

97 Plan of Uxmal, by far the largest Puuc site.

98 The Nunnery Quadrangle
at Uxmal, looking northeast.

Kowalski has been able to work out a partial dynastic history dominated by the figure of Lord Chac, during whose reign the House of the Governor was built, probably as his administrative headquarters.

A causeway or *sacbe* 11¼ miles (18 km) long runs southeast from Uxmal through the small site of Nohpat to Kabah, so presumably the three centers were connected ceremonially if not politically. Kabah is noted for its Codz Poop palace, with an extraordinary façade made up of hundreds of monster-masks, and for its freestanding arch. Sayil, to the south of Kabah, is dominated by a magnificent three-story palace. It has the additional distinction of being thus far the only Puuc site to be completely and intensively mapped; Professor Jeremy Sabloff of the University of Pittsburgh, who headed the project, estimates that about 10,000 people lived in an urban core of 1.7 sq. miles (4.5 sq km), with an additional 7,000 in the zone around this core. To the east of Sayil is Labná, another sizeable Puuc city, with an elaborate freestanding arch (far more impressive than Kabah's), a palace group, and a lofty temple-pyramid.

Etzná is the southernmost of the Puuc sites, and is best known for its five-storied structure which combines features of pyramids and palaces. Presumably its Late Preclassic canal-and-moat system, described in Chapter 2, remained in use throughout the Terminal Classic.

The Terminal Classic at Chichén Itzá

That the Puuc style reached east as well as north is evident at the great site of Chichén Itzá in east-central Yucatán, where a number of buildings at this otherwise Toltec-Maya center closely resemble those to the west, with the proviso that Puuc veneer masonry is seldom present. These are largely located in the southern zone of the city, and include the three-storied Nunnery, the Akab Dzib ('dark writing,' so-called from the reliefs containing glyphic texts on one of the doorways), the Casa Colorada, the Temple of the Three Lintels, and the Temple of the Four Lintels.

99

100

102

101

99 West wing of the Palace at Sayil, Mexico (Puuc culture). Seemingly three-storied, each row of rooms actually rests on a solid rubble core. The vaults have collapsed in the lower 'story.'

Puuc architecture

100 Arch at Labná, a Puuc culture site in Mexico, from a view published by Frederick Catherwood in 1844.

101 East wing of the Nunnery (Puuc culture) at Chichén Itzá, Mexico, from a lithograph by Frederick Catherwood. The masks repeated so many times on this kind of façade are believed to be of the sky-serpent.

102 The five-storied structure at Etzná, Campeche (Late Classic period).

Lintels in the Nunnery and other buildings contain quite extensive hieroglyphic texts, which have been analyzed by David Kelley, Ruth Krochok, Michel Davoust, and other epigraphers. They were inscribed within a very brief period spanning only the second half of the ninth century, and celebrate not the dynastic history of individual kings, as in the southern lowlands, but rather temple dedication rituals carried out by groups of lords, such as bloodletting and drilling of new fire. Many scholars now believe that Chichén Itzá was then governed by what the later Maya chronicles call *mul tepal*, 'joint rule,' seemingly by a group of three (or perhaps four) brothers.

One of these brothers is named Kakupacal, 'Fiery Shield'; the Colonial sources mention a Kakupacal who is described as a valiant Itzá captain, and this raises the question of whether these are the same persons. If so, then the *mul tepal* brothers might have been Itzá Maya, but we will defer the treatment of these enigmatic people until the next chapter. Could the rulers of Terminal Classic Chichén have been Putún? This also is a possibility, since there are distinct iconographic links between the late monuments of Seibal and those of Chichén (even in the Toltec-Maya period), and it will be recalled that there is a strong hint of joint rule in the stelae surrounding Seibal's four-sided temple.

One of the strangest and most intriguing structures ever raised by the Maya is the Caracol ('snail'), located in the Puuc section of Chichén. Once stigmatized by Eric Thompson as a 'two-decker wedding cake on the square carton in which it came,' it is nevertheless one of the outstanding monuments of the Terminal Classic. The Caracol has long been described in the popular literature as an observatory, and this has been proved beyond a shadow of a doubt by measurements taken by the archaeoastronomers Anthony Aveni, Sharon Gibbs, and Horst Hartung. The ancient Maya used lines of sight taken from its platforms and door and window jambs to plot the rising and setting positions of the sun, the moon, and, above all, the planet Venus. As will be seen in Chapter 9, Maya astronomers had a remarkably accurate knowledge of the apparent motion of Venus, and it may be that at least some of that learning came from observations carried out in the Caracol.

The Cotzumalhuapa problem

The Pipil have always been an enigmatic people. Their language is Nahuat, a close relative of Nahuatl, the official tongue of the Aztec, differing mainly from the latter by a substitution of *t* in place of *tl*. Having intruded into the Maya area at some unknown time from an equally unknown region in Mexico, by the Spanish Conquest the Pipil had established a major settlement in a small zone within the well-watered piedmont zone just above the Pacific plain of Guatemala. From traditions recorded in Colonial times, however, it is known that their domain had once extended somewhat to the west into lands later claimed by the Cakchiquel Maya.

This once-Pipil territory is the locus of a vanished civilization which was indisputably Mexican, centering upon the town of Santa Lucía Cotzumal-huapa, in a region which once was famed for its production of cacao, the

The Cotzumalhuapa style

103 A stone relief of the Crab God from El Baúl (Cotzumalhuapa culture). On either side are the Mexican dates 2 Monkey and 6 Monkey. Ht 3 ft 3 in. (1 m).

104 A thin stone head (*hacha*) from El Baúl (Cotzumalhuapa culture). Objects of this sort were probably ball-court markers. Ht *c.* 1 ft (30.5 cm).

105 A ball-player salutes the Moon Goddess. Monument 4 from Santa Lucía Cotzumalhuapa (Cotzumalhuapa culture, end of the Early Classic or beginning of the Late Classic).

chocolate beans used not only for drink but as currency. There are only about a half-dozen Cotzumalhuapan sites known, or perhaps just one large one, for all lie within a tiny area of only 20 square miles. Each is a compact ceremonial center consisting of temple substructures arranged on a single large platform measuring only a few hundred yards on its long axis; structures have earthen cores faced with river cobbles, but stairways and some courts were occasionally covered with dressed stone.

From the evidence of art style and pottery, the Cotzumalhuapan culture must have flourished in the Terminal Classic. A more hard, cruel, and unsympathetic sculptural style can hardly be imagined, or one less Maya in its general aspect. As the late Sir Eric Thompson noted, the Cotzumalhuapan sculptors showed 'a haunting preoccupation with death.' Reliefs of skulls and manikin figures of skeletons are not uncommon. Their second obsession was the rubber ball game. Secure evidence for the game comes from certain stone objects which are frequent in the Cotzumalhuapan zone and in fact over much of the Pacific Coast down to El Salvador. Of these, most typical are the U-shaped stone 'yokes' which represented the heavy protective belts of wood and leather worn by the contestants; and thin heads or *hachas* with human faces, grotesque carnivores, macaws, and turkeys, generally thought to be markers for the zones of the court, but worn on the yoke during post-game

103

104

ceremonies. Both are sure signs of a close affiliation to the Classic cultures of the Mexican Gulf Coast, where such ball-game paraphernalia undoubtedly originated.

Among the relief and in-the-round sculptures of the Cotzumalhuapan sites are representations of some purely Mexican gods: Xipe Totec; the Wind God Ehecatl, shown as a horrifically snouted monster with one extruded eyeball; Tlaloc; Tlalchitonatiuh, god of the rising sun; the Old Fire God, Huehueteotl; and Quetzalcoatl as Feathered Serpent. On some magnificent stelae, ball players wearing 'yokes' and protective gloves reach up to celestial   105 deities, usually the Sun or Moon. From the bodies of gods and men may sprout the fronds and pods of cacao, the apparent source of Cotzumalhuapan wealth.

Not only their religion, but their very calendar was Mexican. The majority of the glyphs on the monuments are recognizable as the kind of day-names prevalent among the peoples of southern Mexico, while the numbers and coefficients are expressed in the Mexican fashion by dots or circles only, without the use of the bar for 'five' so characteristic of the Maya. Again, as in Mexico, individuals (and perhaps gods, too) were identified by the day of their birth.

The creators of the Cotzumalhuapan civilization, then, were not Mayan but Mexican, most likely the Pipil themselves. There are suggestive connections with the Gulf Coast plain, where there is a similar concentration upon the ball game, death, human sacrifice, and the cultivation of cacao. If these were the Pipil, then there might have been an ancient center of Nahuat speakers in southern Veracruz who, as another *pochteca* group, could have invaded the southern Maya area across the Isthmus of Tehuantepec. But the Cotzumalhuapa problem is very far from solved.

The end of an era

Beyond the continuing mystery which surrounds the demise of civilization in the Petén and neighboring regions, there is still much to be learned about the Terminal Classic. In many respects, what transpired in the Puuc area was a replay of the great collapse which had taken place a century earlier in the southern lowlands: for reasons which are yet unclear (but which may include overpopulation and a growing inability of the Puuc rulers to feed their people), all of its cities and lesser centers were virtually abandoned by the end of the tenth century; when first encountered by the Spaniards, they were in ruins.

There was one great exception to this second collapse. To the east of the Puuc, Chichén Itzá was to gather new strength, and to become the largest and perhaps even the most powerful Mesoamerican city of its day, as the transition was made from Classic to Post-Classic.

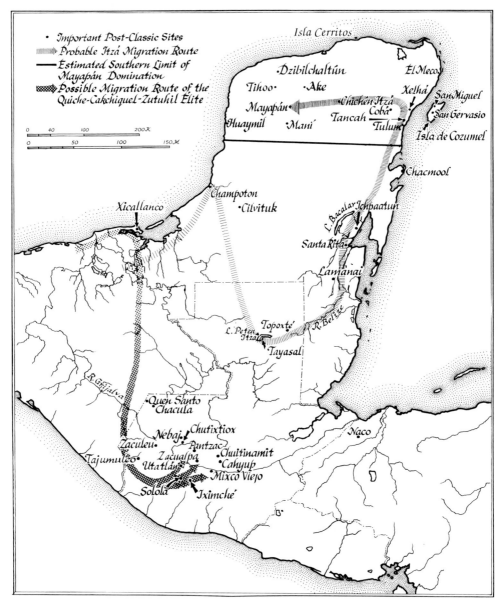

106 Sites of the Post-Classic period and late migration routes.

7·The Post-Classic

By the close of the tenth century the destiny of the once proud and independent Maya had fallen into the hands of grim militarists from the highlands of central Mexico, where a new order of men had replaced the supposedly more intellectual rulers of Classic times. About the events that led to the conquest of Yucatán by these foreigners, and the subsequent replacement of their state by a resurgent but already decadent Maya culture, we know a good deal, for we have entered rather shakily into what might be called history. The traditional annals of the peoples of Yucatán, and also of the Guatemalan highlanders, which were transcribed into Spanish letters early in Colonial times apparently reach back as far as the beginning of our Post-Classic era and are very important sources.

But they should be used with much caution, whether they come to us from Bishop Landa himself, from statements made by the native nobility, or from native lawsuits and land claims. These are often confused and often self-contradictory, above all since native lineages seem to have deliberately falsified their own history for political reasons. Our richest and most treacherous sources are the Katun Prophecies of Yucatán, contained in the so-called Books of Chilam Balam which derive their name from a Maya savant said to have predicted the arrival of the Spaniards from the east. The 'history' which they contain is based upon the Short Count, a cycle of 13 katuns (13 × 7,200 days or 256¼ years),each katun of which was named from the last day, always Ahau, on which it ended. Unfortunately, the Post-Classic Maya thought in purely cyclic terms, so that if certain events had happened in a Katun 13 Ahau, they would recur in the next of the same name. The result is that prophecy and history are almost inextricably entwined in these documents that sometimes read like divine revelation; one such history, for example, begins:

> This is the record of how the one and only god, the 13 gods, the 8,000 gods descended, according to the words of the priests, prophets, Chilam Balam, Ah Xupan, Napuc Tun, the priest Nahau Pech, and Ah Kauil Ch'el. Then was interpreted the command to them, the measured words which were given to them.

The Toltec invasion and Chichén Itzá

Into the vacuum created by the collapse of the older civilizations of central Mexico moved a new people, the Nahua-speaking Toltec, whose northern origins are proclaimed by their kinship with the non-agricultural barbarians called the Chichimec. Shortly after AD 900 they had settled themselves at the key site of Tula under the leadership of a king named Topiltzin, who also claimed the title of Quetzalcoatl or 'Feathered Serpent' (the culture hero of Mexican theology). Prominent among these people were the military orders that were to play such a significant role in later Mexican history – the Eagles, the Jaguars, and the Coyotes – and which paid homage to the war god Tezcatlipoca ('Smoking Mirror') rather than to the more peaceable Quetzalcoatl. According to a number of quasi-historical accounts of great poetic merit, a struggle ensued between Topiltzin Quetzalcoatl and his adherents on the one hand, and the warrior faction on the other. Defeated by the evil magic of his adversary Tezcatlipoca, the king was forced to leave Tula with his followers, most probably in AD 987. In one version well known to all the ancient Mexicans, he made his way to the Gulf Coast and from there set across on a raft of serpents for Tlapallan ('Red Land'), some day to return for the redemption of his people.

Wracked by further internal dissentions and deserted by most of its inhabitants, the Toltec capital was finally destroyed by violence in AD 1156 or 1168, but its memory was forever glorious in the minds of the Mexicans, and there was hardly a ruling dynasty in Mesoamerica in later days which did not claim descent from the Toltec of Tula. The city, which was certainly the administrative center of an empire spanning central Mexico from the Atlantic to the Pacific, has been securely identified as an archaeological site in the state of Hidalgo, some 50 miles northwest of Mexico City, so that a good deal is known about Toltec art and architecture in its place of origin. Everywhere the Toltec went, they carried with them their own very unsympathetic style, in which there is an obsession with the image of the Toltec warrior, complete with pillbox-like headdress with a down-flying bird in front, a stylized bird or butterfly on the chest, and carrying a feather-decorated *atlatl* in one hand and a bunch of darts in the other. Left arms were protected by quilted padding, and the back by a small shield shaped like a round mirror. Prowling jaguars and coyotes, and eagles eating hearts dominate the reliefs which covered their principal temple-pyramid, a testimony to the importance of the knightly orders among these militarists.

Now, it so happens that the Maya historical sources speak of the arrival from the west of a man calling himself Kukulcan (*kukul*, 'feathered,' and *can* 'serpent') in a Katun 4 Ahau which ended in AD 987, who wrested Yucatán from its rightful owners and established his capital at Chichén Itzá. According to the late Maya scholar Ralph Roys, the accounts of this great event are seriously confused with the history of a later people called the Itzá, who moved into the peninsula during the next Katun 4 Ahau, in the thirteenth century, and gave their name to the formerly Toltec site of Chichén. In any case, the Maya credited Kukulcan and his retinue with the introduction of idolatry, but the impressions left by him were generally good, for Bishop Landa states:

> They say he was favorably disposed, and had no wife or children, and that after his return he was regarded in Mexico as one of their gods and called

107 Wall painting from the Temple of the Warriors, Chichén Itzá. Canoe-borne Toltec warriors reconnoiter the Maya coast.

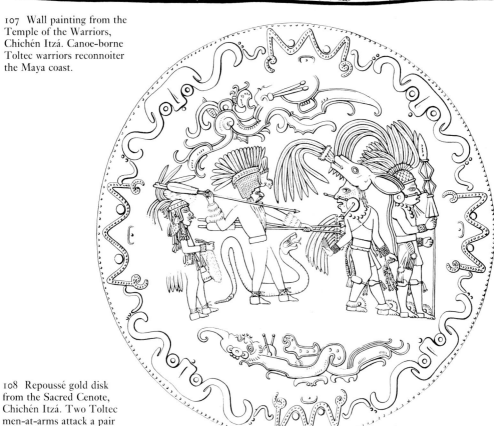

108 Repoussé gold disk from the Sacred Cenote, Chichén Itzá. Two Toltec men-at-arms attack a pair of fleeing Maya. Diam. $8\frac{3}{4}$ in. (22.2 cm).

109 Plan of Chichén Itzá.

110 View of the main monuments at Chichén Itzá, looking northeast from the Nunnery. In the foreground is the Caracol; beyond it to the left, the Castillo or Temple of Kukulcan; and to the right, the Temple of the Warriors.

Quetzalcoatl; and they also considered him a god in Yucatán on account of his being a just statesman.

The goodwill contained in these words is almost certainly due to most of the ruling houses of later times being of Mexican rather than Maya descent, for surely the archaeological record tells us that the conquest of Yucatán by the supposedly peaceful Topiltzin Quetzalcoatl and his Toltec armies was violent and brutal in the extreme. The murals found in the Temple of the Warriors at Chichén Itzá, and the relief scenes on some golden disks fished up from the Sacred Cenote at the same site, tell the same story. The drama opens with the arrival of the Toltec forces by sea, most likely along the Campeche shore, where they reconnoiter a coastal Maya town with whitewashed houses. In a marine engagement in which the Maya come out in rafts to meet the Toltec war canoes, the former suffer the first of their defeats. Then the scene moves to the land, where in a great pitched battle (commemorated in the frescoes of the Temple of the Jaguars) fought within a major Maya settlement the natives are again beaten. The final act ends with 107

108

145

the heart sacrifice of the Maya leaders, while the Feathered Serpent himself hovers above to receive the bloody offering.

The Yucatán taken over by the Toltec exiles was then in its Puuc phase, but following the invasion, Uxmal and most other important Puuc centers must have been abandoned under duress. Chichén Itzá, which in those days seems to have been called Uucil-abnal ('Seven Bushes'), became, under the rule of Topiltzin Quetzalcoatl, the supreme metropolis of a united kingdom, a kind of splendid recreation of the Tula which he had lost. New architectural techniques and motifs were imported from Toltec Mexico and synthesized with Puuc Maya forms. For instance, columns were now used in place of walls to divide rooms, giving an air of spaciousness to halls; a sloping batter was placed at the base of outside walls and platforms; colonnades of pure Tula type were built, which included low masonry banquettes covered with processions of tough Toltec warriors and undulating feathered serpents; and walls were decorated with murals in bands. And everywhere the old Maya monster-masks were incorporated in these new buildings.

For not only was there a synthesis of styles at Chichén Itzá, but also a hybridization of Toltec and Maya religion and society. Jaguar and Eagle knights rub elbows with men in traditional Maya costume and Mexican astral deities coexist with Maya gods. The old Maya order had been overthrown, but it is obvious that many of the native princes were incorporated into the new power structure.

At the hub of Toltec Chichén stands its most important structure, the so-called 'Castillo,' a great four-sided temple-pyramid which Landa tells us was dedicated to the cult of Kukulcan. The corbel-vaulted temple at the summit of the four breathtaking stairways is a curious mixture of indigenous and foreign, monster masks embellishing the exterior, reliefs of tall war captains from Tula being carved upon the jambs of its doors. Inside the Castillo has been discovered an earlier Toltec-Maya pyramid, with beautifully preserved details, such as the chambers of the superstructure which contain a stone throne in the form of a snarling jaguar, painted red, with eyes and spots of jade and fangs of shell. Before it is one of the sculptures called 'chacmools,' reclining figures with hands grasping plate-like receptacles held over the belly, perhaps for receiving the hearts of sacrificed victims. Chacmools are ubiquitous at Tula and at Chichén, and are a purely Toltec invention.

From the Castillo may be seen the Temple of the Warriors, a splendid building resting upon a stepped platform, surrounded by colonnaded halls. It is closely planned after Pyramid 'B' at Tula, but its far greater size and the excellence of the workmanship lavished upon it suggest that the Toltec intruders were better off in Yucatán, where they could call upon the skills of Maya architects and craftsmen. The building is approached on the northwest through impressive files of square columns, which are decorated on all four faces with reliefs of Toltec officers. At the top of the stairs a chacmool gazes stonily out upon the main plaza, while the entrance to the temple itself is flanked by a pair of feathered serpents, heads at the ground and tails in the air. Beyond them can be seen the principal sanctuary with its table or altar supported by little Atlantean Toltec warriors. All interior walls had been

109,110

111

113

112

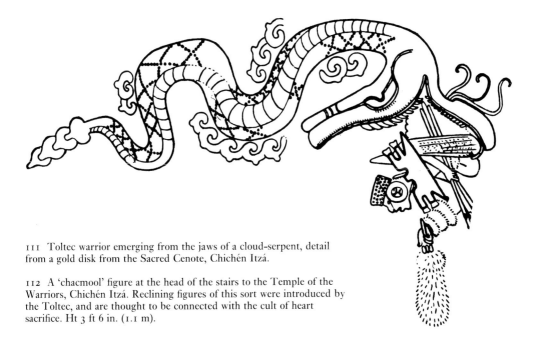

111 Toltec warrior emerging from the jaws of a cloud-serpent, detail from a gold disk from the Sacred Cenote, Chichén Itzá.

112 A 'chacmool' figure at the head of the stairs to the Temple of the Warriors, Chichén Itzá. Reclining figures of this sort were introduced by the Toltec, and are thought to be connected with the cult of heart sacrifice. Ht 3 ft 6 in. (1.1 m).

113 (*opposite*) The Toltec Temple of the Warriors from a doorway of the Castillo, Chichén Itzá. The building is a grandiose replica of Pyramid B at Tula in Mexico, and a symbol of Toltec ascendancy over Yucatán.

114 (*above*) The Toltec Ball Court at Chichén Itzá. With walls 27 ft (8.2 m) high, and an overall length of about 490 ft (149 m), this is the largest court in Mesoamerica. The rings set high on either wall were used in scoring the game.

**Chichén Itzá
architecture**

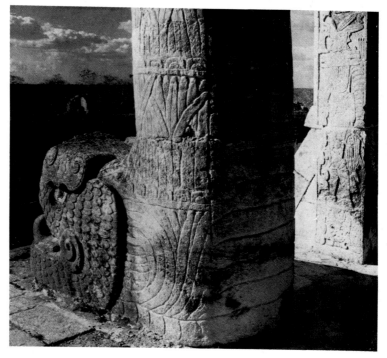

115 Doorway of the Temple of the Jaguars, overlooking the Ball Court, Chichén Itzá. Shown here are one of two Feathered Serpent columns which support the lintel, and a door jamb with a relief figure of a Toltec warrior.

frescoed with lively scenes related to the Toltec conquest of Yucatán (ill. 107).

In 1926, just as restoration of the Temple of the Warriors by the Carnegie Institution staff was near completion, another such structure came to light underneath it, and from this, the Temple of the Chacmool, were recovered relief-carved columns still bearing the bright pigments with which they were painted. Two benches in the temple interior had been painted in a most interesting fashion, one with a row of Toltec leaders seated upon jaguar thrones identical to that in the interior of the Castillo, but the other with Maya nobles seated upon stools covered with jaguar skin, bearing manikin scepters in Maya fashion. Could these have been quisling princes?

The splendid Ball Court of Toltec Chichén is the largest and finest in all Mesoamerica. Its two parallel, upright walls measure 272 ft long and 27 ft high (82.6 by 8.2 m), and are 99 ft (30 m) apart. At either end of the I-shaped playing field is a small temple, the one at the north containing extensive bas-reliefs of Toltec life. That the game was played Mexican-style is shown by the two stone rings set high on the sides of the walls, for a Spanish chronicler tells us that among the Aztec whichever team managed to get the ball through one of these not only won the game and the wager but the clothing of the onlookers. Above the east wall of the court is placed the important Temple of the Jaguars, whose inner walls were once beautifully frescoed with Toltec battle scenes, so detailed and convincing that the artist must have been a witness to the Toltec invasion.

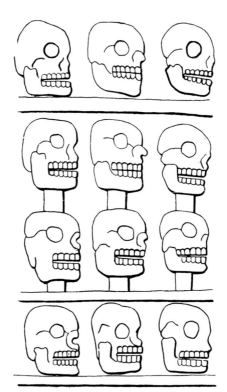

116 (*left*) Toltec relief panel of a jaguar eating a heart, from the Dance Platform of the Eagles, Chichén Itzá. Such a theme is also known at Tula in the Toltec homeland, and is symbolic of the military order of the Jaguars.

117 Bas-relief of skulls skewered on a rack, from the Tzompantli, Chichén Itzá.

Landa describes 'two small stages of hewn stone' at Chichén, 'with four staircases, paved on the top, where they say that farces were represented, and comedies for the pleasure of the public,' surely to be identified with the two Dance Platforms which have their facings covered with themes directly imported from Tula, such as eagles and jaguars eating hearts. Human sacrifice on a large scale must have been another gift of the Toltec, for near the Ball Court is a long platform carved on all sides with human skulls skewered on stakes. The Aztec name given to it, Tzompantli, is certainly apt, for in Post-Classic Mexico such platforms supported the great racks upon which the heads of victims were displayed. Each of the six Ball Court reliefs depicts the decapitation of a ball player, and it is entirely possible that the game was played 'for keeps,' the losers ending up on the Tzompantli.

Chichén Itzá is most renowned not for its architecture, but for its Sacred Cenote, or Well of Sacrifice, reached by a 900-ft-long (274-m) causeway leading north from the Great Plaza. From Landa's pen comes the following:

Into this well they have had, and then had, the custom of throwing men alive as a sacrifice to the gods, in times of drought, and they believed that they did not die though they never saw them again. They also threw into it a great many other things, like precious stones and things which they prized.

Shortly before the Spanish Conquest, one of our Colonial sources tells us that the victims were 'Indian women belonging to each of the lords,' but in the

118 Chamber in the cave of Balankanché, Yucatán. In the center, stalactite and stalagmite have united in an immense pillar; around it were placed Toltec incense burners of pottery and stone.

popular imagination the notion has taken hold that only lovely young virgins were tossed down to the Rain God lurking below its greenish-black waters. The late Dr Hooton, who examined a collection of some fifty skeletons fished up from the Sacred Cenote, commented that 'all of the individuals involved (or rather immersed) may have been virgins, but the osteological evidence does not permit a determination of this nice point.' A goodly number of the skulls turned out to be from adult males, and many from children, while pathology showed that 'three of the ladies who fell or were pushed into the Cenote had received, at some previous time, good bangs on various parts of the head . . . and one female had suffered a fracture of the nose'!

As the great Mayanists Ralph Roys and A. M. Tozzer stressed, the peak of the sacrificial cult at the Sacred Cenote was reached after the decline of Toltec Chichén, and continued into Colonial times and even later. None the less, many of the objects dredged from the muck at the bottom of the Cenote are of Toltec manufacture, including some marvellously fine jades and the gold disks already mentioned. For metals had now appeared in the Maya area, although probably all casting and most working was done elsewhere and imported, the many copper bells and other objects from the well being of Mexican workmanship. From places as far afield as Panama the local lords brought treasures of gold to offer to their Rain God.

108,111

Toltec-style pottery

119 A Toltec effigy jar (Plumbate ware) in the form of the god Itzamná, from Guatemala. Ht 6 in. (15.2 cm).

120 Hands are depicted in black paint on this X-Fine Orange ware jar from coastal Campeche. Together with Plumbate ware, pottery of this kind is a marker for the Toltec presence in the Maya area. Ht *c.* 7 in. (17.8 cm).

121 A Toltec tripod jar (Plumbate ware) from coastal Campeche, Mexico. Produced on the Pacific slopes of Chiapas and Guatemala in Toltec style, this glazed ware was widely traded over much of southern Mesoamerica. Ht 7½ in. (19 cm).

118 The Rain God's cult is also strikingly evident in the underground cavern of Balankanché, located 2½ miles east of Chichén Itzá. In a deep, hot, and humid chamber which they later sealed, the Toltec priests had placed almost 100 incense burners of pottery and stone, most of them at the base of an enormous stalagmitic formation in the center of the chamber. Twenty-six of these are hour-glass in shape, and had been modeled with the goggle-eyed visage of the Mexican Rain God, Tlaloc, and polychromed. Off to one side they had made an offering of 252 miniature *metates* with their *manos*, and it is tempting to speculate whether there might once have been 260 of these, the number of days in the sacred calendar.

119,121 This Toltec occupation has been detected at other places in the Yucatán Peninsula, and is everywhere marked by the presence of the glazed pottery called Plumbate ware, produced in kilns along the Guatemala-Chiapas border area near the Pacific shore. Plumbate vessels must have been made to Toltec taste, for they often take the form of Toltec warriors, but many are simple, pear-shaped vases supported on hollow legs, very much like the carved and painted vessels also associated with the Toltec period in Yucatán.

In 1984 and 1985, a team led by Anthony Andrews and Fernando Robles C. mapped and excavated the tiny island called Isla Cerritos, in the mouth of the Río Lagartos estuary on the north coast of Yucatán. This has proved to be the port of Chichén Itzá, with a seawall pierced by entryways on the exposed side, and with ceramics virtually identical to those of the great Toltec-Maya capital. It will be remembered from Chapter 1 that Yucatán's greatest resource was its coastal salt beds, and Isla Cerritos was certainly strategically located to exploit production and trade in this necessity. But other items were moving along these trade networks, for the excavators encountered obsidian from the mines in central Mexico, turquoise which had probably originated in the American Southwest (a luxury item prized by the Toltec and their cultural heirs the Aztec), and gold from lower Central America.

What finally happened to the Toltec? All indications are that their mighty capital, Chichén Itzá, was abandoned in a Katun 6 Ahau which ended in AD 1224, and they are heard of no more. Another people now take the stage for a brief moment and Maya culture lives a little while longer.

A word of caution should be inserted here. The version of Toltec-Maya history given above is that worked out by the late Ralph Roys, the leading student of Maya ethnohistory of his time, but it is by no means accepted by all Mayanists. The basic problem of dealing with the Short Count chronological system has already been described; this means that other interpretations are possible, but not necessarily probable. A dissenting view which has often cropped up in recent years is that the Toltec of Tula, and the Toltec-Maya of Chichén Itzá, at least in part were contemporary with the terminal Late Classic Maya of the southern lowlands prior to their collapse, and that Tula was more influenced by the Maya than the reverse. Only modern excavations at Chichén Itzá, a site which – despite years of excavations – is still poorly known, will tell us whether this view is tenable, or, more likely, ill-founded. Some of the revisionists have gone so far as to suggest that the 11.16 or

Thompson correlation should be abandoned for one which would make all Classic period Long Count dates $256\frac{1}{4}$ years later, but this is impossible on astronomical and ethnohistoric grounds, and on the evidence of radiocarbon dating.

And just to add to the problem presented by the Early Post-Classic in Yucatán, Drs. Andrews and Robles suggest that it was not the Toltec who established their capital at Chichén as Puuc power waned, but the Itzá themselves, a people they see as emerging from a mosaic of 'westerners' – peoples from the lower reaches of the Usumacinta and Grijalva river systems, like Eric Thompson's Putún Maya. These would have monopolized the salt beds and the coastwise trading routes, eventually consolidating their control over most of the northern peninsula. This theory would not, however, explain the extremely close iconographic links between Chichén Itzá and Toltec Tula, and would relegate most of the ethnohistoric accounts which we have of the Toltec from peoples as diverse as the Aztec and the highland Maya to little more than fiction. The problem remains.

The Itzá and the city of Mayapán

The Toltec may finally have been accepted by the natives of Yucatán, but the Itzá were always despised. Epithets such as 'foreigners,' 'tricksters and rascals,' 'the lewd ones,' and 'people without fathers or mothers' are applied to them by the Maya chronicles, and the phrase 'those who speak our language brokenly' shows that they could not have been Yucatec in origin. Several scholars have suggested that at the beginning of their history the Itzá were a group of Mexicanized Chontal-Maya (that is, Putún) living in Tabasco, where commercial connections with central Mexico were deeprooted. At any rate while the Toltec lorded it over Yucatán, the Itzá were settled in a place called Chakanputún ('savannah of the Putún'), probably Champotón on the coast of Campeche. About AD 1200 they were driven from this town and wandered east across the land, 'beneath the trees, beneath the bushes, beneath the vines, to their misfortune,' migrating through the empty jungles to the region of Lake Petén Itzá, and to the eastern shores of Belize. Finally, this wretched band of warriors found their way up the coast and across to Chichén Itzá, where they settled as squatters in the desolate city, in Katun 4 Ahau (AD 1224–44).

Leading the Itzá diaspora to northern Yucatán was a man who also claimed the title of Kukulcan, like his great Toltec predecessor of the tenth century, and he must have consciously imitated Toltec ideas, such as the cult of the Sacred Cenote, which now reached a peak of intensity. And yet another cult was initiated, that of the Goddess of Medicine, one of the several aspects of Ix Chel, with pilgrims from all over the Northern Area voyaging to her shrine on the island of Cozumel.

In Katun 13 Ahau (AD 1263–83) the Itzá founded Mayapán, some of the tribe remaining behind at Chichén Itzá, which now had lost its old name of Uucil-abnal and taken on its present one (meaning 'mouth of the well of Itzá'). The wily Kukulcan II populated his city with provincial rulers and their families, thus ensuring a dominion over much of the peninsula. However, after his death (or departure), troubles increased, and it was not until about 1283 that Mayapán actually became the capital of Yucatán, after a revolt in which an Itzá lineage named Cocom had seized power, aided by Mexican mercenaries from Tabasco, the Canul ('guardians'). It may have been this sinister Praetorian Guard which introduced the bow-and-arrow to Yucatán.

Mayapán, which is situated in the west central portion of the peninsula, is a residential metropolis covering about $2\frac{1}{2}$ square miles (6.5 sq. km) and completely surrounded by a defensive wall testifying to the unrest of those days. There are over 2,000 dwellings within the wall, and it is estimated that between 11,000 and 12,000 persons lived in the city. At the center of Mayapán is the Temple of Kukulcan, a pitifully shoddy imitation of the Castillo at Chichén Itzá. The colonnaded masonry dwellings of important persons were near this, just as Landa tells us, but dwellings become poorer as one moves away from the center. Each group of thatched-roof houses probably sheltered a family and is surrounded by a low property wall. The city 'pattern' is completely haphazard: there are no streets, no arrangement to be discerned at all, and it seems as if the basically dispersed Maya had been forced by the Itzá to live jam-packed together within the walls in a kind of urban anarchy. No city like it had ever been seen before in the Maya area. On what did the population live? The answer is tribute, for Father Cogolludo tells us that luxury and subsistence goods streamed into the city from the vassals of the native princes whom the Cocom were holding hostage in their capital.

By this time, the Maya were thorough-going idolaters, and the excavators of Mayapán found a proliferation of shrines and family oratories, in which were placed brightly painted pottery incense burners of little artistic merit, representing Mexican gods such as Quetzalcoatl, Xipe Totec (the God of Spring), and the Old Fire God, side-by-side with Maya deities such as Chac the Rain God, the Maize God, and Itzamná (the Maya version of the Old Fire God).

122,123

In an ill-omened era, Katun 8 Ahau (1441–61), fate began to close in upon the Itzá. Hunac Ceel was then ruler of Mayapán, an unusual figure who achieved prominence by offering himself as a sacrifice to be flung into the Sacred Cenote at Chichén, and living to deliver the Rain God's prophecy given him there. The ruler of Chichén Itzá was a man named Chac Xib Chac. According to one story, by means of sorcery Hunac Ceel drove Chac Xib Chac to abduct the bride of the ruler of Izamal, whereupon the expected retribution took place and the Itzá were forced to leave Chichén. Next it was the turn of the Cocom, and a revolt broke out within the walls of Mayapán, stirred up by an upstart Mexican lineage named Xiu which had settled near the ruins of Uxmal. The Maya nobles of Mayapán joined the Xiu, and the Cocom game was up; they were put to death and the once great city was destroyed and abandoned for all time.

Those Itzá who were driven from Chichén Itzá were to be in evidence for several centuries more, however. Once again they found themselves as

Mayapán art

122 Pottery incense burner from a shrine at Mayapán. This effigy of God B, the Rain God Chac, carries a small bowl in one hand and a ball of flaming incense in the other. The censer was painted after firing with blue, green, black, red, white, and yellow pigments. Ht 21½ in. (54.6 cm).

123 Upper part of pottery incense burner from Mayapán, Mexico. God M, Ek Chuah, who was the patron of merchants, is shown here, identifiable from his partly broken, Pinnochio-like nose. Red, blue, and yellow paint had been applied to the censer. Ht 9½ in. (24.1 cm).

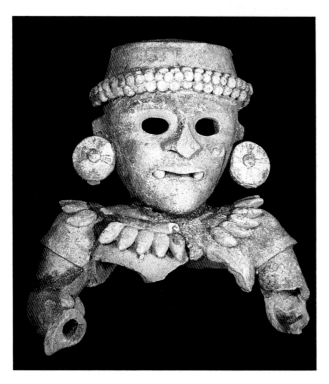

outcasts in the deserted forests, this time wandering back to the Lake Petén Itzá which they had seen in a previous Katun 8 Ahau. On an island in the midst of its waters they established a new capital, Tayasal (a Spanish corruption of *Tah Itzá*), now covered by the city of Flores, chief town of northern Guatemala. Safe in the fastness of an almost impenetrable wilderness, their island stronghold was bypassed by history. Tayasal was first encountered by Hernán Cortés in 1524, while that intrepid conqueror was journeying across the Petén with his army to punish a rebellious insubordinate in Honduras, and he was kindly received by king Canek, whose name was borne by a long line of Itzá rulers. It was not until the seventeenth century that the Spaniards decided something must be done about this last, untamed Maya kingdom, and several missionaries were sent to convert Canek and his people – to no avail.

One of the very last to make the attempt was Fray Andres de Avendaño y Loyola. In 1988 an extraordinary manuscript came to light in Mexico; this is a fragment of a longer document describing the visit by Avendaño, two Franciscan companions, and ten converted Maya to Canek's domain, probably early in 1695. As they waited in a hut in the hostile town of Chakan, on the lake's western shore, a breathtaking sight met their eyes. From the east came a great, wedge-shaped flotilla of canoes,

> all of them adorned with many flowers and playing much music with sticks and with drums and wooden flutes. And seated in one larger than all was the king of the Itzás, who is the Lord Canek, which means the star twenty serpent.

The last of the Maya kings wore a crown of gold, and gold disks in his ears from which golden pendants hung down to his shoulders. He had bands of pure gold on his arms and golden finger-rings, and his blue sandals were covered with golden bells. Over his blue tunic he wore a long, white cape, also edged with blue, emblazoned with the hieroglyph of his name.

Canek did not succumb to the Franciscans' arguments. But two years later, Spanish arms succeeded where peaceful missions had repeatedly failed. It seems almost beyond belief that Tayasal fell to the Spaniards only in 1697, and that while students at Harvard College had been scratching their heads over Cotton Mather's theology, Maya priests 2,000 miles away were still chanting rituals from hieroglyphic books.

The independent states of Yucatán

With Mayapán gone, the whole peninsula reverted to the kind of political organization that had been the rule in Classic times, six centuries earlier. In place of a single, united kingdom were now sixteen rival statelets, each jealous of the power and lands of the other, and only too eager to go to war in asserting its claims. The culture of the times, for whatever it was worth, was Maya, for much of what the Mexicans had brought was already forgotten and traditional Maya ways of doing things were substituted for imported habits.

There are few archaeological sites which can be assigned to this final phase,

124

124 The independent states of the Northern Area on the eve of the Spanish Conquest.

although the life of the times is well described by Landa and other early post-Conquest writers who were able to question natives who had actually participated in that culture. We are sure that there were one or more major towns within each province, but these were chosen by the Spaniards for their settlements and most are buried under centuries of Colonial and more recent constructions.

One site which was untouched, however, is Tulum, a small town in the province of Ecab founded in the Mayapán period. Spectacularly placed on a cliff above the blue-green waters of the Caribbean, Tulum is surrounded by a defensive wall on three sides and by the sea on the fourth. Probably no more than five or six hundred persons lived there, in houses concentrated on artificial platforms arranged along a sort of 'street.' The principal temple, a miserable structure called the Castillo, and other important buildings are

125

0 10 20 30 40 50   100 M

125 Plan of the walled town of Tulum, on the Caribbean coast of the Yucatán Peninsula.
A, Castillo; *B*, Temple of the Frescoes; *C*, Temple of the Diving God.

clustered together near the sea. On the upper façades of many of these dwarfish structures, which are of strikingly slipshod workmanship, are plaster figures of winged gods descending from above. Wall paintings have been found on both the interiors and outer surfaces of some temples, but the best preserved are in the two-storied Temple of the Frescoes. Like the murals of the Late Post-Classic center of Santa Rita in northern Belize (discovered by Dr Thomas Gann in 1894 and subsequently destroyed), the style of these is less Maya than Mixtec, undoubtedly influenced by the pictorial manuscripts of that gifted people from the hilly country of Oaxaca. Yet the content of the Tulum frescoes is native Maya, with scenes of gods such as Chac and various female divinities performing rites among bean-like vegetation. In one, the Rain God sits astride a four-legged beast, for which there can be but one explanation: they had seen, or heard tell of, Spaniards riding on horseback. Not only Tayasal, then, but also Tulum must have lived for a while beyond the Conquest, protected by the dense forests of Quintana Roo.

The Central Area in the Post-Classic

As was mentioned in the last chapter, not all of the lowland Maya centers and populated regions suffered total decline and abandonment with the Classic collapse, although most certainly did. In fact, Cobá in the northeast had a virtual renaissance in the Post-Classic, as Tulum-style superstructures were built on top of Classic pyramids. In the Central Area certain towns, including

126 Temple of the Frescoes, Tulum, from the west, a photograph taken prior to 1923, before the walled site had been cleared. The temple is noted for its wall paintings carried out in a hybrid Mixtec-Maya style. Inset panels over the doorways contain stucco 'diving god' figures, while stuccoed faces at the corners of the lower story suggest its dedication to the god Itzamná.

127 Detail of a wall painting in the Temple of the Frescoes at Tulum. An aged goddess, probably Ix Chel, carries two images of the god Chac.

Tayasal, were founded and flourished after AD 1200 on islands in the chain of lakes that extends across the eastern Petén almost to the Belize border. Lamanai, the ancient port town on the New River, saw much construction during the Post-Classic, and was occupied well into the Colonial era as a church built in the sixteenth century (and abandoned in the next) testifies.

Maya-Mexican dynasties in the Southern Area

In the mountain valleys of highland Guatemala, there were numerous independent nations on the eve of the Conquest, but the Quiché and Cakchiquel were the greatest of these. All indications are that they and their lesser neighbors, the Tzutuhil and Pokomam, had been there since very early times. And yet they claimed in their own histories that they had come from the west, from Mexico. As the Annals of the Cakchiquels relate:

> From the setting sun we came, from Tula, from beyond the sea; and it was at Tula that arriving we were brought forth, coming we were produced, by our mothers and fathers, as they say.

This claim may have been pure wishful thinking, similar to that of many Americans who would have liked their forebears to have stepped off the *Mayflower* in 1620. The great authority on Quiché Maya culture and history, Dr Robert Carmack, traces the *actual* origin of the Quiché elite not to the Toltec diaspora of the late tenth and eleventh centuries, but to a much later incursion of Toltecized Chontal-Nahua speakers (in other words, Putún Maya) from the Gulf Coast border region of Veracruz and Tabasco. These 'forefathers' would have arrived as small but very formidable military bands similar to the Japanese samurai, and terrorized the native Quiché-Cakchiquel highlanders. Gradually they established an epi-Toltec state, complete with a ruling line claiming descent from Quetzalcoatl. Many of the elite's personal names, as well as names of early places, objects, and institutions, seem to be Chontal rather than Quiché; and they introduced into the Guatemalan highlands many Nahua words for military and ritual matters.

128   The *conquistadores* have described the splendor of their towns, such as Utatlán, the Quiché capital which was burned to the ground by the terrible Pedro de Alvarado, or the Cakchiquel center Iximché. These sites were placed in defensive positions atop hills surrounded by deep ravines, and are completely Mexican down to the last architectural detail. Typically, the principal building is a large double temple with two frontal stairways, much like the Great Temple of the Aztec in Tenochtitlan, and there usually is a well-made ball court near by, for we know from the Popol Vuh that the highlanders were fond of that game. Lastly, all buildings are covered in Mexican fashion with flat beam-and-mortar roofs, the corbel principle being unknown here.

129   Best preserved of these late highland centers is Mixco Viejo, capital of the brave Pokomam nation; the almost impregnable site, surrounded by steep gorges, fell to Alvarado and two companies of Spanish infantry only through treachery.

128 Group C, Chuitinamit, Guatemala, looking west; restoration drawing by Tatiana Proskouriakoff. The Quiché built an impressive stronghold here after driving out the Pokomam Maya. A typically Mexican feature of the late highland centers is the double pyramid in the middle of the group. In the background can be seen a ball court.

Utatlán (Gumarcaj in Quiché Maya) is the best known of these highland capitals, both archaeologically and ethnohistorically. In it, there was a fundamental social cleavage between the lords and their vassals: these were castes, in the strictest sense of the term. The former were the patrilineal descendants of the original warlords; they were sacred, and surrounded by royal emblems. The vassals served as foot-soldiers to the lords, and while they could and did receive military titles through their battlefield prowess, they were still subject to sumptuary laws. Merchants had a privileged status, but they had to pay tribute. In addition, the free population included artisans and serfs (a growing class of rural laborers). Slaves comprised both sentenced criminals and vassal war captives; in general, only captive lords were considered fit for sacrifice, or for consumption in cannibalistic rites.

There were twenty-four 'principal' lineages in Utatlán, closely identified with the buildings or 'Big Houses' in which they (the lords) carried out their affairs. The functions carried out in them were ceremonial lecturing; the giving of bride-price; and eating and drinking associated with marriages between the lineages. The Quiché state was headed by a king, a king-elect, and two 'captains,' but there was also a kind of quadripartite rule (known also in Yucatán) embodied in four chiefs, one from each of the four major Utatlán lineages.

Documentary evidence unique for the ancient Maya enables us to

129 Group B, Mixco Viejo, Guatemala, looking east. The ruins of the Pokomam capital are surrounded on all sides by tremendously precipitous ravines. To take the town from its defenders, Alvarado's Spanish army had to advance up a steep path along which only two abreast could move, under a hail of rocks and poisoned arrows. This is the main group of the site, dominated by the usual double temple.

associate specific ruined temples at Utatlán with gods revered by the Quiché. The major cult structures faced each other across a plaza, and were dominated by the Temple of Tojil, a Jaguar deity connected with the sun and with rain. In the same plaza was the circular temple dedicated to the Feathered Serpent, while the Ball Court of Utatlán represented the Underworld. There was a palace elaborating the idea of the Big Houses in honor of Utatlán's ruling lineage, the Cawek ('Rain') dynasty; other Big Houses can be identified as the range structures so typical of highland towns. Perhaps we have a clue here to the functions played by the 'palaces' in Classic sites of the southern lowlands.

The Spanish Conquest

'The raised wooden standard shall come!' cried the Maya prophet Chilam Balam, 'Our lord comes, Itzá! Our elder brother comes, oh men of Tantun! Receive your guests, the bearded men, the men of the east, the bearers of the sign of God, lord!'

The prediction came true in 1517, when Yucatán was discovered by Hernández de Córdoba, who died of wounds inflicted by Maya warriors at Champoton. The year 1518 saw the exploratory expedition of Grijalva, and that of the great Hernán Cortés in 1519, but Yucatán was for a while spared as the cupidity of the Spaniards drew them to the gold-rich Mexico. The Spanish Conquest of the northern Maya began only in 1528 under Francisco de Montejo, on whom the Crown bestowed the title of Adelantado. But this was no easy task, for unlike the mighty Aztec, there was no overall native authority which could be toppled, bringing an empire with it. Nor did the Maya fight in the accepted fashion. Attacking the Spaniards at night, plotting ambushes and traps, they were jungle guerrillas in a familiar modern tradition. Accordingly, it was not until 1542 that the hated foreigners managed to establish a capital, Mérida; even so revolt continued to plague the Spaniards throughout the sixteenth century.

The reduction of the Southern Area was largely the accomplishment of the resourceful but cruel Pedro de Alvarado, who arrived in Guatemala in 1523 fresh from his Mexican triumphs with cavalry, footsoldiers, and native auxiliaries. By 1541, the year of his death, the Quiché and Cakchiquel kingdoms had fallen under the Spanish yoke, and indigenous resistance was largely at an end.

But the Maya are, for all their apparent docility, the toughest Indians of Mesoamerica, and the struggle against European civilization never once halted. In 1847 and again in 1860 the Yucatec Maya rose against their white oppressors, coming very close the first time to taking the entire peninsula. As late as 1910 the independent chiefs of Quintana Roo were in rebellion against the dictatorial regime of Porfirio Díaz, and only in the last few decades have these remote Maya villagers begun to accept the rule of Mexico. Likewise the Tzeltal of highland Chiapas have repeatedly risen, most notably in 1712 and 1868. The Cholan-speaking regions west of Lake Izabal in Guatemala were feared by missionaries and soldiers alike as 'The Land of War,' and the pacification of these Maya took centuries. The survival of the Itzá on their island Tayasal is a case in point; another is that of the Lacandón, still relatively independent. No, the Maya were never completely conquered, but their civilization and spirit were seemingly broken. As a poem from one of the books of Chilam Balam puts it:

> Eat, eat, thou hast bread;
> Drink, drink, thou hast water;
> On that day, dust possesses the earth;
> On that day, a blight is on the face of the earth,
> On that day, a cloud rises,
> On that day, a mountain rises,
> On that day, a strong man seizes the land,
> On that day, things fall to ruin,
> On that day, the tender leaf is destroyed,
> On that day, the dying eyes are closed,
> On that day, three signs are on the tree,
> On that day, three generations hang there,
> On that day, the battle flag is raised,
> And they are scattered afar in the forests.

8·Maya Life on the Eve of the Conquest

While we have until this moment been dealing mainly with the pots, jades, and ruins of a once-great people, we actually know a good deal more than this about the daily life of the Maya, particularly of the natives of Yucatán on the eve of the Conquest. For it is our good fortune that the early Spanish missionaries were accomplished scholars, and that owing to their eagerness to understand the nations they wished to convert to the Cross they have left us with first-class anthropological accounts of native culture as it was just before they came. So it is upon this foundation that we must interpret the archaeological remains of the Post-Classic Maya – and the Maya of the Classic as well.

The farm and the chase

Maya agriculture, which has been described in some detail in Chapter 1, was the foundation of their civilization. Maize, beans, squashes, chile peppers, cotton, and various kinds of root crops and fruit trees were cultivated. That the pre-Conquest lowlanders usually prepared their plots by the slash-and-burn method is certain, but exactly how large trees were felled prior to the adoption of copper axes in the Post-Classic (and of steel ones in Colonial days) is unclear; perhaps they were merely ringed and left to die. The times of planting were under the control of a kind of farmer's almanac of which we apparently have examples in the codices. According to Landa, fields were communally owned and jointly worked by groups of twenty men, but this may not be very close to the real picture, as we shall see.

In Yucatán, the Maya stored their crops in above-ground cribs of wood, but also in 'fine underground places' which might well be the *chultunob* so common in Classic sites. The Spanish sources consistently fail to mention tortillas or flat cakes (*pec uah*) for the lowland Maya; while a few clay griddles have been found in Post-Classic occupations in sites like Lamanai, these may have been used to toast cacao beans rather than tortillas. However, other ways of preparing maize are mentioned in the sources. These include *saca'*, a corn-meal gruel which was taken with chile pepper as the first meal of the day; *keyen*, a mixture of water and sour dough carried in gourds to the fields for sustenance during the day; and the well-known tamales (*ceehel uah*), which turn up in food offerings found painted on Late Classic ceramics. The peasant cuisine (we know little of that current among the elite class) was largely confined to such simple foods and to stews compounded from meat and vegetables, to which were added squash seeds and peppers.

130, 131 (*left*) Woman grinding maize on a *metate*, from a Late Classic figurine from Lubaantún, Belize. (*right*) Huntsman slaying deer, on a Late Classic figurine from Lubaantún, Belize.

'Cash crops' were of prime importance to Yucatán. Cotton was widely grown, for the province was famed for its textiles which were exported over a very large area. Along river drainages in southern Campeche, Tabasco, and Belize and on the Pacific slope of Guatemala groves of cacao trees were planted, but in the north these were restricted to the bottoms of filled-in *cenotes* and other natural depressions. The cacao bean from this tree provided chocolate, the preferred drink of the Mesoamerican ruling classes, but well into Colonial times the beans served as a form of money in regional markets; so precious were they that the Maya traders encountered off the coast of Honduras by Columbus were said to have snatched up any that had dropped as though it was their own eyes that had fallen to the canoe bottom.

Every Maya household had its own kitchen garden in which vegetables and fruit trees were raised, and fruit groves were scattered near settlements as well. Papaya, avocado, custard apple, sapodilla, and the breadnut tree were all cultivated, but many kinds of wild fruits were also eaten, especially in times of famine.

There were several breeds of dogs current among the Maya, each with its own name. One such strain was barkless; males were castrated and fattened on corn, and either eaten or sacrificed. Another was used in the hunt. Both wild and domestic turkeys were known, but only the former used as sacrificial victims in ceremonies. As he still does today, the Maya farmer raised the native stingless bees, which are kept in small, hollow logs closed with mud plaster at either end and stacked up in A-frames, but wild honey was also much appreciated.

The larger mammals, such as deer and peccary, were hunted with the bow-and-arrow in drives (though in Classic times the *atlatl*-and-dart must have been the principal weapon), aided by packs of dogs. Birds like the wild turkey, partridge, wild pigeon, quail, and wild duck were taken with pellets shot from blowguns. A variety of snare and deadfalls are shown in the Madrid Codex, especially a trap for armadillo.

131

167

In Yucatán, fishing was generally of the offshore kind, by means of sweep and drag nets and hook-and-line, but fish were also shot with bow-and-arrow in lagoons. Inland, especially in the highland streams, stupefying drugs were pounded in the water, and the fish taken by hand once they had floated into artificial dams; one of the beautifully incised bones from Late Classic Tikal shows that this was also the practice in the Petén. Along the coasts the catch was salted and dried or roasted over a fire for use in commerce.

Among wild products of the lowland forests of great cultural importance to the Maya was *pom*, the resin of the copal tree, which (along with rubber and chewing gum!) was used as incense – so holy was this that one native source describes it as the 'odor of the center of heaven.' Another tree produced a bark for flavoring *balché*, a 'strong and stinking' mead imbibed in vast amounts during festivals.

Industry and commerce

Yucatán was the greatest producer of salt in Mesoamerica. The beds extended along the coast from Campeche, along the lagoons on the north side of the peninsula, and over to Isla Mujeres on the east. The salt, which Landa praised as the 'best . . . which I have ever seen in my life,' was collected at the end of the dry season by the coastal peoples who held a virtual monopoly over the industry, although at one time it was entirely in the hands of the overlord of Mayapán. A few localities inland also had salt wells, such as the Chixoy valley of Guatemala, but it was sea salt that was in most demand and this was carried widely all over the Maya area. Other valuable Yucatecan exports were honey, cotton mantles, and slaves, and one suspects that it was such industrial specialization which supported the economy, not maize agriculture.

Further regional products involved in native trade were cacao, which could only be raised in a few well-watered places, quetzal feathers from the Alta Verapaz, flint and chert from deposits in the Central Area, obsidian from the highlands northeast of Guatemala City, and colored shells (particularly the thorny oyster) from both coasts. Jade and a host of lesser stones of green color were also traded, most originating in the beds of the Motagua River, but some which appeared on the market could well have been looted from ancient graves.

The great majority of goods traveled by sea since roads were but poor trails and cargoes heavy. This kind of commerce was cornered by the Chontal Maya, or Putún, such good seafarers that Thompson calls them 'the Phoenicians of Middle America.' Their route skirted the coast from the Aztec port of trade in Campeche, Xicallanco, around the peninsula and down to Nito near Lake Izabal, where their great canoes put in to exchange goods with the inland Maya. However, a special group of traders traveled the perilous overland trails, guided by the North Star and under the protection of their own deity, Ek Chuah, the Black God. Markets (*kiuic*) are rarely mentioned where the lowland Maya are concerned, in contrast with Mexico where they were so large that the Spaniards were astonished, and it is probable that they were unimportant since there was little cause for heavy subsistence to change hands in this very uniform land. But we are told by one source that highland Guatemalan markets were 'great and celebrated and very rich,' and these have persisted to this very day.

It was this trade that linked Mexico and the Maya, for they had much to exchange – especially cacao and the feathers of tropical birds for copper tools and ornaments – and it was probably the smooth business operations conducted by the Chontal that spared the Maya from the Aztec onslaught that had overwhelmed less cooperative peoples in Mesoamerica.

The life cycle

Immediately after birth, Yucatecan mothers washed their infants and then fastened them to a cradle, their little heads compressed between two boards in such a way that after two days a permanent fore-and-aft flattening had taken place which the Maya considered a mark of beauty. As soon as possible, the anxious parents went to consult with a priest so as to learn the destiny of their offspring, and the name which he or she was to bear until baptism.

The Spanish Fathers were quite astounded that the Maya had a baptismal rite, which took place at an auspicious time when there were a number of boys and girls between the ages of three and twelve in the settlement. The ceremony took place in the house of a town elder, in the presence of their parents who had observed various abstinences in honor of the occasion. The children and their fathers remained inside a cord held by four old and venerable men representing the Chacs or Rain Gods, while the priest performed various acts of purification and blessed the candidates with incense, tobacco, and holy water. From that time on the elder girls, at least, were marriageable.

In both highlands and lowlands, boys and young men stayed apart from their families in special communal houses where they presumably learned the arts of war, and other things as well, for Landa says that the prostitutes were frequent visitors. Other youthful diversions were gambling and the ball game. The double standard was present among the Maya, for girls were strictly brought up by their mothers and suffered grievous punishments for lapses of chastity. Marriage was arranged by go-betweens and, as among all peoples with exogamous clans or lineages, there were strict rules about those with whom alliances could or could not be made – particularly taboo was marriage with those of the same paternal name. Monogamy was the general custom, but important men who could afford it took more wives. Adultery was punished by death, as among the Mexicans.

Ideas of personal comeliness were quite different from ours, although the friars were much impressed with the beauty of the Maya women. Both sexes had their frontal teeth filed in various patterns, and we have many ancient Maya skulls in which the teeth have been inlaid with small plaques of jade. Until marriage, young men painted themselves black (and so did warriors at all times); tattooing and decorative scarification began after wedlock, both men and women being richly elaborated from the waist up by these means.

Slightly crossed eyes were held in great esteem, and parents attempted to induce the condition by hanging small beads over the noses of their children.

Death was greatly dreaded by all, the more so since the deceased did not automatically go to any paradise. Ordinary folk were buried beneath the floors of their houses, their mouths filled with food and a jade bead, accompanied by idols and the things which they had used while alive. Into the graves of priests they are said to have placed books. Great nobles, however, were cremated, a practice probably of Mexican origin, and funerary temples were placed above their urns; in earlier days, of course, inhumation in sepulchers beneath such mausoleums was the rule. To the Cocom dynasty of Mayapán was reserved the practice of mummifying the heads of their defunct lords, these being kept in the family oratories and fed at regular intervals.

Society and politics

The ancient Maya realm was no theocracy or primitive democracy, but a class society with strong political power in the hands of an hereditary elite. To understand the basis of the state in sixteenth-century Yucatán, we have to go right to the heart of the matter, to the people themselves.

In Yucatán, every adult Maya had two names. The first came to him from his mother, but could only be transmitted from women to their offspring, that is, in the female line. The second derived from the father, and similarly was exclusively passed on in the male line. There is now abundant evidence that these two kinds of name represented two different kinds of cross-cutting and coexistent descent groups: the matrilineage and the patrilineage. There were approximately 250 patrilineages in Yucatán at the time of the Conquest, and we know from Landa how important they were. For instance, they were strictly exogamous, all inheritance of property was patrilineal, and they were self-protection societies, all members of which had the obligation to help each other. Titles deriving from early Colonial times show that they had their own lands as well, which is probably what Landa meant when he said that all fields were held 'in common.' As for the matrilineage, it probably acted principally within the marriage regulation system, in which matrimony with the father's sister's or mother's brother's daughter was encouraged, but certain other kinds forbidden.

Now, while among many more primitive people such kin groups are theoretically equal, among the Maya this was not so, and both kinds of lineage were strictly ranked; to be able to trace one's genealogy in both lines to an ancient ancestry was an important matter, for there were strongly marked classes. At the top were the nobles (*almehen*, meaning he whose descent is known on both sides), who had private lands and held the more important political offices, as well as filling the roles of high-ranking warriors, wealthy farmers and merchants, and clergy. The commoners were the free workers of the population, probably, like their Aztec cousins, holding in usufruct from their patrilineage a stretch of forest in which to make their *milpas*; but in all likelihood even these persons were graded into rich and

132

poor. There is some indication of serfs, who worked the private lands of the nobles. And at the bottom were the slaves who were mostly plebeians taken in war, prisoners of higher rank being subject to the knife. Slavery was hereditary, but these menials could be redeemed by payments made by fellow members of one's patrilineage.

133

By the time the Spaniards arrived, political power over much of the inhabited Maya area was in the hands of ruling castes of Mexican or Mexican-influenced origin. Yucatecan politics was controlled by such a group, which of course claimed to have come from Tula and Zuyuá, a legendary home in the west. In fact, any candidate for high office had to pass an occult catechism known as the 'Language of Zuyuá.' At the head of each statelet in Yucatán was the *halach uinic* ('real man'), the territorial ruler who had inherited his post in the male line, although in an earlier epoch and among the highland Maya there were real kings (*ahauob*) who held sway over wider areas. The *halach uinic* resided in a capital town and was supported by the products of his own lands, such as cacao groves worked by slaves, and by tribute.

The minor provincial towns were headed by the *batabob*, appointed by the *halach uinic* from a noble patrilineage related to his own. These ruled through local town councils made up of rich, old men, led by an important commoner chosen anew each year among the four quarters which made up the settlement. Besides his administrative and magisterial duties, the *batab* was a war leader, but his command was shared by a *nacom*, a highly tabooed individual who held office for three years.

The Maya were obsessed with war. The Annals of the Cakchiquels and the Popol Vuh speak of little but intertribal conflict among the highlanders, while the sixteen states of Yucatán were constantly battling with each other over boundaries and lineage honor. To this sanguinary record we must add the testimony of the Classic monuments and their inscriptions. From these and from the eye-witness descriptions of the *conquistadores* we can see how Maya warfare was waged. The *holcanob* or 'braves' were the footsoldiers; they wore cuirasses of quilted cotton or of tapir hide and carried thrusting spears with flint points, darts-with-*atlatl*, and in late Post-Classic times, the bow-and-arrow. Hostilities typically began with an unannounced guerrilla raid into the enemy camp to take captives, but more formal battle opened with the dreadful din of drums, whistles, shell trumpets, and war cries. On either side of the war leaders and the idols carried into the combat under the care of the priests were the two flanks of infantry, from which rained darts, arrows, and stones flung from slings. Once the enemy had penetrated into home territory however, irregular warfare was substituted, with ambuscades and all kinds of traps. Lesser captives ended up as slaves, but the nobles and war leaders either had their hearts torn out on the sacrificial stone, or else were beheaded, a form of sacrifice favored by the Classic Maya.

132 (*right above*) Person of high rank in a palanquin, from a graffito incised on a wall at Tikal.

133 (*right below*) Standing captive, incised on a bone from the Temple I tomb, Tikal (Late Classic period).

9·Maya Thought and Culture

As in almost all the early civilizations of which we have record, it is extremely difficult to separate primitive scientific knowledge from its ritual context, but this should not lead one to suppose that a people like the Maya or the Sumerians had not evolved a considerable body of empirically derived information about the natural world. As we shall see, arithmetic and astronomy had reached a level comparable to that achieved by the ancient Babylonians and surpassing in some respects that of the Egyptians; but one should not exaggerate. Science in the modern sense was not present. In its place we find, as with the Mesopotamian civilizations, a combination of fairly accurate astronomical data with what can only be called numerology, developed by Maya intellectuals for religious purposes.

None the less, our knowledge of ancient Maya thought must represent only a tiny fraction of the whole picture, for of the thousands of books in which the full extent of their learning and ritual was recorded, only four have survived to modern times (as though all that posterity knew of ourselves were to be based upon three prayer books and *Pilgrim's Progress*). These are written on long strips of bark paper, folded like screens and covered with gesso. Pictorial representations on Classic Maya funerary pottery show that in Classic times the codices had jaguar-skin covers, and were painted by scribes using brush or feather pens dipped in black or red paint contained in cut conch-shell inkpots.

135

According to the early sources, the Maya books contained histories, prophecies, songs, 'sciences,' and genealogies, but our four examples are completely ritual, or ritual-astronomical, works compiled in the Northern Area during the Post-Classic. The Dresden Codex is the finest, and measures 8 inches high and 11¾ ft long (20.3 by 358.2 cm); while some of its content was certainly copied from Late Classic sources, some of the iconography of the Dresden has been shown by Karl Taube to be Aztec-influenced, so that it must date in its present form to just before the Conquest. The Madrid and the very fragmentary Paris codices are much poorer in execution than the Dresden but probably similar in date. Thompson even suggested that a Spanish priest might have obtained the Madrid Codex at Tayasal.

134,142

134 (*opposite*) The Dresden Codex is the most beautiful of the surviving folding-screen books of the Maya. Written on a long strip of bark paper, each page coated with fine stucco, much of it is concerned with 260-day ritual counts divided up in various ways, the divisions being associated with specific gods. The texts immediately above each deity contain their names and epithets. Ht 8 in. (20.3 cm).

135 Rabbit God writing in a folding-screen codex with jaguar-skin covers. Detail from a Late Classic cylindrical vase in codex style, northern Petén or southern Campeche. Eighth century AD.

136 In 1971 there was exhibited at the Grolier Club in New York a fourth Maya book which has since been labeled the 'Grolier Codex'; it once belonged to a private collector in Mexico and on circumstantial evidence seems to have been found in a wooden box in a cave near Tortuguero, Chiapas, within the past three decades. Unfortunately in very bad condition, it comprises about one half of a twenty-page table concerned with the Venus cycle. Although its authenticity was vigorously disputed by Thompson, the radiocarbon date of AD 1230 from its paper is fully consistent with the Toltec-Maya style in which the glyphs and associated deities are drawn. It is now considered genuine, thus making the Grolier the earliest of the four pre-Conquest Maya manuscripts.

To these must be added the Classic Maya inscriptions. And then we have a great deal of very valuable information on Maya ritual in the early post-Conquest accounts, and in various esoteric texts like the Books of Chilam Balam, written in Maya but transcribed into Spanish letters. From all these documents it can readily be seen that Maya life was deeply imbued with religious feeling, and that ritual behavior gave meaning and a sense of security to all strata of Maya society.

The universe and the gods

The idea of cyclical creations and destructions is a typical feature of Mesoamerican religions, as it is of Oriental. The Aztec, for instance, thought that the universe had passed through four such ages, and that we were now in the fifth, to be destroyed by earthquakes. The Maya thought along the same lines, in terms of eras of great length, like the Hindu *kalpas*. There is a suggestion that each of these measured 13 baktuns, or something less than 5,200 years, and that Armageddon would overtake the degenerate peoples of the world and all creation on the final day of the thirteenth. Thus, following the Thompson correlation, our present universe would have been created in 3114 BC, to be annihilated on 23 December AD 2012, when the Great Cycle of the Long Count reaches completion.

136 Pages from the Grolier Codex, a Toltec-Maya book dealing with the planet Venus.

Maya cosmology is by no means simple to reconstruct from our very uneven data, but apparently they conceived of the earth as flat and four-cornered, each angle at a cardinal point which had a color value: red for east, white for north, black for west, and yellow for south, with green at the center. The sky was multi-tiered, and supported at the corners by four Bacabs, Atlantean gods with the appropriate color associations. Alternatively, the sky was held up by four trees of different colors and species, with the green ceiba or silk-cotton tree at the center. Each of the thirteen layers of heaven seems to have had its own god, that of the uppermost being the *muan* bird, a kind of screech-owl. The underworld was nine-layered with nine corresponding 'Lords of the Night'; this cold, unhappy place was the final destination of most Maya after death, and through it passed the heavenly bodies such as the sun and moon after they had disappeared below the horizon.

Classic art and the Post-Classic codices suggest that the flat earth was thought of as the back of a monstrous crocodile resting in a pool filled with water-lilies. Its counterpart in the sky was a double-headed serpent, a concept probably stemming from the fact that the word for sky, *caan*, is a homonym of the word for snake. On the body of the sky-serpent are marked not only its own sign, crossed bands, but also those of the sun, moon, Venus, and other celestial bodies.

137

WHITE — NORTH

BLACK — WEST   GREEN   RED — EAST

YELLOW — SOUTH

137 Glyphs for the world directions and associated colors.

Exceedingly little is known about the Maya pantheon. That their Olympus was peopled with a bewildering number of gods can be seen in the eighteenth-century manuscript, 'Ritual of the Bacabs,' in which 166 deities are mentioned by name, or in the pre-Conquest codices where more than thirty can be distinguished. This theogonic multiplicity results in part from the gods having many aspects. Firstly, in the case of certain gods, each was not only one but four individuals, separately assigned to the color-directions. Secondly, a number seem to have had a counterpart of the opposite sex as consort, a reflection of the Mesoamerican principle of dualism, the unity of opposite principles. Thirdly, some seem to have had young and old aspects, or (especially in Classic times) fleshed and fleshless guises. Fourthly, there was no clear dividing line between humans and animals, or even between species of animals, so that many supernaturals combine these elements in fantastic ways. And lastly, every astronomical god had an Underworld avatar, as he died and passed beneath the earth to reappear once more in the eastern sky.

While some Maya sources speak of a one-and-only god (Hunab Ku) who was incorporeal and omnipotent, the supreme deity was surely Itzamná ('Lizard House'), pictured as an aged man with Roman nose in the codices, the inventor of writing and patron of learning and the sciences. His wife was Ix Chel, 'Lady Rainbow,' the old goddess of weaving, medicine, and childbirth; she was also the old Moon Goddess, and the snakes in her hair and

138

the claws with which her feet and hands are tipped prove her the equivalent of Coatlicue, the Aztec mother of gods and men. All the other gods, including the Bacabs, were apparently the progeny of this pair.

The Sun God, Kinich Ahau, is very similar to Itzamná in the codices, and may have been one of his aspects. On his night journey beneath the earth, he becomes the Jaguar God of the Underworld of fearsome aspect, often pictured on Classic monuments. It is believed that a young, half-naked lady prominent in the Dresden Codex represents the Moon Goddess, a younger variant of Ix Chel known as Ix Ch'up ('The Woman'), perhaps the consort of Kinich Ahau. Other celestial deities were the North Star, and various guises of Venus.

At the corners of the world were the benevolent Chacs, the Rain Gods, each of different color but all deeply venerated by the Maya who saw them as manifested in thunder and lightning bolts. There were also the quadruple Bacabs, each of whom presided over one quarter of the 260-day period in turn.

Further, there were patrons of the classes and professions. Heading this list is Kukulcan, god of the ruling caste; introduced after the Classic collapse, his cult reached a peak in Toltec times. Several war gods were venerated by the soldiers, some of them clearly deified heroes famed for their conquests. For the merchants and cacao growers there was Ek Chuah, with black face and Pinocchio nose, but there were also patron deities of hunters, fishers,

138 Some gods of the Maya pantheon with their name glyphs, from the Dresden Codex. *a*, Death God; *b*, Chac, the Rain God; *c*, North Star God; *d*, Itzamná; *e*, Maize God; *f*, Sun God; *g*, Young Moon Goddess; *h*, Kauil; *i*, Ek Chuah, the Merchant God; *j*, Ix Chel, Old Moon Goddess and Goddess of Medicine.

beekeepers, tattoo artists, comedians, singers and poets, dancers, lovers, and even suicides. Less easy to deal with are gods who may have been connected with the idea of lineage and descent; one of these is God K or Kauil, whose face with baroquely branching nose can be seen on the ceremonial bars and manikin scepters brandished by persons of high rank on Classic monuments. On Kauil's forehead is a mirror with a tube in it which emits smoke, and one leg has in place of a foot the head and body of a dragon-like serpent; he is thus cognate with the snake-footed Tezcatlipoca ('Smoking Mirror') of the Aztecs. Since the latter was the chief god of the royal house, so must Kauil have been the patron of the Maya lords.

The Classic Maya Underworld

It is now clear that an important function of Classic Maya pictorial ceramics, whether painted or carved, was funerary, which is hardly surprising considering that their final destination was as food containers in the tombs and graves of the honored dead. The Maya Underworld, which is the subject matter dealt with in these remarkable scenes, was known as Xibalbá, 'Place of Fright.' Part of a very complex mythology concerning it and its dread denizens has been miraculously preserved in the Popol Vuh manuscript, discovered among the Quiché Maya in the nineteenth century. This great Underworld epic was probably formulated during the Late Preclassic. It centers upon the doings of two sets of twins, young lords who are summoned in turn to Xibalbá by its horrible rulers (these bear the names of mortal diseases). The first pair, Hun Hunahpu and Vucub Hunahpu (1 Ahau and 7 Ahau in the lowland calendar), are forced to endure various houses of torture, and are finally defeated in a ball game, to suffer death by decapitation.

The Xibalbans hang up Hun Hunahpu's head in a calabash tree. One day, a young Underworld princess named Lady Blood happens by and holds up her hand to the head, which spits into it. She becomes pregnant, and is banished in disgrace to the earth's surface, where she enters the house of the malevolent old mother of Hun Hunahpu (surely Ix Chel, the old moon and ancestress). There Lady Blood gives birth to Hunahpu and Xbalanque, the glorious Hero Twins. These grow up to be great ballplayers and blowgunners, as well as tricksters. Through skill and subterfuge they defeat not only a monstrous and arrogant anthropomorphic bird named Vucub Caquix (a theme celebrated on several Classic ceramics), but also their jealous half-brothers Hun Batz and Hun Chuen, whom they turn into Monkey-men. These latter become the patrons of scribes, artists, musicians, and dancers for all the Maya, including those of Post-Classic Yucatán.

139   The Hero Twins are also summoned, like their father and uncle, to the Underworld to play ball with the angry Xibalbans. In a virtual 'Harrowing of Hell,' they turn the tables on the rulers and defeat them, eventually rising up through the surface of the earth to the sky, where they reach apotheosis as the sun and the moon (or, as Thompson believed, the sun and Venus). This was the sacred paradigm for the rulers of the Maya realm, who must have believed that like Hunahpu and Xbalanque, they would never suffer total

139 Plate in codex style, from northern Guatemala or southern Campeche. Eighth century AD. In the center, the Maize God (Hun Hunahpu) emerges from the split surface of the earth, depicted as a turtle carapace, as he is resurrected by his Hero Twin sons, Hunahpu (left) and Xbalanque (right). The latter pours water from a jar to ensure the sprouting of the corn.

extinction in Xibalbá. As for the Twins' father, Hun Hunahpu, iconographic research by Karl Taube has shown that he was none other than the Maize God, his severed head symbolizing the harvested ear of corn, and the maize seed planted beneath the surface arising from Xibalbá in resurrection, to reach fruition in the fields of our own world.

It is thus no surprise to find incredibly explicit pictorial references to the Underworld epic on Classic Maya pottery. The entire epic, of which the Popol Vuh preserves only a fragment, must have been written in codices which would have been the equivalent of the Egyptian Book of the Dead.   140

The iconography of Xibalbá is rich and complex. Heading the pantheon are three aged divinities – God L, who wears an owl headdress and smokes a cigar; God N, ruler of the year's end, who can be identified with the quadruple Pauahtuns, directional divinities who stood at the four corners of the Underworld and held up the earth; and God D or Itzamná, here in his role as a chthonic deity. Also present in Xibalbá are the Jaguar God of the

140 Rollout of a Late Classic cylindrical vase, probably from Naranjo, Guatemala. This is a night scene of God L (right) in his Underworld palace, at the creation of our present era. Facing him are six major lords of Xibalbá, including the Jaguar God of the Underworld and GI (Chac Xib Chac).

Underworld, whose face was emblazoned on Maya war shields, and the rain deity Chac Xib Chac or GI, whose chief role seems to have been the sacrifice of gods and men by decapitation.

Hunahpu and Xbalanque often appear in ceramic scenes, the former marked by the black spots of death and the latter by patches of jaguar skin over face and body; there are wonderful representations of Vucub Caquix being shot with blowguns by one or both Twins. These youths were considered divine rulers of the dead right into the Colonial era, and Professor David Kelley has even suggested that the very name 'Palenque,' the great Maya site which is significantly located in the west, region of death, might be a corruption of 'Xbalanque.' It may be significant that the known Emblem Glyphs of Palenque feature a bone or one of two animal skulls as their main element.

Funerary ceramics tell of an even stranger obsession of the Classic elite. This was the taking of ceremonial enemas by means of a leather or rubber syringe-bag fitted with a bone tube. The aged Pauahtun himself was often the recipient, administered at the hands of a beautiful young consort. The exact substance injected remains in doubt, but the vases show the liquid was kept in wide-mouthed jars and had froth on top. This suggests the intoxicating *balché* mead, and we do know from Aztec accounts of the Huaxtec, linguistic relatives of the Maya, that those people habitually intoxicated themselves by means of 'wine' enemas. On the other hand, Dr Peter Furst has pointed to the widespread custom in lowland South America of administering powerful hallucinogens in enemas, and has documented the custom among the contemporary Huichol of western Mexico (who use the potent *peyote* or spineless cactus buttons for the infusion). Incidentally, the otherwise unexplained bone tubes found in Classic Maya tombs and graves probably represented the surviving remains of the enema apparatus.

Deep caverns have always been conceptual entrances to Xibalbá for past and present Maya. One such cave, now named Naj Tunich, was discovered in 1979 by local residents in karst terrain near Poptún, in the southeastern Petén. The cave is huge, measuring 2,790 ft (850 m) deep along its longest passage. It has ancient walls, Late Classic burials, and terminal Late Preclassic pottery, but it was apparently extensively looted before archaeologists could get to it. The importance of Naj Tunich lies in its extensive hieroglyphic texts (altogether comprising about 400 glyphs) and scenes, all executed in carbon black on the cave walls. The latter include depictions of the ball game, amorous activities which are probably of a homosexual nature, and Maya deities, which not unexpectedly include the Hero Twins,

141

141 Section of paintings and hieroglyphic texts from the walls of Naj Tunich cave, Guatemala. The figure at top left may be a musician, seated near his conch-shell trumpet. At bottom left is a ballplayer, complete with protective belt and knee-pad; this is probably Hunahpu, one of the Hero Twins in the Popol Vuh story. Late Classic, eighth century AD.

Hunahpu and Xbalanque. The style of the writing and painting is closely related to Late Classic vases in 'codex style,' and must have been carried out by one or more artists or scribes skilled in the production of Maya books.

Rites and ritual practitioners

In contrast to that of the Aztec, the late Post-Classic Maya clergy was not celibate. Sons succeeded their fathers to the office, although some were second sons of lords. Their title, Ah Kin ('He of the Sun') suggests a close connection with the calendar and astronomy, and the list of duties outlined by Landa makes it clear that Maya learning as well as ritual was in their hands. Among them were 'computation of the years, months, and days, the festivals and ceremonies, the administration of the sacraments, the fateful days and seasons, their methods of divination and their prophecies, events and the cures for diseases, and their antiquities and how to read and write with the letters and characters . . .,' but they also kept the all-important genealogies. During the prosperity of Mayapán, an hereditary Chief Priest resided in that city whose main function seems to have been the overseeing of an academy for the training of candidates for the priesthood, but in no source do we find his authority or that of the priests superseding civil power.

The priest was assisted in human sacrifices by four old men, called Chacs in honor of the Rain God (recalling the sacrificial role of the Classic rain deity Xib Chac), who held the arms and legs of the victim, while the breast was opened up by another individual who bore the title of Nacom (like the war leader). Another religious functionary was the Chilam, a kind of visionary shaman who received messages from the gods while in a state of trance, his prophecies being interpreted by the assembled priests.

Every single Maya ritual act was dictated by the calendar, above all by the 260-day count. These sacred performances were imbued with symbolic meaning. For instance, the numbers 4, 9, and 13 and the color-directions appear repeatedly. Before and during rituals food taboos and sexual abstinence were rigidly observed, and self-mutilation was carried out by jabbing needles and sting-ray spines through ears, cheeks, lips, tongue, and the penis, the blood being spattered on paper or used to anoint the idols. On the eve of the Conquest such idols were censed with copal and rubber as well as ritually fed. Human sacrifice was perpetrated on prisoners, slaves, and above all on children (bastards or orphans bought for the occasion). Nevertheless, before the Toltec era, animals rather than people may have been the more common victims, and we know that such creatures as wild turkeys, dogs, squirrels, quail, and iguanas were considered fit offerings for the Maya gods.

Our understanding of the Yucatecan ritual round is crippled by Landa's sporadic inability to distinguish between what he called 'movable feasts,' *i.e.* rites determined by the 260-day count, and those geared to the nineteen months of the 365-day Vague Year. But apparently the greatest ceremonies had to do with the inauguration of the New Year. These took place in every community within the Uayeb, the five unnamed and unlucky days at the

142

142 New Year ceremonies in the Dresden Codex. Below, the Death God sacrifices before the New Year image; middle, the idol of Itzamná in the temple; above, the Opossum God carries out the image of the Maize God to a shrine at the entrance of the town.

close of the previous year, and involved the construction of a special road (perhaps like the Classic 'causeways') to idols placed at a certain cardinal point just outside the town limits; a new direction was chosen each year in a four-year counterclockwise circuit. There were all sorts of omens, good or bad, for every year, but an inauspicious augury could be offset by expiatory rites, such as the well-known fire-walking ceremony in which priests ran barefoot over a bed of red-hot coals.

Throughout the year, there were agricultural rites and ceremonies for such important economic groups as hunters, beekeepers, fishermen, and artisans, probably geared to the 260-day count if we may rely on the testimony of the Madrid Codex, which seems mainly devoted to such matters. Increase of game, abundance of honey, and wax, and so forth were the purpose of these activities, which so often take the form of the 'sympathetic magic' defined by Sir James Frazer, for instance compelling the rain to fall by having the Chacs empty water from pots onto a fire.

Despite past claims that Classic Maya societies were organized as theocracies, that is, as states ruled by priests, there is not the slightest evidence for the existence of priests in Classic times! That role was seemingly played by the elite – the rulers and nobility – and by the scribes. David Stuart has recently isolated in Classic ceramic texts the title for scribe (*ah dzib*) and has demonstrated that on one vase ascribed to Naranjo, the scribe/artist had signed his name as a royal prince from that city. And the discovery at Copán of a magnificent scribal palace, complete with Monkey-man God sculptures, shows the exalted status that these devotees of Hun Batz and Hun Chuen occupied in ancient times. Probably all knowledge of writing, the calendar, astronomy, and the esoteric world of the supernatural was in their hands. The institution of priesthood must therefore have been introduced to the Maya by the Toltec.

The Classic elite were obsessed with blood, both their own and that spilled by high-ranking captives. Hieroglyphic and iconographic studies, particularly by David Joralemon and David Stuart, have shown the supreme significance of ritually shed blood by the Classic Maya rulers and their families. This was drawn at calendrically important intervals by men from the penis, and from the tongue by their wives. The penis-perforator was usually a stingray spine or bone 'awl' and seems to have been ritually adorned and deified. Scenes on stelae once thought to have been concerned with water or maize kernels cascading from the lowered hands of rulers are now known to portray blood dripping from their mutilated members. Thus, 'blood' signified noble lineage and descent, as it traditionally did in Europe.

Numbers and the calendar

Otto Neugebauer, the historian of science, considers positional, or place-value, numeration as 'one of the most fertile inventions of humanity,' comparable in a way with the invention of the alphabet. Instead of the clumsy, additive numbers used by the Roman and so many other cultures of the world, a few peoples have adopted 'a system whereby the position of a number symbol determines its value and consequently a limited number of symbols suffices to express numbers, however large, without the need for repetitions or creation of higher new symbols.'

143 The Maya operated with only three such symbols: the dot for one, the bar for five and a stylized shell for nought. Unlike our system adopted from the Hindus, which is decimal and increasing in value from right to left, the Maya was vigesimal and increased from bottom to top in vertical columns. Thus, the first and lowest place has a value of one; the next above it the value of twenty; then 400; and so on. It is immediately apparent that 'twenty' would be written with a nought in the first place and a dot in the second, although it also had a symbol of its own. Professor Sánchez has demonstrated the ease

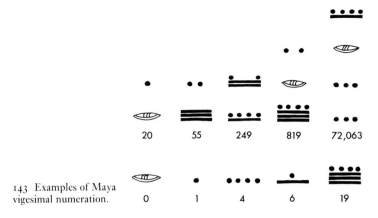

143 Examples of Maya vigesimal numeration.

with which calculations like addition and subtraction could be carried out in the system, but has also suggested in contradiction to others that multiplication and division, although not mentioned in the sources, would also have been possible.

And what kind of calculations were made, and for what purposes? Landa says that the purely vigesimal notation was used by merchants, especially those dealing in cacao, and he mentions that computations were performed 'on the ground or on a flat surface' by means of counters, presumably cacao beans, maize grains and the like. But the major use to which Maya arithmetic was put was calendrical, for which a modification was introduced: when days were counted, the values of the places were those of the Long Count, so that while the first two places had values of one and twenty respectively, the third was thought of as a *tun* of 360 days (18 × 20), and so on up the line. For operating within their incredibly involved calendar, which among other things included the permutation of the Long Count with the 52-year Calendar Round, the Maya scribes found it necessary to construct tables of multiples; in the Dresden Codex, such tables include multiples of 13, 52, 65, 78, and 91 (the nearest whole number approximating one quarter of a year). Fractions find no place in their system – they were always trying to reach equations of cycles in which all numbers are integers, *e.g.* 73 × 260 days equals 52 × 365 days.

There are several kinds of dates expressed on the Classic Maya monuments and in the Dresden manuscript. Leading off a typical Classic inscription is the Initial Series, a Long Count date preceded by an Introductory Glyph with one of the nineteen month-gods infixed. This is immediately followed by the day reached in the 260-day count, and, after an interval filled by several other glyphs, the day of the month (365-day count). The intervening glyphs indicated which of the nine gods of the underworld is ruling over that day (in a cycle of nine days), and lunar calculations which will be considered later.

However, this is not the whole story, for there are usually a number of other dates on the same monument. These are reached by Distance Numbers, which tell one to count forwards or backwards by so many days

144

a   b   c   d   e   f

144 Glyphs for the cycles of the Long Count. *a*, Introducing Glyph; *b*, baktun; *c*, katun; *d*, tun; *e*, uinal; *f*, kin.

from the base date, and while the intervals are usually of modest length, in a few examples these span millions of years. And then there are Period Ending dates in the inscriptions, which commemorate the completion of a katun, half-katun ('lahuntun,' that is, ten tuns), quarter-katun ('hotun'), or tun. As an example one might cite the katun ending 9.18.0.0.0, which was celebrated all over the Central Area. 'Anniversaries' also dot the Classic inscriptions; these are Calendar Round dates falling at intervals of so many katuns or tuns from some date other than the above-mentioned Period Ending Dates.

Why this apparent obsession with dating and the calendar? What do all the dates on the Classic monuments mean? They were formerly explained as the work of priests working out the positions of calendrical and celestial cycles in a religion which was essentially the worship of time itself. As we shall see, an utterly different explanation is not only possible, but probable.

The sun and the moon

To the Maya the round of 365 days – 18 months of 20 days plus the 5 extra days of the Uayeb – was as close to the solar year as they cared to get. This 'Vague Year' began among the Yucatec of Landa's time on 16 July (Julian calendar – the Gregorian was not to appear until 1582). Yet the earth actually takes about $365\frac{1}{4}$ days to complete its journey about the sun, so that the Vague Year must have continually advanced on the solar year, gradually putting the months out of phase with the seasons. We know that none of the Maya intercalated days on Leap Years or the like, as we do, and it has been shown that more sophisticated corrections thought to have been made by them are a figment of the imagination. Yet their lunar inscriptions show that they must have had an unusually accurate idea of the real length of the Tropical Year.

Curiously, the Maya went to far greater trouble with the erratic moon. In the inscriptions, Initial Series dates are followed by the so-called Lunar Series, which contains up to eight glyphs dealing with the cycles of that body. One of these records whether the current lunar month was of 29 or 30 days, and another tells the age of the moon on that particular Long Count date. Naturally, the Maya, like all civilized peoples, were faced with the problem of coordinating their lunar calendar with the solar, but there is no indication that they used the 19-year Metonic cycle (on which the 'Golden Number' in the Book of Common Prayer is based). Instead, from the mid-fourth century

145 Glyphs for the earth and the heavenly bodies in the codices. *a*, *Caan*, the Sky; *b*, *Kin*, the Sun; *c*, solar eclipse; *d*, *U*, the Moon; *e*, *Nohoch Ek*, Venus; *f*, *Cab*, the Earth; *g*, believed to be Mars.

AD each center made its own correction to correlate the two. However, in AD 682 the scribes of Copán began calculating with the formula 149 moons = 4,400 days, a system which was eventually adopted by almost all the Maya centers. In our terms, they figured a lunation to average 29.53020 days, remarkably close to the actual value 29.53059!

Of great interest to Mayanists and astronomers alike have been the eclipse tables recorded on seven pages of the Dresden Codex. These cover a cycle of 405 lunations or 11,960 days, which conveniently enough equals 46 × 260 days – a kind of formula with which the Maya were deeply concerned, for such equations enabled them to coordinate the movements of the heavenly bodies with their most sacred ritual period. The ancients had found out, at least by the mid-eighth century AD but possibly much earlier, that lunar and solar eclipses could only occur within plus or minus 18 days of the node (when the moon's path crosses the apparent path of the sun); and this is what the tables are, a statement of when such events were likely. They also seem to have been aware of the recession of the node (or at least of its effect over long periods of time), and Eric Thompson suggested that the tables were constructed anew every half-century or so.

The celestial wanderers and the stars

Venus is the only one of the planets for which we can be absolutely sure the Maya made extensive calculations. Unlike the Greeks of the Homeric age, they knew that with the Evening and Morning Stars they were dealing with the same object. For the apparent, or synodical, Venus year they used the figure of 584 days (the actual value is 583.92, but they were close enough!), divided into four periods of varying length – Venus as Morning Star, disappearance at superior conjunction, appearance as Evening Star, and disappearance at inferior conjunction. After five Venus 'years' its cycle met with the solar round, for $5 \times 584 = 8 \times 365 = 2,920$ days. Such an eight-year table can be found in the Dresden Codex and in the recently discovered Grolier Codex.

Some have questioned whether the movements of planets other than Venus were observed by the Maya, but it is hard to believe that one of the Dresden tables, listing multiples of 78, can be anything other than a table for Mars, which has a synodic year of 780 days; or that the Maya intellectuals could have overlooked the fact that 117, the product of the magic numbers 9 and 13, approximates the length of the Mercury 'year' (116 days). The Classic inscriptions suggest that Jupiter was of interest to them. They were, of course, astrologers not astronomers, and all these bodies which were seen to wander against the background of the stars must have influenced the destiny of prince and pauper among the Maya.

Potentially the most significant new breakthrough along these lines has been the confirmation by Floyd Lounsbury of Yale University of the exact correlation between the Maya and Christian calendars, long a bone of contention. Any valid correlation has to fit two historical facts: one is that Bishop Landa stated that 16 July, AD 1553 (Julian) was the Calendar Round day 12 Kan 1 Pop in the late Yucatecan Maya calendar (this would have been 11 Akbal 1 Pop in the Classic system); the other is that the Spanish Conquest of Yucatán began in a katun which ended on a day 13 Ahau. The two currently rival correlations are one which would have this correspond to the Long Count date 11.3.0.0.0 13 Ahau – espoused by some archaeologists working in Yucatán, but impossible since it violates the Landa equation – and one corresponding to 11.16.0.0.0 13 Ahau, long championed by Eric Thompson.

That Thompson was correct is demonstrated not only by this and other historical information from Post-Classic Yucatán, but also by the Dresden Codex itself. The eclipse predictions tables of this book forecast a solar eclipse on 9.16.4.10.8 12 Lamat 1 Muan; given the first Thompson correlation (he successively advocated three during his lifetime, each a day apart from the other), this would be 8 November AD 755 in the Julian calendar – the precise date of a lunar-solar conjunction! No other correlation satisfies this requirement. Furthermore, Lounsbury has shown that the base number of the Venus Table as given in the Dresden Codex (9.9.9.16.0 1 Ahau 18 Kayab) is contrived; as usual with such carefully chosen dates, it contains many integral multiples of important calendrical components. 1 Ahau was important throughout Mesoamerica as the conceptual heliacal rising of the deified Venus (that is, its rising just ahead of the sun on the eastern horizon following its disappearance in inferior conjunction).

This contrived base date had been projected backwards in time from the *real* base of the Dresden Venus Table, namely 10.18.9.15.0. Using the first Thompson correlation again, this was 20 November AD 943, a red-letter day on which *both* Venus and Mars rose heliacally with each other in the east, on a day 1 Ahau 18 Kayab. Such an extraordinarily rare celestial event must have seared itself into the Maya astronomical mind.

With the correlation now fixed, it should be possible, by consulting modern astronomical tables, to test the hypothesis, long held by David Kelley, that the Classic Maya inscriptions contain references to the heavenly bodies, above and beyond the lunar data which customarily follow initial Long Count dates on Maya stelae. Lounsbury has found confirmation of this hypothesis at the famous site of Bonampak, renowned for its murals. The Long Count position of the date associated with the great battle scene corresponds to 6 August, AD 792 (Gregorian); the tables tell us that this date was marked by the Inferior Conjunction of Venus, by a zenith passage of the sun (as it passes directly overhead on its way to its winter 'home'), and by the conjunction of Venus with the star Regulus.

That Venus played a sanguinary role among the Maya similar to that of Mars in the western Old World can be seen in the glyph for war: a Venus sign over another element, sometimes the Emblem Glyph of the site attacked. The date selected by the Bonampak astronomers for this martial action was, in the words of Professor Lounsbury, 'apparently seen as a propitious date for the undertaking, the outcome of which was such as to confirm the opinion.' Likewise, the first visibility of Venus as Evening Star on 3 December, AD 735, set off an attack on the southern Petén site of Seibal by Dos Pilas, leading to the capture of its ruler the next day. This unfortunate was kept alive for another twelve years, finally being sacrificed at a ritual ball game timed for an inferior conjunction of Venus. 'Star Wars' indeed!

Jupiter was also taken into account by the Classic Maya: the accession, at age forty-nine, and apotheosis twenty-one years later of the great Palenque ruler Chan-Bahlum was set by the planet's second station (the end of its retrograde or east-to-west movement against the background of the stars).

The astronomer Anthony Aveni and the architect Horst Hartung have determined that the ancient Maya used buildings and doorways and windows within them for astronomical sightings, especially of Venus. At Uxmal, for instance, all buildings are aligned in the same direction, except the House of the Governor. A perpendicular taken from the central doorway of this structure reaches a solitary mound about $3\frac{1}{2}$ miles away; Venus would have risen precisely above the mound when the planet reached its southerly extreme in AD 750. In collaboration with Sharon Gibbs, they have shown that in the case of the Caracol at Chichén Itzá, the whole building is aligned to the northerly extremes of Venus at about AD 1000, as is a diagonal sightline in one of the windows of the tower top; another diagonal sightline matched the planet's setting position when it attained its maximum southerly declination.

The Chaldean and Egyptian astrologers divided up the sky in various ways, each sector corresponding to a supposed figure of stars, so as to check the march of the sun as it retrogrades from sector to sector through the year, and to provide a star clock for the night hours. The zodiac of Mesopotamia is the best known of such systems. Did the Maya have anything like it? On this subject there was previously little agreement, but Linda Schele, David

Kelley, and their colleagues are now convinced of its existence. The subject is indeed complex, but in brief the Maya seem to have conceived of the Milky Way as both a great World Tree with its crocodile-headed base in the south, and as the mystic road along which souls walk into the Underworld. Crossing the Milky Way at the constellation Scorpio (seen as a scorpion by both the Maya and ourselves) is the ecliptic, the apparent path of the sun, moon, and planets as they move against the background of stars.

In Maya iconography, the ecliptic appears as a two-headed sky-serpent, its body marked with astronomical signs; a stylized form of the creature can be seen in the 'ceremonial bars' carried by Classic rulers. It has been recognized for years that two much-damaged pages of the Paris Codex show a scorpion, a peccary, and other beings pendant from the sky-serpent, and a similar series appears sculpted on the Nunnery at Chichén Itzá. From Bishop Landa's account, we know that the Yucatec Maya called the zodiacal constellation Gemini *ac*, 'peccary,' just one of a number of clues that the zodiac was present among these people.

The nature of Maya writing

146 Notable advances have been made in epigraphy, and it is probably not exaggerating to say that as much as 85 percent of the total body of Classic Maya inscriptions can now be 'read' – 'read' in the sense that we understand their meaning with some precision if not always how they were pronounced in Maya. This means that the ancient Maya are now the only truly historical civilization in the New World, with records going back to the third century after Christ.

Forty years ago, however, it could truly be said that few studies had made such little advancement with so much effort as the decipherment of the Maya script. This is not to say that a great deal was not understood, but there is a difference between unraveling a meaning for a sign, and matching it with a word in a Mayan tongue. Progress was most rapid on those glyphs which were of mainly calendrical or astronomical significance. For instance, by the mid-nineteenth century the Abbé Brasseur de Bourbourg had discovered Landa's *Relación*, from which he was able to recognize day glyphs and interpret the bar-and-dot numeration in the codices. It was quickly discovered that Maya writing was to be read in double columns from left to right, and top to bottom. At the turn of the century all of the following had been correctly deciphered by scholars in Europe and America: the zero and 'twenty' signs, the world directions and the colors, Venus, the months (also in Landa), and the Long Count. In a remarkable collaboration between astronomers and epigraphers, the mysteries of the Lunar Series had been unveiled by the early 1930s. But after these intellectual triumphs, fewer and fewer successes were scored, leading a few pessimists such as Sylvanus Morley and Eric Thompson to the quite unfounded claim that there was little else in these texts but calendrical and astronomical mumbo-jumbo.

It is generally accepted among linguists that all writing systems express the utterances of a particular language. Earlier generations of scholars once held

146 Tablet of the 96 Hieroglyphs, from Palenque. A very long text of the Late Classic period, marking the first katun anniversary of the accession to the throne by Sun Lord Kuk ('Quetzal') in AD 764. The text is completely historical, containing Kuk's pedigree.

that some early scripts, such as Chinese and Egyptian, were 'ideographic' in that they expressed thoughts directly without the intervention of language, but this has proved to be a delusion. All, we now realize, have a strong phonetic component (they denote sounds), no matter how pictorial some of the signs may look. Yet, even in heavily phonetic scripts including our own alphabetic one, there are some signs (for instance, our mathematical notation) which are purely semantic and can be 'read' in any tongue on earth.

True writing emerged simultaneously with the evolution of complex societies in various parts of the Old World. All these early scripts are *logographic*: that is, they have a large number of *logograms*, signs standing for parts of words or (less commonly) whole words, along with phonetic and semantic ('meaning') signs to help in their reading. In logographic writing, semantic and phonetic elements are usually complexly intertwined, sometimes in a single hieroglyph or 'character,' and the logograms themselves require a certain degree of memorization, so such scripts were always more easy to read than to write. In Chinese (and in ancient Sumerian) the auxiliary semantic signs accompany logograms or phonetic signs to indicate the class of things the referred item belongs to (such as 'wood,' 'water,' and so on). These are not used in some scripts, but phonetic signs are universally employed to indicate the pronunciation of a logogram.

Behind the phonetic signs in all logographic systems is the principle of the *rebus*. While many logograms may have originated as pictures of actual objects, as in Egypt and China, most of the nouns and verbs in a language are more abstract and thus not so easily visualized. But here the scribe could take a pictorial logogram and exploit it for its sound value alone, as the sign for 'fire' could be utilized in English as a sign meaning to 'fire' or sack a subordinate. As children we have all run across such examples of rebus or

147 The Maya 'alphabet' according to Bishop Landa.

148 (*right*) Phonetic-syllabic readings of Maya signs given by Y. V. Knorosov, and emended by others.

puzzle writing as 'I saw Aunt Rose,' expressed by pictures of an eye, a saw, an ant, and a rose flower. The Mixtec and Aztec used such writing to record personal and place names, and it was apparently the only kind of script they knew.

In many ancient logographic scripts, the phonetic component takes the form of a syllabary, in which each sign represents a complete syllable (usually a consonant followed by a vowel), although each of the 'pure' vowels will have its own sign. This is the case with the *kana* syllabary of Japanese, which gives the grammatical endings for Chinese-derived logograms expressing word roots. Some peoples have eschewed logograms altogether or relegated them to minor importance, and have constructed totally syllabic systems; the two most famous examples are the Linear B syllabary of Bronze Age Greece, and the Cherokee syllabary invented in the nineteenth century by Sequoyah.

The ultimate reduction to an almost completely phonetic script is the alphabet, perfected by the Greeks from a script handed to them by their Phoenician trading partners in the eastern Mediterranean. In the alphabet, all of the phonemes – the smallest distinctive units of speech – become separately indicated, instead of appearing together as syllables.

With these preliminary remarks, what kind of a system do we then find in the Maya script? Bishop Landa has given to us his famous 'alphabet' in which some twenty-nine signs are presented. Several extremely distinguished Maya scholars have stumbled badly in trying to read the codices and the inscriptions with Landa's treacherous 'ABC,' while some have gone so far as to declare it a complete fraud. A more careful examination suggests that this is really not an alphabet in the usual sense. For instance, there are three signs

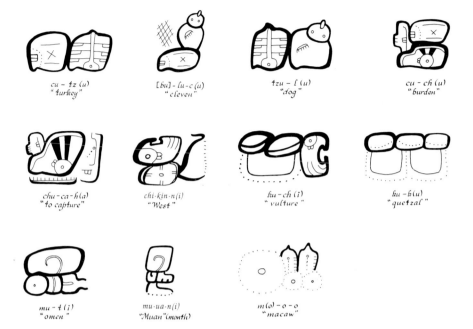

cu – tz (u)
"turkey"

[bu] – lu-c (u)
"eleven"

tzu – l (u)
"dog"

cu – ch (u)
"burden"

chu – ca – h(a)
"to capture"

chi-kin-n(i)
"West"

ku – ch (i)
"vulture"

ku – k(u)
"quetzal"

mu – t (i)
"omen"

mu-ua-n(i)
"Muan"(month)

m(o) – o – o
"macaw"

for 'A,' two for 'B,' two for 'L.' Secondly, several signs are quite clearly glossed as syllables of the consonant-vowel sort, i.e. *ma, ca,* and *cu.* We shall consider this important point later.

After the almost complete failure of decipherments along the strictly phonetic lines suggested by the Landa 'alphabet, a diametrically opposite line was taken by many authorities, namely that the script was purely 'ideographic,' with perhaps a few rebus signs imbedded in the texts from time to time. That is to say, any one sign could have as many referents or associations as the priests could think up, and that only they could read the holy signs, which in general character were more ritualistic than linguistic. There is a striking resemblance between this position and that of the would-be decipherers of the Egyptian script before the great discoveries of Champollion.

This resemblance was not lost upon the Russian epigrapher Yuri 148
Knorosov, a student of Egyptian hieroglyphic writing. In 1952, he began publishing a series of studies which re-opened the question of the Landa 'alphabet' and the possibility of phoneticism in the Maya script. About 287 signs, not including variants, appear in the codices. If the system were completely alphabetic, then the language of the texts would have contained this many phonemes; if purely syllabic, then there would have been about half this number of phonemes. Both are linguistic impossibilities. On the other hand, if all signs were semantic – representing units of meaning only – then the script represented an incredibly small number of ideas, certainly not enough for civilized communication. With this in mind, Knorosov presented convincing evidence that the Maya were writing in a mixed, logographic

system in which phonetic and semantic elements were combined as in Sumerian or Chinese, but that they also had a fairly complete syllabary.

Knorosov's starting point was Landa's 'ABC.' Thompson had already demonstrated that the bishop's native informant had mistaken his instructions, that is, he gave the Maya sign not for the letter itself, but for the names of the letters; see, for instance, the first 'B,' which shows a footprint on a road – 'road' is *be* in Yucatec, and this is exactly what the Spaniards call that letter. But the point is that this is really a partial and much flawed syllabary, not an alphabet, and Knorosov was able to show that words of the very frequent consonant-vowel-consonant (CVC) sort were written with two syllabic signs standing for CV-CV, the final vowel (usually the same as the first) not being pronounced. The proof of phonetic-syllabic writing is, of course, in the reading, and a number of Knorosov's readings have been confirmed by the contexts in which the signs appear in the codices, especially by the pictures which accompany various passages of text.

If this were all that needed to be done, it would be a simple job to read the Maya hieroglyphs, but the semantic dimension is very much there. There is strong evidence that phonetic complements were often attached to logograms to help in their reading, either prefixed as a representation of the initial sound of the sign, or postfixed as the final consonant; the recognition of these has notably advanced the process of decipherment. Phonetic redundancy of this sort was already being practiced in the Classic; for example, David Kelley was the first to notice that the name of the great Palenque ruler Pacal ('Hand-shield') could be written either as a picture of a hand-shield, or phonetically as *pa-cal-l(a)*, or both.

Although ridiculed by Thompson and his followers, Knorosov's phonetic approach is now universally utilized by Maya epigraphers. Since the initial work of Knorosov and Kelley, the recognition of phonetic construction in the script has proceeded at such a pace that epigraphers are now in general agreement on over 140 signs that have phonetic value (some of them, of course, allographs for one and the same syllable). It is also now recognized that in Maya, as in many ancient scripts, a number of signs are polyvalent, that is, a particular sign may have more than one phonetic reading, and it may also be read for its logographic value.

The content of Maya writing

All four codices deal exclusively with religious and astronomical matters, as is quite obvious from the pictures of gods associated with the texts, from the tables, and from the high frequency of passages geared to the 260-day count. Thus, we have in these texts little more than short phrases of esoteric significance, surely to be read in an archaic Yucatec, which often seem to match passages in the Books of Chilam Balam.

What, then, of the subject matter of the inscriptions? Until quite recently, the prevailing opinion was that this was in no way different from that of the books; and further, that all those dates recorded on the monuments were witnesses to some sort of cult in which the time periods themselves were

149 Some Emblem Glyphs from the Classic monuments. *a*, Tikal; *b*, Naranjo; *c*, Yaxchilán; *d*, Piedras Negras; *e*, Palenque; *f*, Seibal; *g*, Copán; *h*, Quiriguá.

deified. The great John Lloyd Stephens was of a different mind, writing about Copán:

> One thing I believe, that its history is graven on its monuments. No Champollion has yet brought to them the energies of his enquiring mind. Who shall read them?

The discovery within the last few decades of the historical nature of the monumental inscriptions has been one of the most exciting chapters in the story of New World archaeology.

It began in 1958, when Heinrich Berlin published evidence that there was a special kind of sign, the so-called 'Emblem Glyph,' associated with specific archaeological sites, and recognizable from the same kind of glyphic elements which appear affixed to each. Thus far, the Emblem Glyphs for a number of Classic centers – including Tikal, Piedras Negras, Copán, Quiriguá, Seibal, Naranjo, Palenque, and Yaxchilán – have been surely identified. Berlin suggested that these were either the names of the cities themselves or of the dynasties which ruled over them, and proposed that on the stelae and other monuments of these sites their histories might be recorded.

The next breakthrough was by Tatiana Proskouriakoff of the Carnegie Institution, who analyzed thirty-five dated monuments from Piedras Negras. The arrangement of stelae before structures she found was not random; rather, they fell into seven groups. Within a single such group, the time span covered by all the dates on the stelae is never longer than an average lifetime, which immediately raised the possibility that each group was the record of a single reign. This has now proved to be so. The first monument in a series shows a figure, usually a young man, seated in a niche above a platform or plinth; on this stela two important dates are inscribed. One is associated with a glyph like an animal's head with a toothache, and has been shown to record

149

150*b*

150 Historical glyphs in the monumental texts. *a*, Birth Glyph;
b, Accession Glyph; *c*, 'Shield Jaguar'; *d*, 'Bird Jaguar'; *e*, prefix for
female names and titles.

the accession to power of the young man; the other appears with the 'up-
ended frog' glyph and is that same person's date of birth. Later monuments
in a particular group celebrate marriages and the birth of offspring, and
Proskouriakoff was able to identify the signs for personal names and titles,
particularly of women who are quite prominent in Classic Maya sculpture.
Military victories were also marked with great frequency, especially if an
important enemy happened to have been taken captive by the ruler.

Thus, the figures which appear in Classic reliefs are not gods and priests
but dynastic autocrats and their spouses, children, and subordinates. As the
records for one reign come to an end, the next begin with the usual accession
motif. Among the more complete documents which we have for the temporal
dynasties which ran the ancient Maya centers are the inscriptions carved on
the many stone lintels of Yaxchilán; from these Proskouriakoff reconstructed
the history of the extremely militant 'Jaguar' dynasty, which ruled the site in
the eighth century AD. The record begins with the exploits of a lord called
'Shield Jaguar'; he was succeeded in AD 752 by 'Bird Jaguar' (both these
names recall the double names of the Yucatec – matronymic followed by
patronymic), who was probably his son. As an example of how much of the
writing that accompanies the reliefs celebrating the victories of this ruler can
151   now be read or at least interpreted, we have Lintel 8 of Yaxchilán, which
begins with a Calendar Round date falling in AD 755. Below this is
Knorosov's *chucah* or 'capture' glyph, then a glyph resembling a jeweled
skull, which is obviously the name of the prisoner on the right. Above right,
the second glyph is that of the Bird Jaguar himself (the figure with spear),
beneath which is the Emblem Glyph of Yaxchilán.

Of special interest are those inscriptions which indicate the interference of
some centers with the destinies of others. For instance the Yaxchilán
Emblem Glyph appears with one of the most prominent women in the
Bonampak frescoes, and, thanks to a royal marriage, the glyph for Tikal

Kan-Toc

7 Imix

14 Tzec

chucah
(he
captured)

"Jeweled
Skull"

2nd
captive

u bac
(his
captive)

Bird-
Jaguar

Yaxchilán
Emblem
Glyph

2nd captive   "Jeweled Skull"

151 Lintel 8, Yaxchilán. A record of the capture of 'Jeweled Skull' and one other enemy by 'Bird Jaguar' and a companion.

appears quite frequently on monuments at Naranjo. Piedras Negras is not far downstream from Yaxchilán, and the famous Lintel 3 from that site is now believed to show a Yaxchilán ruler presiding over a council called in the late eighth century to choose a successor to the Piedras Negras throne.

In 1973, Linda Schele and Peter Mathews were able to announce at a conference in Palenque that they had worked out the dynastic record of all the Palenque rulers going back to AD 465; this record has later been refined by them and Floyd Lounsbury. Thanks to their research, we can now place such important figures as Pacal and Chan-Bahlum in relation to the stupendous art and architecture that was created for them. Palenque, like Yaxchilán had entered into the realm of history.

Important glyphs now known to relate to dynastic affairs include the signs for events such as battles (the 'star-shell' glyph), inauguration or 'seating' in office, ritual blood-letting, and death and burial, in addition to the birth and accession glyphs. As one would expect with ruling families obsessed with noble lineage and marriage affiliation, there are a number of relationship glyphs which have recently been recognized, such as 'child of father,' 'child of mother,' 'child of parent,' and 'wife' (atan in Maya), as well as a sign expressing the relationship (unpleasant in the extreme) between a local dynast and an important captive whom he had taken.

Thanks to advances in Maya dynastic history, scholars are now gaining some idea of how the Central Area was governed in Classic times. From earliest times until the Classic downfall and the coming of the Toltec to

152 Political geography of the Central Maya Area at AD 790, based on the distribution of cities with Emblem Glyphs. Boundaries are only approximate. The southern lowlands were characterized by rival city-states, with none having hegemony over the rest.

Yucatán, there was never any overall authority among the ancient Maya. Based upon the analysis of sites with Emblem Glyphs, the epigrapher Peter Mathews has drawn a political geography of the Central Area during the Classic which bears a striking resemblance to post-Mayapán Yucatán: this was no 'Old Empire,' to use Morley's outdated phrase, but a series of city-states with constantly shifting alliances and hostilities. By the last centuries of the Classic, the highest goal of these lineage-proud dynasts was to capture the ruler of a rival city-state in battle, to torture and humiliate him (sometimes for years), and then to subject him to decapitation following a ball game which the prisoner was always destined to lose.

152

If this is all history, then why the Lunar Series and the calculations far into the past and future? Because the Classic Maya elite believed in astrology, and must have consulted their scribes for lunar and other cosmic auguries at every important civil event, as did the Babylonians, Etruscans, Egyptians, and many other peoples of the Old World. There is a logic to astrology which not only the ancients have found compelling – Kepler and Newton did likewise – so we need not condemn the Maya for their beliefs. Another Maya concern was with lineage, and we find figures and dates on some monuments which can only refer to distant ancestors.

Thus, Berlin showed that the dates in inscriptions of the Temple of the Cross at Palenque fall into three groups. The first are so ancient that they could only be referring back to deified ancestors of a legendary epoch; the next may have to do with distant progenitors of a more intermediate time; and the third are connected with contemporary historical events.

It will be remembered that the tablet of the Temple of the Cross celebrates the accession to the throne by Lord Chan-Bahlum following the death of his predecessor, Lord Pacal, in AD 683. Now, Pacal was born on a day 8 Ahau in the 260-day count. The very earliest date on the tablet is 3,722 years earlier, and also falls on a day 8 Ahau, which in itself is suspicious. Professor Lounsbury has demonstrated that on this initial date, a mythical ancestress was born, but in addition the interval between her birth and that of Pacal – 1,359,540 days – is an integral multiple of seven different important Maya periods, including the synodic period of Mars! It is inescapable that the initial date was thus contrived to fit the needs of numerology and astrology, thus intertwining religion, genealogy, and history in the characteristic Maya style.

A century and a half ago, John Lloyd Stephens had called for a Champollion to decipher the Maya inscriptions. It was not until the second half of the twentieth century that such a decipherment took place, but it has been the work of not one mind, but of many, with Proskouriakoff and Knorosov taking the lead. In recent years, a group of young epigraphers has forged ahead with new readings which throw light on entirely unexpected areas of ancient Maya culture.

One of these is what has come to be known as 'name-tagging,' the labeling of objects with their names and with the names of their owners. The first known case of this concerns a pair of ground obsidian ear spools from a Classic period royal tomb at Altun Ha, Belize. Peter Mathews showed that the texts incised on each read *u tup(a)*, 'his ear spool,' followed by the ruler's name.

In 1972, I discovered that there is a formulaic, repetitive hieroglyphic text on Classic Maya ceramics, usually placed below the rim, which I christened the Primary Standard Sequence (or PSS). I hypothesized that this was some sort of funerary chant (since these vessels are almost always in burial contexts), but a younger generation of Mayanists has found otherwise: Stephen Houston, David Stuart, and Karl Taube have shown that part of the PSS describes the form of the vessel as well as its contents (such as chocolate or atole, a white maize gruel). This breakthrough received striking confirmation with an unusual screw-top jar from an Early Classic tomb at Río Azul: the painted text on it said that it contained chocolate (written *ca-ca-u(a)*, 'cacao'), and subsequent tests carried out by the Hershey Company proved that this had indeed been the case.

On a few Maya vases the Classic artist-scribes went one step further, by signing their own works of art, a custom otherwise unknown in Mesoamerica. And on one vase known to have been painted in Naranjo, the artist gave his pedigree, noting that his mother was a princess of Yaxhá, while his father was none other than Naranjo's king. Among the ancient Maya, it seems, artists and scribes belonged to the very highest stratum of a rigidly ranked society. David Stuart, who made this remarkable discovery, has gone on to find the signatures of individual sculptors on carved reliefs from several Usumacinta cities; in some instances, several artists worked on the same relief, which they all signed in their distinctive hands.

Name-tagging was not confined to portable objects only. The Maya who lived in these cities named many other things in the man-made and natural worlds. At Copán, for example, it has been found by Linda Schele, David Stuart, and Nikolai Grube that stelae, altars, buildings, and even plazas received proper names. This raises the question of whether the Emblem Glyphs brought to light by Berlin are toponyms or the names of ruling lineages. There are now cogent reasons to think that the former is the case. For one thing, the affix group attached to the variable main sign of an Emblem Glyph is read as *ch'ul ahau* in Cholan Maya, giving the reading 'Holy Lord of —' for the entire sign. For another, toponyms have now been found to be widespread in Maya inscriptions of the Classic period (there are even toponyms for supernatural places), and some of these show up as main signs in Emblem Glyphs.

These young epigraphers have opened a window into the supernatural world of the Maya by another decipherment. The glyph in question appears often in ceramic texts as something possessed by 'Holy Lords,' that is, rulers of cities. It is read as *uay*, a term that remains in use among highland Maya groups for an individual's alter-ego spirit or soul, conceived as an animal counterpart (which might be anything from a jaguar to a mouse). According to the ceramic texts and accompanying images, each ruler had such a *uay*, often a fantastic chimera combining the features of two or three animals, with whom he was in a special kind of relationship.

Uay has a further meaning of 'sleep' in some Mayan tongues, and it is possible that such mystic contacts were made in dreams; it is certainly suggestive that a few inscriptions point to certain Classic buildings as 'sleeping places,' where Maya kings may have sought out these spirits, like the vision quest of native North Americans.

Thanks to research being carried out by Linda Schele, David Freidel, and their colleagues and students, we are journeying even further into the mythological and supernatural world that was so important to the Maya. Using epigraphic, astronomical, and ethnographic data, they are beginning to understand how the Classic Maya conceived of the cosmological events associated with the act of creation on 13 August, 3114 BC, when the universe was put in motion: the raising of the heavens from the primordial sea, the setting of three hearth stones in the sky, and the creation of the Milky Way as both a cosmic monster and as a world tree – all to be followed by the birth of the gods.

The modern decipherment has thus opened up realms of Maya thought and behavior that were undreamt of by earlier generations of archaeologists, and has established a bridge to the thought-systems of millions of modern Maya whose culture has survived centuries of oppression.

10·The Enduring Maya

The six million or so Maya alive in the world today are survivors: they have endured repeated cycles of conquest that continue unabated even today. What have kept the Maya people culturally and even physically viable are their hold on the land (and that land on them), a devotion to their community, and an all-pervading and meaningful belief system. It is small wonder that their oppressors have concentrated on these three areas in incessant attempts to destroy them as a people, and to exploit them as a politically helpless labor force. As the novelist and anthropologist Oliver La Farge put it over a half century ago, 'from the Conquest until recently there has been a steady drive, with some reversals, to destroy the Indian ownership of large blocks of land which forms the physical and economic base of tribal solidarity and of freedom from the necessity to work for non-Indians.'

La Farge, largely drawing on Guatemalan data, saw five broad stages in the history of the Maya since the initial invasion of their lands by the Spaniards. The first is the *Conquest Period*, from 1524 until the end of the sixteenth century. This was a violent era, shattering Indian cultural structures – although some native polities, particularly in the Petén, were not subdued until the close of the following century. The next stage was *Colonial Indian*, which lasted until 1724, at which time the Spanish Crown abolished the *encomienda* system, an oppressive institution which had given Spanish land barons total right to Indian forced labor in return for the supposed conversion of the natives to the Christian religion. It was a time when Spanish and Christian elements were absorbed wholesale into the fabric of Maya life and somewhat altered to fit the pattern of native culture; many Maya traits were destroyed or mutilated, while others were greatly changed.

During the *Transition Period*, lasting until the colonies broke away from Spain about 1820, life became more tolerable for the Maya, as Spanish control slowly relaxed, and suppressed Maya cultural traits re-emerged. It was during this time that traditional Maya patterns took on the form that they retain today.

Recent Indian I was ushered in by the independence of Mexico and Guatemala, and persisted until the 1870s or 1880s; while La Farge saw this as an era of smooth integration between Spanish and Maya elements, with relative tranquility, this is true only for the Guatemalan highlands under the country's pro-Indian Conservative government. A different story could be told in Chiapas, with major Indian revolts, and in Yucatán, with the Caste Wars in which the Maya came close to crushing their white overlords.

From 1880 until today we are in *Recent Indian II*, marked by a new tide of intervention in Indian life, and with concerted efforts by governments to force the Maya to become laborers on cash-crop plantations as part of the world market system. Travelers to Guatemala City may drive along the 'Avenida de la Reforma,' but they surely will not know what the 'reform' was: the abolition by President Rufino Barrios of Indian communal lands, and the imposition of a system to supply forced labor from the Maya highlands to the newly-established coffee *fincas* of the Pacific piedmont zone. Bitter revolts against this injustice took place, but they were put down by the Liberal government of Barrios with a ferocity that foreshadowed more modern developments. Such imposed seasonal migrations were absent in the Yucatán Peninsula, but on the great sisal (*henequén*) plantations which covered much of the north, rock-bottom wages and debt peonage were the rule.

This last period was marked by the emergence of a new cross to be born by the Maya: the invasion of their lands, villages, and towns by a class of *ladinos*, hispanic or hispanicized citizens who occupied all the lucrative and politically powerful positions in largely Maya territories; they were the shopkeepers, the labor majordomos, the schoolteachers, the judiciary, the Catholic priests. They spoke Spanish rather than the Indian 'dialects' (as the Maya languages were pejoratively thought of), they dressed in Western clothes, and they generally held themselves to be superior to the native peoples. It is a situation which persists.

The new Spanish order

To understand the processes of conflict, accommodation, and integration that have gone on among the Maya since the Conquest, it is necessary to understand what the Spaniards introduced. First and foremost were epidemic diseases previously unknown in the New World, such as smallpox, influenza, and measles. It is generally agreed among scholars that these produced a holocaust unparalleled in the world's history: within a century, 90 percent of the native population had been killed off, including that of the Maya area. Smallpox, in fact, had reached the Guatemalan highlands even before the arrival of Pedro de Alvarado, and it is a wonder that the weakened Maya put up the defense that they did.

Over the next two centuries, then, the Spaniards were able to impose their own cultural pattern on regions that had been devastated by disease. By order of Church and Crown, the scattered populations were 'reduced,' that is, concentrated into villages and towns on the Spanish pattern, where they could be better controlled and converted. These new settlements were laid out on the grid plan, with rectilinear streets, a central plaza, and a church, a settlement type still to be seen throughout the Maya area. Along with the church, the seat of religious power, there was usually a building housing the *Ayuntamiento*, the civil government run by, or under the thumb of, Spaniards or *ladinos*; and, later on, a *ladino*-run store.

Catholicism brought its priests, its rituals, and its saints, and was usually the principal agent of acculturation. One of its most successful institutions was the *cofradía* (confraternity or brotherhood), adopted enthusiastically throughout the highlands, each dedicated to the care and honor of a particular saint. There are twelve of these brotherhoods, for instance, among the Ixil of the Nebaj region, and they play a crucial role in the ritual life of these people. The Christian sacrament of baptism introduced another element into native social life, namely that of *compadrazgo* or co-godparenthood, which formalizes bonds of friendship between adult Maya.

There was, of course, a great deal of syncretism between Spanish and Maya religious institutions and beliefs, since in many respects they were so similar. Both burned incense during rituals, both had images which they worshiped, both had priests, and both conducted elaborate pilgrimages set by their respective calendars. Thus, when the Tzotzil Maya of Zinacantan make pilgrimages to crosses set up on holy mountains, it is really irrelevant to ask if this is a Maya or Spanish custom: to the Tzotzil, both cross and ancestral mountain are a unity.

But the European invaders brought with them more than their civil and religious order: they imposed an economic order as well. Iron and steel tools replaced chipped or ground stone ones, and the Maya took readily to the Spaniards' axes, machetes, and billhooks, which in the lowlands enabled them to cope with the forest as they never had before. Cattle, pigs, and chickens began to replace game as the main source of meat in the diet, although the Maya never took to the heavy use of lard and oil which was such a prominent feature of the Spanish cuisine. The invaders brought in citrus trees, watermelons, and other welcome crops, but the sugarcane and coffee (the latter largely supplanting the native cacao) introduced as cash crops were a mixed blessing as they led to the plantations that put economic shackles on the Maya.

Perhaps the most destructive of these introduced elements was distilled alcohol. The Maya had always used alcohol in their rituals – *chicha* or maize beer in the highlands, and *balché* (a flavored mead) in the lowlands, but they were unprepared for the power of the Spaniards' *aguardiente*, and many despondent Maya sought relief or oblivion in strong drink, a habit encouraged by the *ladino* majordomos and store owners who often controlled their destiny.

On the plus side, though, was the Roman alphabet, initially used by the earlier missionaries to write down sermons and the like in the native languages. It was not long before educated Maya were using it to transcribe their own ritual and historical texts, which had previously existed in hieroglyphic form, an activity which was probably conducted in secret. To this we owe the preservation of the great Quiché epic – the Popol Vuh – and the Yucatec Maya Books of Chilam Balam. In Yucatán, there has always been a strong tradition of native literacy, still kept by men who occupy the office of *ah dzib*, 'scribe.' It was probably such specialists who produced the large body of surviving letters in Yucatec exchanged between leaders of the Caste Wars of the 1840s and 50s.

In all of this, the various Maya groups have clearly assimilated and altered many disparate foreign, and even threatening, elements to fit their own cultural patterns inherited from the pre-Conquest era. Take the marimba, a percussion instrument of ultimately African origin, but introduced to Guatemala in colonial times. Today it appears as a typically 'Maya' instrument in native performances, both religious and secular; so assimilated is it that many tourists believe that it must be pre-Columbian.

The highland Maya, yesterday and today

Anthropologists and other social scientists agree that about half of Guatemala's population of eight million is Maya; most of these live in the central and western highlands of the country, the eastern part having been subject to heavy Spanish migration and consequent 'ladinoization' over the centuries. Another million Maya, mainly Tzotzil and Tzeltal, occupy the adjacent Chiapas highlands. All of these populations are rapidly growing and expanding, in spite of Guatemala's recent history of terror.

The highland Maya economy is both a part of, and separate from, the economies of the modern nation-states of Mexico and Guatemala. Most Maya households engage in corn farming, and many produce crafts for local consumption or for sale in Indian-run markets, but in many areas the men must travel long distances to work in the lowlands for part of the year on coffee fincas, cotton plantations, and the like. One of the most striking features of the Maya lands in Guatemala, apart from the magnificent landscape, is the vast network of markets and trade routes linking them, producing – as one anthropologist called it – a kind of 'penny capitalism.' These markets can sometimes be spectacular, like the ones at Sololá and Santiago Atitlán, near Lake Atitlán, with their row upon row of colorfully garbed Maya women selling produce of all kinds.

It is typical of the Maya highlands that each village will have its own distinctive style of dress. The skirts of the women are usually machine-made, *ikat* wrap-arounds, but their embroidered cotton blouses or *huipiles* mark them as members of a particular community. Recent studies made by Walter 'Chip' Morris have shown that the designs on them are not merely decorative, but rather illustrate a complex iconographic system based on native and sometimes Christian cosmology. The men, in contrast, wear clothing more or less based on Spanish modes of dress, but even this has been transformed into something distinctive to the community: Sololá men, for example, wear short black-and-white jackets with frogging, but on the back of each is a great emblematic bat, while the Tzotzil men of Zinacantan are clad with broad-brimmed, beribboned straw hats, ponchos, and high-backed sandals recalling those of the Classic Maya.

The old Maya Calendar Round has survived to an extraordinary degree in the highlands. Among peoples like the Ixil and the Quiché, the 260-day count is an integral part not only of native ritual, but of their everyday life, as it was among their distant ancestors. Wherever it is found, there are shaman-priests or 'day-keepers' whose job it is to keep track of the round of days, and to conduct rituals for individuals and the whole community in accord with its dictates. The most dramatic of these is the great Eight Monkey or *Guajxaquip Bats*, held in the Quiché community of Momostenango every 260 days. On the day of that name, tens of thousands of Indians gather at dawn at altars formed of mounds of broken pottery; there, over 200 shamans act as intermediaries between individual petitioners and the supreme deity *Dios Mundo* ('God World'). Prayers are made for forgiveness for past sins, and requests that some boon be granted, while each individual adds a potsherd to the pile.

An important function of all highland shamans is divination. This is sometimes done through the mechanism of the 260-day count, and sometimes by means of casting certain red seeds or maize kernels, both practices deeply rooted in the pre-Spanish past.

The Tzotzil Maya of Zinacantan

The resilience of the contemporary highland Maya when left in relative peace to work out their own destinies in a changing world is well-exemplified by the Tzotzil of Zinacantan, a community that was intensively studied over a period of years by a Harvard project directed by Evon Vogt.

The approximately 12,000 Zinacantecos live in a landscape of rugged mountains; over a thousand occupy the ceremonial center within a densely occupied valley, while the rest are scattered in outlying hamlets. The Zinacanteco world is conceived of as a large quincunx, with four corners and a 'navel of the earth' in the middle – actually a low, rounded mound in the ceremonial center. This all rests on the shoulders of the *Vaxak-Men*, the four-corner gods; when one of these shifts his burden, there is an earthquake. The sky above is the domain of the sun, moon, and stars. While the sun, 'Our Holy Father,' is associated in Zinancanteco cosmology with God the Father or Jesus Christ, the moon is thought to be one with the Virgin Mary.

153 Mountains and hills located near settlements are the homes of ancestral deities, 'fathers and mothers'; these supernaturals are pictured as elderly Zinacantecos, living eternally in their mountain abodes, and are referred to constantly in prayers and rituals conducted in their honor; they are sustained by offerings of black chickens, candles, incense, and liquor. Many Mayanists, incidentally, are convinced that these holy, ancestral mountains are directly analogous to the temple-pyramids of the Classic Maya cities, which celebrated the cult of the dead and presumably deified royal ancestors.

Almost of equal weight in Zinacanteco religious life is the Earth Lord – thought of as a fat, greedy *ladino*! – who dwells in caves, limestone sinks, and waterholes. He owns all the waterholes, and controls and produces lightning and rain.

The most sacred objects in Zinacantan are the wood or plaster images of the saints. These have their own legends and associated beliefs (not always the same as those in official hagiographies), and most are kept in three churches in the center.

The Zinacanteco people, on their lowest level of social organization, live in patrilocal, extended families, which in turn are grouped into local patrilineages or *sna*. Each *sna* maintains a series of cross shrines on nearby mountains, for communicating with the ancestral deities, and in caves, for

153 A Tzotzil Maya shaman from Zinacantan prays for the soul of a patient at a mountain shrine; in the background is another sacred mountain resembling an ancient Maya pyramid.

communicating with the Earth Lord. Two to over a dozen patrilineages form a waterhole group (waterholes are highly sacred), and in turn keep up their own series of cross shrines; a particular hamlet will be made up of several waterhole groups.

It will be remembered that the Spaniards imposed a civil hierarchy on each Maya group, and this persists in the ceremonial center of Zinacantan, with strictly ranked officials who are elected to three-year terms. But the more important hierarchy, as can be seen in native communities throughout the New World, is religious. Some of the people with religious power are shamans or 'seers,' of whom there are over 250, almost all adult males. Of overwhelming significance to the community is the system of ranked religious offices which functions on the *cargo* principle, in which each office is conceptualized as 'bearing a burden' (or *cargo*, in Spanish). Within this hierarchy, which fulfills the function of the confraternities found elsewhere, there are 61 positions grouped into four levels of seniority. All *cargo*-holders must reside in the center for the duration of the office, and as they rise through the ranks, their expenses grow increasingly exorbitant. After occupying the most senior rank, a Zinacanteco can expect to retire as a poor but highly honored individual. This was a 'burden' indeed!

Zinacanteco rituals require formalized eating and drinking, and often large processions to sacred places. The abiding concern with rank shows up in how individuals are placed in these activities. There are many rituals for the curing and well-being of individuals; these often involve a person's innate soul or *ch'ulel*, as well as his or her animal counterpart (every Zinacanteco has such an alter-ego, all of which live together in corrals within a 9,200-foot-high extinct volcano).

There are waterhole and lineage rituals, as well as frequent ceremonies conducted in the ceremonial center by *cargo*-holders. But the greatest of all are the end-of-the-year/New Year *cargo* rites, which reach their culmination in the latter half of January in celebrations held in honor of St Sebastian. Like the myths which surround this Roman saint – themselves the result of four centuries of syncretism – these dramatic ceremonies show a heady mixture of Christian and Maya-pagan elements. Much of the action is pure theater, with actors ritually impersonating jaguars, 'Blackmen,' and Spanish men and women. The entire religious drama is clearly directed towards renewal of the universe and of the community, and ends with the transfer of the sacred objects of office to a new set of *cargo*-holders.

As Professor Vogt has said of these Zinacantan Maya, 'they are a shrewd people, and have not retreated from the encroachment of *ladino* civilization. What is most valued and most vital to the culture has been reinforced, for the ritual life is, if anything, more intensified and elaborated than ever before.'

The Yucatec Maya

The Spanish conquest of Yucatán was a protracted and by no means completely successful process, and it ended with Spanish control being confined to the northern third of the peninsula, along with portions of the west and east coasts. The foreign overlords lived in *villas* with European administrative machinery and the usual grid plan; around and between them were hundreds of Maya communities which were forced to pay *encomienda* tribute and more-or-less forced labor, as well as to give up their 'idolatry.'

The ethnohistorian Grant Jones has documented that to the south and east lay a huge area inhabited by tens of thousands of Maya who had refused to submit to this oppression; this included most of the Petén and Belize, the east coast of the peninsula, and the region to the south of Campeche. At the heart of these defiant lands was Tah Itzá (or Tayasal) which, as we have seen in Chapter 8, only surrendered to Spanish arms in 1697. Various attempts to colonize the region by the Spaniards failed time and time again, one reason being, as Professor Jones has found, that vast numbers of Yucatec Maya were arriving from the north where they had fled the terrible *encomienda* system.

As a result, the eastern part of the peninsula – including most of what later became the Mexican Territory of Quintana Roo – remained a bastion of Maya independence until very recent times.

The War of the Castes
As in the highlands, the achievement of independence by the modern nation-states that control the Maya meant not a betterment of conditions for the latter, but worsening. The cruelty and misery of the sisal plantations and cattle ranches of Yucatán were amply documented in the books of John Lloyd Stephens, who saw them at first hand. The storm that became known to rich Yucatecan whites as the 'War of the Castes' broke out in 1847, not long after Stephens' visit when almost all the Maya of the peninsula took up arms against the hated whites. Eventually, the government troops held only Mérida, some towns along the coast, and the main road leading from Campeche. The Conquest had been reversed!

The dénouement of this story is well known: when the time came for the Indians to plant corn in their *milpas*, the native army disintegrated. Nonetheless, in 1850 a new element was introduced into the conflict. This took place in Chan Santa Cruz, a native village in central Quintana Roo, where a miraculous 'Talking Cross' began to prophesy a holy war against the whites. Bolstered by arms and other military equipment received from the British in Belize, the Maya of the region, now formed into quasi-military companies and inspired by messianic zeal, once more battled the armies of the oppressors. Fighting was not to end until 1901, when Federal forces under General Ignacio Bravo took Chan Santa Cruz. But Mexican government control gradually faded away during the ensuing decades, Talking Crosses proliferated, and the Maya of Quintana Roo went their own way (I saw a Talking Cross inside the Castillo at Tulum as late as 1948). Only the frantic development of tourism over the last 25 years has managed to spell the doom of Maya culture in this part of the peninsula.

The Maya of Chan Kom
Located in just about the center of the Yucatán Peninsula, during the 1930s when it was the focus of a study by the anthropologists Robert Redfield and Alfonso Villa Rojas, Chan Kom was the typical Yucatec Maya village. It has been since 'modernized' considerably, but settlements like Chan Kom as it then was can yet be found throughout the peninsula. With its houses of white-washed walls and thatched roofs, and its women in spotlessly white *huipils* edged with colorful embroidery, it offered a picture of rural tranquility belied by the turbulent history of victors and vanquished in the Maya lowlands.

Like their counterparts in Zinacantan, most of the Chan Kom Maya were and are maize farmers, but here they practice lowland slash-and-burn, shifting cultivation rather than the fixed-field systems of the highlands. There is the usual Spanish-style municipal government, but nothing like the religious hierarchy that is so striking among people like the Tzotzil. Two types of religious specialists practice here and in other traditional Yucatec

Maya settlements. One is the *Maestro Cantor*, a layman who nevertheless knows the Catholic prayers which may be used in Christian rituals like baptism, weddings, and funerals. The other is seemingly imbued with far greater spiritual and perhaps real power: this is the *h-men*, 'he who does or understands things' – that is, the shaman. *H-menob* are found all over the peninsula, even in large cities like Mérida, but they are an integral part of the agricultural rituals so vital to rural life. Even though the traditional Maya 260-day calendar has disappeared in Yucatán, these specialists still play an important role in divination and prophecy, using their crystals to scry the future.

The supernatural world is ever-present in Chan Kom and in the outlying fields and forest. At the four entrances to the village are four pairs of crosses and four *balam* ('jaguar') spirits, watching to keep evil away from the householders. The benevolent yet feared *balamob* also act as guardians of the cornfields. There are many *Chaacob*, Rain Gods descended from the Classic and Post-Classic deity Chac, visualized as old men on horseback, led by St Michael Archangel. Other supernaturals invoked in agricultural rites are deities of the forest in which the farmer must clear his plot, gods of the bees, and guardians of deer and cattle. Evil winds loose in the world can attack one and cause sickness; also to be avoided are the *aluxob*, leprechaun-like dwarves with large hats who bring misfortune.

Judging from the intensity of farming rituals in Yucatán, anxiety centered on subsistence must be far higher than in the highlands; as we have seen in Chapter 1, the peninsula has generally thin soils, and rainfall is far more sparse than in the south. Underlying the ceremonies performed in the *milpas* of Chan Kom farmers is the idea that 'what man wins from nature, he takes from the gods.' The nature gods must be asked for favors, and they must be repaid through prayers and offerings, including sacred foods and the first-fruits of the harvest.

These foods are those not consumed in ordinary life: stacks of bean-smeared tortillas cooked in the *pib* or pit, *balché* mead, *sacá* (sacred maize gruel), broth made from fowls, and sacrificed animals. About every fourth year, an individual farmer will sponsor an *u hanli col* ('dinner of the *milpa*') rite, conducted by a *h-men* at a rustic altar set with these holy foods and drink.

The largest and most dramatic of the Yucatec Maya agricultural ceremonies is the *Ch'a-chaac*; its purpose is to bring rain during times of drought, and thus involves the entire community. The participants are only men, who withdraw for several days to the place on the village's outskirts where the *Ch'a-chaac* is to held. The rite begins after the *h-men* has consulted his *zaztun* or crystal. The altar is covered with fowl, venison, and the sacred breadstuffs and drink, all set out in predetermined order; under the altar, and tied to its legs, are four boys, who croak like the *uo* frogs which are harbingers of rain in the Maya lowlands. Off to one side is an older man, chosen to impersonate the *Kunku-chaac*, the chief of the rain gods, holding in one hand the calabash from which he unleashes rain on the cornfields, and in the other a wooden knife symbolizing the lightning that accompanies downpours.

The Maya *h-menob* have other duties as well, most importantly to cure sickness, which the people of Chan Kom generally hold to come from evil winds and the evil eye; for this, curing rituals are held which include the usual offerings to the gods. As with their highland counterparts, these shamans also engage in divination, either by using their magic crystals, or by separating out cast maize kernels by groups of four (the outcome depending upon whether the number of piles is odd or even, or the remainder odd or even). Witchcraft is an omnipresent danger; the witch takes the form of animal alter-ego or *uay* (see Chapter 9), and may be male or female. The witch visits sleeping individuals like the incubus of European folklore, and through illicit sex saps that person's strength.

The Lacandón

Visitors to the site of Palenque may encounter near the entrance two or three Maya men with long hair and wearing long, white robes, selling bows and arrows especially made for the tourist trade. These are Lacandón, members of a stubbornly independent tribal group that some say number about 250, and others place at about 500 (a discrepancy that may arise from the fact that some choose to live as *ladinos* for part of the year).

The Lacandón inhabit three small villages in what was once a vast rain forest in eastern Chiapas. Historically, they almost certainly originated as one of the Yucatec-speaking refugee groups who chose to flee to the jungle fastnesses at the base of the peninsula rather than submit to Spanish rule. While most Lacandón have been converted to fundamentalist Christianity, some have remained fiercely conservative, preserving many elements of the old Maya religion; these latter still make pilgrimages to the ruined temples of Yaxchilán, invoking the gods with their incense-filled pottery censers. At one time they hunted and farmed in an unbroken, high-canopied forest; this was set aside for them in the 1970s by presidential decree, an edict which was soon abrogated, releasing lumber companies to sack its valuable timber. The lumber trucks were followed by an army of landless peasants, largely impoverished Tzeltal Maya from the highlands, who cut down what remained of the jungle. The final stage in the death of the Lacandón forest has been the conversion of peasant holdings to great cattle *fincas*, supplying beef to feed Americans' hunger for hamburgers.

The great terror

The greatest and bloodiest episode in the 'cycles of conquest' that have befallen the Maya since the arrival of the Spaniards began on 29 May 1978 in the Kekchí-speaking town of Panzós in the Department of Alta Verapaz, Guatemala. There, a unit of the Guatemalan army opened fire on a group of Indians peacefully protesting the government's refusal to award them land titles. Over one hundred men, women, and children were immediately killed.

Worse yet for the highland Maya, a second element had entered the picture: the Guerrilla Army of the Poor, which had chosen to base their anti-government operations in the western part of the highlands. Consisting largely of Marxist *ladinos*, the guerrillas looked upon traditional Maya culture as an obstacle to the proletarian revolution which they intended to bring about. Nevertheless, the Indian villagers had little choice but to give them support in the way of food and shelter.

Retribution by the Guatemalan government, its army, and its police came swiftly: under a series of military regimes, the official security forces and governmental death squads unleashed a reign of terror against the Maya that was almost unprecedented in its ferocity. It is estimated by anthropologists like George Lovell of Queen's University in Kingston (Ontario) that over one million Maya were displaced. According to a report by the National Academy of Sciences of the United States, approximately 150,000 people were killed, and an additional 40,000 'disappeared' – almost all of these being Maya. By the end of the terrible decade of the 1980s, 35,000 Indian refugees were living in camps in Mexico, and thousands had fled to the United States.

This was indeed ethnocide, if not genocide, on a grand scale. Uprooted communities were forced into 'model villages' (a move recommended by American military advisors), where able-bodied men were, and still are, required to perform service in civil patrols. For hundreds of thousands of Quiché, Ixil, Mam, and other Maya, the traditional ties with the land had finally been shattered. As these immense disruptions took place, fundamentalist Christian missionaries from the United States, with government support, began to make vast numbers of converts among Guatemala's Maya. With whole villages undergoing mass baptism, the effect on the traditional structure of Maya life (the confraternities and *cargo* system, for instance) may well be imagined.

Will the Maya survive? They have been under attack from every side: from the army and death squads in Guatemala, from mass tourism and the destruction of the tropical forest in Mexico, from *ladino* encroachments on their lands everywhere. These almost intolerable pressures have resulted in vast dislocations and migrations throughout the Maya area. But there are signs of hope for them. In Guatemala, many Maya intellectuals have realized that to survive, various Maya linguistic groups, heretofore separate, must come together to save their language and culture. And many more Maya now know that they can stand up to terror by speaking out: Rigoberta Menchú, a Quiché Maya woman who lost most of her family to the death squads, did so – for which she was awarded the Nobel Peace Prize for 1992.

The Yucatec Maya of the Talking Cross villages in Quintana Roo prophesy a coming Great War, an Armageddon when (as they told Paul Sullivan) a new king will awaken in Chichén Itzá, along with thousands of petrified beings from a past creation, and a petrified Feathered Serpent will come to life and inflict havoc on the creatures of this creation. Messianic predictions like this will surely crop up again and again as pressures on the Maya intensify. Yet the Maya are actually increasing, not dwindling, in numbers, and a heightened awareness that they are all one people with a glorious past, and an adaptability to future change, may help them survive for centuries into the future.

Further Reading

There is no up-to-date, comprehensive bibliography on the ancient, Colonial, and contemporary Maya; it might number almost 10,000 entries. Here I have tried to concentrate on those articles and volumes which I have found most useful in the preparation of this book, and which might be of interest to those wishing to follow certain topics further. Two important series specializing in Maya culture should be consulted: *Estudios de Cultura Maya*, published since 1961 by the Seminario de Cultura Maya, Universidad Nacional Autónoma de México; and *Research Reports on Ancient Maya Writing*, issued since 1985 by the Center for Maya Research, Washington, D.C.

ADAMS, RICHARD E. W. (ed.). *The Origins of Maya Civilization*. Albuquerque 1977. (Fifteen essays, but already outdated by recent excavations in the Petén and Belize.)

ANDREWS, ANTHONY P. *Maya Salt Production and Trade*. Tucson 1983. (Thorough study of an important Maya industry.)

ANDREWS, E. WYLLYS IV, and E. WYLLYS ANDREWS V. 'Excavations at Dzibilchaltún, Yucatán, Mexico', *Middle American Research Institute, Tulane University*, Publication 48. New Orleans 1980.

ANDREWS, E. WYLLYS V 'The early ceramic history of the lowland Maya', in *Vision and Revision in Maya Studies*, ed. F. S. Clancy and P. D. Harrison, 1–19. Albuquerque 1990. (Establishes the sequence for the Middle Preclassic in the lowlands.)

AVENI, ANTHONY F. *Skywatchers of Ancient Mexico*. Austin 1980. (The clearest introduction to Maya astronomy.)

BARRERA VÁSQUEZ, ALFREDO, and SYLVANUS G. MORLEY. 'The Maya chronicles', *Carnegie Institution of Washington, Contributions to American Anthropology and History*, no. 48. Washington 1949. (Yucatec Maya prophetic history based on the Books of Chilam Balam.)

BAUDEZ, CLAUDE-FRANÇOIS, and PIERRE BECQUELIN. *Les Mayas*. Paris 1984. (Lavishly illustrated introduction to the Maya by two French specialists.)

BAUDEZ, CLAUDE-FRANÇOIS, and SYDNEY PICASSO. *Lost Cities of the Maya*, London and New York 1992. (Low-priced paperback on history of Maya discovery.)

BENSON, ELIZABETH P. *The Maya World*. Revised edition. New York 1977.

——, (ed.). *City-States of the Maya: Art and Architecture*. Denver 1986. (Five essays on Maya cities, including Late Preclassic Edzná and El Mirador, and Terminal Classic Uxmal.)

BENSON, ELIZABETH P., and GILLETT G. GRIFFIN (eds.). *Maya Iconography*. Princeton 1988. (Pioneering essays on Maya art and epigraphy.)

BERLIN, HEINRICH. 'El glifo "emblema" en las inscripciones mayas', *Journal de la Société des Américanistes*, vol. 47 (1958), 111–9. (Article that presaged the historical approach to the inscriptions.)

BRICKER, VICTORIA R. *Grammar of Mayan Hieroglyphs*. New Orleans 1986. (The application of linguistics to Maya decipherment.)

CANBY, PETER. *Heart of the Sky: Travels Among the Maya*. New York 1992. (First-hand account by a journalist of the dilemma and tragedy of the modern Maya.)

CARMACK, ROBERT M. *Quichean Civilization*. Berkeley and Los Angeles 1973. (Overview of the Post-Classic Quiché Maya of Guatemala.)

——, *The Quiché Maya of Utatlán*. Norman 1981.

——, (ed.). *The Maya Indians and the Guatemalan Crisis*. Norman 1985. (Eye-witness accounts and interpretive essays dealing with the official violence directed against the Maya of Guatemala.)

CARR, ROBERT F., and JAMES E. HAZARD. 'Map of the Ruins of Tikal, El Petén, Guatemala', *Tikal Reports*, no. 11. Philadelphia 1961.

CHAMBERLAIN, ROBERT S. 'The conquest and colonization of Yucatán', *Carnegie Institution of Washington*, publ. 582. Washington 1948.

CHASE, ARLEN F., and PRUDENCE M. RICE (eds.). *The Lowland Maya Postclassic*. Austin 1985. (19 essays covering all aspects of the subject, up to the fall of Tayasal in 1697.)

CLANCY, FLORA S., and PETER D. HARRISON (eds.). *Vision and Revision in Maya Studies*. Albuquerque 1990. (A potpourri of essays, covering subjects from subsistence to epigraphy.)

CLARK, JOHN E. 'The beginnings of Mesoamerica: aopologia for the Soconusco Early Formative', in *The Formation of Complex Society in Southeastern Mesoamerica*', ed. W. R. Fowler, Jr., 13–26. Boca Raton 1991. (Summary article on the precocious development of settled life along the Pacific Coast of Chiapas and Guatemala.)

COE, MICHAEL D. *The Maya Scribe and His World*. New York 1973. (Iconographic and epigraphic study of Maya vases, along with a description of the Grolier Codex.)

——, 'Early steps in the evolution of Maya writing', in *Origins of Religious Art and Iconography in Preclassic Mesoamerica*, ed. H. B. Nicholson, 107–22. Los Angeles 1976.

——, *Breaking the Maya Code*. London and New York 1992. (The history of the Maya decipherment.)

COE, MICHAEL D., and RICHARD A. DIEHL. *In the Land*

of the Olmec, 2 vols. Austin 1980. (Excavations and human ecology at the Olmec site of San Lorenzo Tenochtitlán.)

COE, MICHAEL D., and KENT V. FLANNERY. *Early Cultures and Human Ecology in South Coastal Guatemala*. Washington 1967. (Early Preclassic investigations.)

COE, WILLIAM R. 'Tikal, Guatemala, and emergent Maya civilization', *Science*, vol. 147, no. 3664 (1965), 1401–19.

——, *Tikal, a Handbook of the Ancient Maya Ruins*. Philadelphia 1967.

COGGINS, CLEMENCY C., and ORRIN C. SHANE (eds.). *Cenote of Sacrifice: Maya Treasures from the Sacred Well at Chichén Itzá*. Austin 1984. (Catalogue of objects recovered from the cenote at the turn of the century.)

COLBY, BENJAMIN N., and LORE M. COLBY. *The Daykeeper: The Life and Discourse of an Ixil Diviner*. Cambridge, Mass., 1981. (Account of shamanistic practices among the contemporary Ixil of the north-central highlands.)

CULBERT, T. PATRICK (ed.). *The Classic Maya Collapse*. Albuquerque 1973. (Contains all of the old and most of the new theories about the downfall of the Classic Maya civilization.)

DANIEN, ELIN C., and ROBERT J. SHARER (eds.). *New Theories on the Ancient Maya*. Philadelphia 1992. (20 essays prepared for a centennial symposium at The University Museum.)

FASH, WILLIAM L. *Scribes, Warriors and Kings: The City of Copán and the Ancient Maya*. London and New York 1991. (Authoritative introduction to this important city, combining archaeology, iconography, and dynastic analysis.)

FERGUSON, WILLIAM M., and JOHN Q. ROYCE. *Maya Ruins of Mexico in Color*. Norman, Oklahoma 1977. (Color photographs taken from a light airplane of many important Maya sites.)

——, *Maya Ruins in Central America in Color*. Albuquerque 1984.

FLANNERY, KENT V. (ed.). *Maya Subsistence*. New York 1982. (Essays presented at a conference in memory of the Mayanist Dennis Puleston.)

FOX, JOHN W. *Quiché Conquest: Centralism and Regionalism in Highland Guatemalan State Development*. Albuquerque 1978. (Argues for the Gulf Coast origin of the Post-Classic Highland elites.)

GENDROP, PAUL. *Los estilos Río Bec, Chenes y Puuc en la arquitectura maya*. Mexico 1983. (A well-illustrated overview of this part of the Maya lowland development.)

GRUBE, NIKOLAI. 'Die Entwicklung der Mayaschrift'. *Acta Mesoamericana*, Band 3. Berlin 1990. (The evolution of Maya script.)

HAMMOND, NORMAN. *Ancient Maya Civilization*. New Brunswick and Cambridge, England 1982.

——, (ed.). *Social Process in Maya Prehistory*. London and New York 1977. (Contains 25 essays, including three on the Maya collapse.)

HANKS, WILLIAM F., and DON S. RICE (eds.). *Word and Image in Maya Culture*. Salt Lake City 1989. (Results of a symposium, with 24 essays on Maya linguistics, writing, and iconography.)

HANSEN, RICHARD D. 'The Maya rediscovered: the road to Nakbé'. *Natural History*, May 1991, 8–14. New York. (Investigations at a great, Late Preclassic city.)

——, 'El proceso cultural de Nakbé y el área del Petén nor-central: las épocas tempranas', in *V Simposio de Investigaciones en Guatemala*, 81–96. Guatemala City 1992.

HARRIS, JOHN F., and STEPHEN K. STEARNS. *Understanding Maya Inscriptions: A Hieroglyphic Handbook*. Philadelphia 1992. (A useful guide to the Maya calendar and the inscriptions for the neophyte.)

HARRISON, PETER D., and B. L. TURNER II (eds.). *Pre-Hispanic Maya Agriculture*. Albuquerque 1978.

HAY, CLARENCE L., *et al* (eds.). *The Maya and Their Neighbors*. New York 1940. (A now-classic *festschrift* dedicated to the great Mayanist Alfred M. Tozzer.)

HELLMUTH, NICHOLAS M. *Tikal, Copán Travel Guide*. St. Louis 1978. (A well-illustrated introduction to Maya ruins in Guatemala and Honduras.)

HOUSTON, STEPHEN D. *Maya Glyphs*. London 1989. (Concise overview of Maya epigraphy, including recent advances.)

JONES, GRANT D. *Maya Resistance to Spanish Rule: Time and History on a Colonial Frontier*. Albuquerque 1989. (Documentary history of the independent Maya of southern Yucatán and the Petén.)

——, 'The Canek Manuscript in ethnohistorical perspective'. *Ancient Mesoamerica*, vol. 3, no. 2 (1992), 243–68.

JUSTESON, JOHN S., *et al*. *The Foreign Impact on Lowland Mayan Language and Script*. New Orleans 1985.

JUSTESON, JOHN S., and LYLE CAMPBELL (eds.). *Phoneticism in Mayan Hieroglyphic Writing*. Albany 1984. Essays presented at a watershed conference on Maya epigraphy, marking general acceptance of the Knorosov approach.)

KATZ, S. H., M. L. HEDIGER, and L. A. VALLEROY. 'Traditional maize processing in the New World'. *Science*, vol. 184, 765–73. (Stresses the importance of the 'nixtamalization process' in the Mesoamerican diet.)

KELLEY, DAVID H. *Deciphering the Maya Script*. Austin and London 1976. (Updates Thompson's 1950 work, but now, due to the fast pace of the decipherment, somewhat out-of-date itself.)

KERR, JUSTIN. *The Maya Vase Book*. Vols. 1–3. New York 1989–92. (A continuing series, presenting rollouts of Maya vases, accompanied by important essays on ceramic iconography and epigraphy.)

KIDDER, ALFRED V., JESSE L. JENNINGS, and EDWIN M. SHOOK. 'Excavations at Kaminaljuyú, Guatemala', *Carnegie Institution of Washington*, publ. 561. Washington 1946. (Excavation of Early Classic Esperanza tombs.)

KNOROSOV, YURI V. 'The problem of the study of the Maya hieroglyphic writing', *American Antiquity*, vol. 23, no. 3 (1958), 284–91. (First American publication of Knorosov's revolutionary approach to the glyphs.)

——, 'Selected chapters from "The Writing of the Maya Indians"', translated by Sophie D. Coe. *Russian Translation Series, Peabody Museum of Archaeology and Ethnology, Harvard University*, vol. 4. Cambridge, Mass., 1967.

KOWALSKI, JEFF K. 'Lords of the Northern Maya: dynastic history in the inscriptions'. *Expedition*, vol. 27, no. 3 (1985), 50–60. (Historical texts from the Puuc sites.)

——, *The House of the Governor: A Maya Palace at*

Uxmal, Yucatán, Mexico. Norman 1987. (Important architectural and iconographic study of a major administrative building of the Puuc.)

LEÓN-PORTILLA, MIGUEL. *Time and Reality in the Thought of the Maya.* Boston 1973. (An interpretive study of Maya religion and philosophy.)

LOTHROP, SAMUEL K. 'Tulum, an archaeological study of the east coast of Yucatán', *Carnegie Institution of Washington*, publ. 335. Washington 1924.

LOUNSBURY, FLOYD G. 'Maya numeration, computation, and calendrical astronomy', *in Dictionary of Scientific Biography*, vol. 15, supplement I (1978), 759–818. (Full account of these subjects, written for the advanced student.)

——, 'Astronomical knowledge and its uses at Bonampak, Mexico', in *Archaeo-astronomy in the New World*, ed. A. F. Aveni, 143–68. Cambridge 1982. (Identification of an astronomically-determined war.)

LOWE, GARETH W., THOMAS E. LEE, and EDUARDO E. MARTÍNEZ. 'Izapa: an introduction to the ruins and monuments', *Papers of the New World Archaeological Foundation*, no. 31. Provo 1973. (Definitive study of the type site of the Izapan civilization.)

MACNEISH, RICHARD., S. J. K. WILKERSON, and A. NELKEN-TURNER. *First Annual Report of the Belize Archaic Archaeological Reconnaissance.* Andover 1989.

MARCUS, JOYCE. *Emblem and State in the Classic Maya Lowlands.* Washington 1976. (Hypothetical political organization of the Classic Maya, based upon the distribution of Emblem Glyphs.)

MATHENY, RAY T. (ed.). 'El Mirador, Petén, Guatemala: an interim report', *Papers of the New World Archaeological Foundation*, no. 45. Provo 1980. (Investigations at the largest Late Preclassic city.)

MATHENY, RAY, et al. 'Investigations at Edzná, Campeche, Mexico', *Papers of the New World Archaeological Foundation*, no. 46. Provo 1980 and 1983.

MAUDSLAY, ALFRED P. *Biologia Centrali-Americana, Archaeology.* Text and 4 vols. of plates. London 1889–1902. (Magnificent photographs and drawings of Maya monuments and cities; a milestone in the history of Maya research.)

MCGEE, R. JON. *Life, Ritual and Religion Among the Lacandón Maya.* Belmont 1990.

MENCHÚ, RIGOBERTA. *I, Rigoberta Menchú.* London 1984. (First-hand account of the terror inflicted on the Maya of Guatemala, by the winner of the 1992 Nobel Prize for Peace.)

MILLER, ARTHUR G. *On the Edge of the Sea: Mural Painting at Tancah-Tulum, Quintana Roo.* Washington 1982. (Post-Classic art in the eastern Yucatán peninsula.)

MILLER, MARY ELLEN. *The Art of Mesoamerica from Olmec to Aztec.* London and New York 1986. (Excellent introduction to Mesoamerican culture as a whole.)

——, *The Murals of Bonampak.* Princeton 1986.

MILLER, MARY and KARL TAUBE. *The Gods and Symbols of Ancient Mexico and the Maya: An Illustrated Dictionary of Mesoamerican Religion.* London and New York 1993.

MORLEY, SYLVANUS G. 'The inscriptions of Peten', *Carnegie Institution of Washington*, publ. 437, 5 vols. Washington 1937–8.

MORLEY, SYLVANUS G., and GEORGE W. BRAINERD. *The Ancient Maya.* Fourth edition, revised by Robert J.

Sharer. Stanford 1983. (Extensively revised, with a useful new chapter on language and writing.)

MORRIS, EARL H., et al. 'The Temple of the Warriors at Chichén Itzá, Yucatán', *Carnegie Institution of Washington*, publ. 406, 2 vols. Washington 1931.

MORRIS, WALTER F., JR. *Living Maya.* New York 1987. (The text emphasizes the weaver's art, and has photographs of the contemporary Maya of Chiapas.)

PARSONS, LEE A. *Bilbao, Guatemala*, 2 vols. Milwaukee 1967–9. (Description and excavation of a major Cotzumalhuapan site.)

——, 'The origins of monumental stone sculpture of Kaminaljuyú, Guatemala, and the southern Pacific coast', *Dumbarton Oaks Studies in Pre-Columbian Art and Archaeology*, no. 28. Washington 1986. (Study of a major body of Late Preclassic sculpture.)

PENDERGAST, DAVID M. *Excavations at Altún Ha, Belize, 1964–1970.* Toronto. Vol. 1, 1979. Vol. 2, 1982.

——, 'Lamanai, Belize: summary of excavation results, 1974–1980', *Journal of Field Archaeology*, vol. 8, no. 1 (1981), 29–53.

POHL, MARY (ed.). 'Prehistoric Lowland Maya Environment and Subsistence Economy', *Papers of the Peabody Museum of Archaeology and Ethnology*, vol. 77. Cambridge, Mass., 1985. (Agriculture and use of faunal resources among the ancient Maya.)

POLLOCK, H. E. D. 'The Puuc: an Architectural survey of the hill country of Yucatan and northern Campeche, Mexico', *Memoirs of the Peabody Museum of Archaeology and Ethnology, Harvard University*, vol. 19. Cambridge, Mass., 1980. (Indispensable for the study of the Puuc cities.)

POLLOCK, H. E. D., et al. 'Mayapán, Yucatán, Mexico', *Carnegie Institution of Washington*, publ. 619. Washington 1962. (The account of Itzá history in Chapter 7 is largely based upon the Roys essay.)

PROSKOURIAKOFF, TATIANA. 'An album of Maya architecture', *Carnegie Institution of Washington*, publ. 558. Washington 1946. (Reconstructions of Maya cities by this artist-archaeologist.)

——, 'A study of Classic Maya sculpture', *Carnegie Institution of Washington*, publ. 593. Washington 1950. (Stylistic dating of Maya monuments.)

——, 'Historical implication of a pattern of dates at Piedras Negras, Guatemala', *American Antiquity*, vol. 25, no. 4 (1960), 454–75. (A now classic paper which established the historical nature of the Maya inscriptions.)

——, 'The lords of the Maya realm', *Expedition*, vol. 4, no. 1 (1961), 14–21. (A less technical treatment of the 1960 paper.)

RECINOS, ADRIAN, and DELIA GOETZ. *The Annals of the Cakchiquels. Title of the Lords of Totonicapán.* Norman 1953. (English translation of important documents pertaining to pre-Conquest peoples of the Guatemalan highlands.)

REDFIELD, ROBERT, and ALFONSO VILLA ROJAS. *Chan Kom, a Maya Village.* Chicago 1962. (Classic study of a Yucatec Maya community.)

REED, NELSON. *The Caste War of Yucatán.* Stanford 1964. (Documentary history of the great 19th-century uprising by the Yucatec Maya.)

ROBERTSON, MERLE GREENE. *The Sculpture of Palenque.* 4 vols. Princeton 1983–91. (The most complete survey of the sculpture of any Maya city, magnificently illustrated.)

——, (gen. ed.). *Palenque Round Table Series (Mesa Redonda de Palenque)*. Nos. 1–2, Pebble Beach, Calif., 1974–76. No. 3, Palenque 1979. Nos. 4–5, San Francisco 1985. No. 6, Norman 1991. (Much of the recent information on Maya iconography and epigraphy has appeared in this indispensable series.)

Roys, Ralph L. 'The Book of Chilam Balam of Chumayel', *Carnegie Institution of Washington*, publ. 438. Washington 1933. (Annotated translation of the most important native Colonial-period text from the Maya lowlands.)

——, 'The Indian background of Colonial Yucatán', *Carnegie Institution of Washington*, publ. 548. Washington 1943. (Documentary study of Late Post-Classic Yucatán.)

——, 'The political geography of the Yucatán Maya', *Carnegie Institution of Washington*, publ. 613. Washington 1957. (Should be read in conjunction with the above.)

Ruppert, Karl, J. Eric S. Thompson, and Tatiana Proskouriakoff. 'Bonampak, Chiapas, Mexico', *Carnegie Institution of Washington*, publ. 602. Washington 1955. (Reproduces Antonio Tejeda's copies of the murals.)

Ruz Lhuillier, Alberto. *El Templo de las Inscripciones, Palenque*. Mexico City 1973. (Excavation report on Pacal's tomb.)

Sanchez, George I. *Arithmetic in Maya*. Austin 1961. (A mathematician's suggestions on how the Maya may have calculated.)

Schele, Linda. *Maya Glyphs: the Verbs*. Austin 1982. (Identification of event glyphs, and how they conformed to Mayan morphology and syntax.)

——, *Notebook for the Maya Hieroglyph Workshop*. Austin 1992. (Broad survey of Maya epigraphy, with emphasis on texts relating to the creation of the universe.)

Schele, Linda, and David Freidel. *A Forest of Kings. The Untold Story of the Ancient Maya*. New York 1990. (Major work, presenting Maya history through the ages as told by the Maya inscriptions and iconography.)

Schele, Linda, and Mary E. Miller. *The Blood of Kings: Dynasty and Ritual in Maya Art*. Fort Worth 1986, London 1992. (The definitive statement of what is now known about Maya art and culture.)

Schocken, Wolfgang A. *The Calendar of the Maya*. Boston 1960. (Succinct account by a specialist on ancient calendars.)

Sharer, Robert J. (ed.). 'Quiriguá Project 1974–1979', *Expedition*, vol. 23, no. 1, 5–10.

——, (ed.). *Quiriguá Reports I, II*. Philadelphia 1979, 1983.

Shook, Edwin M., and Alfred V. Kidder. 'Mound E–III–3, Kaminaljuyú, Guatemala', *Carnegie Institution of Washington, Contributions to American Anthropology and History*, no. 53. Washington 1952. (Excavation of rich Miraflores period tombs.)

Smith, A. Ledyard. 'Uaxactún, Guatemala: excavations of 1931–7', *Carnegie Institution of Washington*, publ. 588. Washington 1950.

Smith, Robert E. 'Ceramic sequence at Uaxactún, Guatemala', *Middle American Research Institute*, publ. 20, 2 vols. New Orleans 1955. (Established the archaeological chronology of the southern Maya lowlands.)

Stephens, John L. *Incidents of Travel in Central America, Chiapas, and Yucatán*, 2 vols. New York 1841. (With the 1843 work, both illustrated by Frederick Catherwood, brought the Maya civilization to the attention of the outside world; still eminently readable.)

——, *Incidents of Travel in Yucatán*, 2 vols. New York 1843.

Stuart, David. 'Ten Phonetic Syllables', *Research Reports on Ancient Maya Writing*, no. 14. Washington 1987. (A major epigraphic advance, building on the methodology pioneered by Knorosov.)

Stuart, George E. 'Maya art treasures discovered in caves', *National Geographic*, vol. 160, no. 2 (1981), 220–36. (The cave drawings of Naj Tunich.)

——, 'Quest for decipherment: a historical and biographical survey of Maya hieroglyphic investigation', in *New Theories on the Ancient Maya*, ed. E. C. Danien and R. J. Sharer, 1–63. Philadelphia 1992.

Stuart, George E., and Gene S. Stuart. *The Mysterious Maya*. Washington 1977. (Popular account of the ancient and modern Maya.)

Sullivan, Paul. *Unfinished Conversations: Mayas and Foreigners Between Two Wars*. New York 1989. (Perceptive account of the extraordinary dialogue in the 1930s between the Maya of Quintana Roo and the Carnegie archaeologists based at Chichén Itzá.)

Tate, Carolyn E. *Yaxchilán: The Design of a Maya Ceremonial Center*. Austin 1992.

Taube, Karl A. 'The major gods of ancient Yucatán', *Dumbarton Oaks Studies in Pre-Columbian Art and Archaeology*, no. 32. Washington 1992. (Definitive study of Maya religious iconography.)

Tedlock, Barbara. *Time and the Highland Maya*. Albuquerque 1982. (Herself an initiated day-keeper, the author shows how the ancient calendar functions in Quiché life and society.)

Tedlock, Dennis. *Popol Vuh*. New York 1985. (The definitive edition of the greatest piece of Native American literature, and the key source for the understanding of pre-Conquest Maya iconography and thought.)

Teeple, John E. 'Maya astronomy', *Carnegie Institution of Washington, Contributions to American Archaeology*, no. 2. Washington 1930. (Teeple solved the puzzle of the lunar calculations in the inscriptions.)

Thompson, J. Eric S. 'Maya hieroglyphic writing. Introduction', *Carnegie Institution of Washington*, publ. 589. Washington 1950. (A monumental survey of Maya calendrics, religion, and astronomy, but written before the adoption of the historical and phonetic approaches to the glyphs.)

——, *A Catalog of Maya Hieroglyphs*. Norman 1962. (Covers glyphs of both the monuments and codices, and now in universal use.)

——, 'Trade relations between the Maya highlands and lowlands', *Estudios de Cultura Maya*, vol. 4, 13–49. Mexico City 1964.

——, *Maya History and Religion*. Norman 1970. (Contains first-class studies of Maya ethnohistory. Especially important for its treatment of the Putún Maya.)

Tozzer, Alfred M. 'Chichén Itzá and its Cenote of Sacrifice', *Memoirs of the Peabody Museum of Archaeology and Ethnology, Harvard University*, vols. ii, 12. Cambridge, Mass., 1957.

——, (ed.). 'Landa's Relación de las Cosas de Yucatán', *Papers of the Peabody Museum of Archaeology and Ethnology, Harvard University*, vol. 18. Cambridge, Mass., 1941. (Thanks to the extensive notes which accompany Landa's text, this is virtually an encyclopedia of Maya life.)

VILLACORTA, J. ANTONIO and CARLOS A. *Códices mayas*. Guatemala 1930. (Three of the four Maya hieroglyphic books reproduced by line drawings in a useful edition.)

VOGT, EVON Z. *Zinacantan: A Maya Community in the Highlands of Chiapas*. Cambridge, Mass., 1969. (A classic study of the contemporary Tzotzil Maya.)

WEAVER, MURIEL PORTER. *The Aztecs, Maya, and Their Predecessors*. Second edition. New York 1981. (Has detailed coverage of Mesoamerica as a whole.)

WILLEY, GORDON R. 'The Altar de Sacrificios excavations: general summary and conclusions', *Papers of the Peabody Museum of Archaeology and Ethnology*, vol. 74, no. 3. Cambridge, Mass., 1973.

——, 'General summary and conclusions', in 'Excavations at Seibal', *Memoirs of the Peabody Museum of Archaeology, Harvard University*, vol. 17, no. 4. Cambridge, Mass., 1990. (Seibal was a huge Classic city on the Pasión, with important Preclassic and Terminal Classic components.)

——, *et al.* 'Prehistoric Maya settlements in the Belize Valley', *Papers of the Peabody Museum of Archaeology and Ethnology, Harvard University*, vol. 54. Cambridge, Mass. (A pioneering work on Maya settlement pattern.)

WILLEY, GORDON R., and PETER MATHEWS (eds.). 'A consideration of the Early Classic period in the Maya lowlands', *Institute for Mesoamerican Studies*, publ. 10. Albany 1985. (Combines archaeological and epigraphic evidence.)

ZIMMERMAN, GÜNTER. *Die Hieroglyphen der Maya-Handschriften*. Hamburg 1956. (A catalog of the glyphs in the codices, still useful.)

List of Illustrations

All maps were drawn by Mrs Jean Zallinger and Mr Peter Zallinger. Other drawings are by the author, unless otherwise indicated.

Index